THERE'S A YACHT MORE TO LIFE

Loving, Working and Playing in Paradise

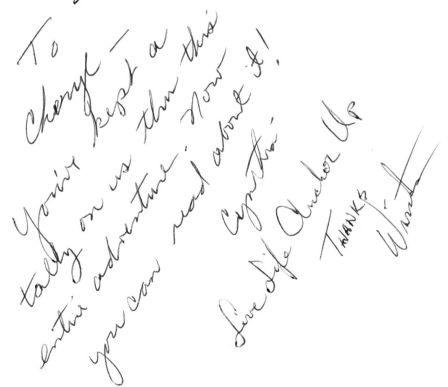

To —
Cheryl —
You've kept a this
tally on us thru this
entire adventure. Now
you can read about it!
Cynthia

Live Life Anchor Up
THANKS
Winston

The Real Life Adventures of Our Career Makeover

Cynthia Zvanut Hovey and Winston A. Hovey

Copyright © 2018 WinCyn Partners
All rights reserved.
www.WinCynBook.com

Barringer Publishing, Naples, Florida
www.barringerpublishing.com
Cover, graphics, layout design by Linda Duider

ISBN: 978-0-9989069-6-6

Library of Congress Cataloging-in-Publication Data
There's A Yacht More To Life
Loving, Working and Playing in Paradise

Printed in U.S.A.

There is nothing more enticing, disenchanting and enslaving than the life at sea.

— Joseph Conrad

Dedication

To Sandra,
the reason we're here

To Judith,
who helped us weather the storms

To Andrea and Jason,
for cheering us on

Our dream of an adventurous career in
paradise started with our vacations to the British
Virgin Islands and U.S. Virgin Islands.

As yacht crew we toured them almost weekly. Hassle
Island in St. Thomas, USVI; Roadtown, Tortola and Saba
Rock off Virgin Gorda in the BVI were our home bases,
but each island holds a special place in our hearts.

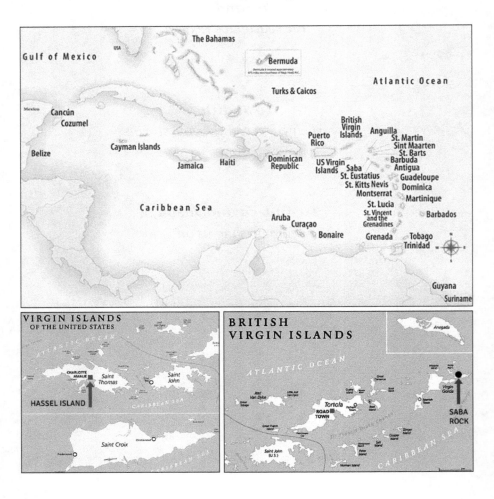

Contents

Part Two: Kissing Frogs and Paying Dues

Part Three: Yacht Enough

Foreword

by Judith Keltner Anthony

Winston and Cynthia transformed their love of the sea and global travel into a mutual second career. Cynthia, vice president of a large San Diego public relations firm, and Winston, a Canadian engineer from the Maritime Provinces, with a seagoer's heritage, met in 1990 on Windansea Beach, in La Jolla, California. Whetted by their annual Caribbean sailing vacations and spurned by a company layoff, together they meshed a new career strategy: "perma-vacationing" with salary. Their primary goal: adventure.

Ingenuity and flexibility epitomize Cynthia and Winston's lifestyle. They traded their glass condo on Windansea Beach for a grass hut in the British Virgin Islands. The hut was soon followed by a sunset-colored beach house, with no electricity and no running water, and then to U.S. Virgin Islands' Hassel Island, where their residency brought the island population to a whopping nine.

Their tropical career has taken them through every adventure outlined in their favorite book about island life, *Don't Stop the Carnival*. Combine hurricanes, whale sightings, island legends, and Caribbean archaeology with their thirty-day Pacific crossing, honeymoon rafting the Colorado River through the Grand Canyon, ten thousand-mile Harley Davidson trips, and sailing Antigua's Classic Yacht Race, and you have a rich backdrop against which their storytelling abounds.

Acquiring dual U.S. Coast Guard captain's licenses and transitioning from island landlubbers to running multimillion-dollar mega yachts, Winston and Cynthia have been captain and chef on luxury sailing and motor yachts in the Pacific, Atlantic, Caribbean, Gulf of Mexico, and all facets of the Intracoastal Waterway. They've run yachts from Mexico to Alaska and from Trinidad to Martha's Vineyard. (A mega yacht is generally privately owned, measures over twenty-four meters long and carries a professional crew.)

Beginning with their first island job running water makers and managing cooks for a tiny "Jimmy Buffet style" restaurant to sharing culinary skills and proven ability in navigation, maintenance, management, and hospitality on multimillion-dollar yachts, this couple's career is a colorful example of how to become "perma-vacationers" and get paid for it.

From corporate careers to running mega yachts, Winston and Cynthia's story may inspire you. If they could get their dream job, why can't you?

Preface

The idea for this book came from a bright-eyed, curly-haired seven-year-old vacationing aboard a yacht we were running. "You guys are so lucky," she said with wide-eyed envy. "You guys get to go on *everybody's* vacation!"

Whenever Winston and I talk with strangers, which is often in our line of work, we're asked what we do for a living. "We run luxury yachts, taking people on their vacations." Inevitably the next question is: "How in the world did you get that job?"

It was a watery and windy path, but this book is that story.

When we decided to pursue our dream of an adventurous career and move to the Caribbean, our biggest challenge was dispersing almost everything we owned—all our "stuff." After accomplishing that, we took a deep breath, packed six UPS boxes and moved—via two planes, one ferry, and one runabout boat—to a grass hut with a tiny, island bar. Twenty-five years later, we've morphed from running that island bar into a career running multimillion-dollar yachts, all with the freedom of "no stuff."

Winston and I have worked (and played) in many of the splendid places people vacation. And we've done it all, with only two pairs of shoes, a handful of shorts and T-shirts, and, oh, yes, our foul-weather gear.

Giving up our stuff to pursue our dream career made us free, but there's a *yacht* more to our story. The words are Winston's and mine together, anchored by quotes from my favorite mentor, author Richard Bach. Read about our journey, then trust yourself and try your own.

Cynthia Zvanut Hovey

Acknowledgments

Our story unfolds over twenty-five years. The journey we undertook while putting it on paper was an adventure itself, recalling all the places and people who've crossed our ever-winding path. We've changed names to protect the innocent, but every incident is based on true happenings and is recounted to the best of our ability.

We want to thank everyone who provided input, reminding us of situations we'd let slip under the waves. We also thank my meticulous sister, Suzanne Lagomarcino, my author sister, Deborah Drake, my wise and creative St. Louis coworker, Jackie Engle, Winston's dear friend, Richard Blakley, and gypsy author, Laura Melvin, for their precious time and dedicated help editing our manuscript.

And thank you to Jeff Schlesinger of Barringer Publishing and his team for their diligent pursuit of artistry in publishing *There's a Yacht More to Life*.

Part One:

Adjusting Our Sails

*Don't let making a living
get in the way of having a life.*

1990 - 2000

Chapter 1
The Travel Bug Bites

You are lead through your lifetime by the inner learning creature, the playful spiritual being that is your real self.

—Richard Bach

Winston and Cynthia eastbound for the next twenty-eight days, delivering a sailboat from Hawaii to San Diego.

San Diego, British Virgin Islands, Hawaii, New Zealand
January 1990—May 1994

In January, 2001, we got the shocking news. Fired? How could we possibly be fired?

This was our dream job, living aboard a yacht and taking people on sailing vacations in the most beautiful waters of the Caribbean. We were perma-vacationers with full-time pay. We'd been crewing sailboats successfully for almost two years, hosting over fifty charters,

1

with hundreds of happy guests. Our critiques were outstanding. Not one complaint—not from our employer, fellow crewmembers or charter guests. How could we possibly be fired?

We lived here, in this foreign country—the British Virgin Islands. We had lived here for seven years, from 1994 til now, 2001. We'd lived full-time on this yacht for the past year and a half. It was our home. Now we were being forced to leave? Where were we supposed to go? Didn't they understand we wanted to do this job for the rest of our lives? Didn't they know we loved this job, and our guests loved us? We'd received 'thank you' gifts, long letters of recommendation and lavish gratuities. How in the world did we go from our corporate lives and all our "stuff" to running that dilapidated beach bar to attaining our ultimate dream job as yacht crew—only to have it ripped from under us?

Shocked, we thought about all the water—eleven years of our lives together—that had passed under the bridge before we were suddenly homeless . . .

Little did we know, we'd still be in the yachting business almost twenty years later. But we didn't know that then. Heartbroken, we reminisced about our beginnings, way back in 1990 . . .

Windansea Rendezvous

"You seem like the kind of girl who'd love the Caribbean," Winston had mused, the first time I met him, back in May, of 1990. With that seemingly off-the-cuff statement, this tall, straight-backed, white side-burned guy projected our next twenty-five years together without having a clue. From strangers at Windansea Beach, in La Jolla, California, to lovers in the British Virgin Islands six months later, that begins our story. Meeting on that beach was fate.

Raised playing on rivers and lakes, and nowhere near a beach, I'm a Midwesterner born the middle child of five of loving parents, in Lakewood, Ohio, and raised in St. Charles, Missouri, near St. Louis.

I first fell in love with travel, in 1972, when my then-husband, Jim, and I drove toddler, Andrea, and newborn, Jason, from our two-year, army life in Tacoma, Washington, back to our home, in St. Charles, by way of San Diego and the western desert of Texas. We traveled those thirty-four hundred miles, with everything we owned—two babies, in a polo green Volkswagen bug, crowned with one huge, lumpy bundle of belongings, precariously strapped on, with a worn, drab, army tarp and a slew of ugly knots.

The ocean grabbed my soul as we were driving the coastline from the northwest water's edge to the beaches, of Southern California; I stood on a San Diego beach named Windansea and vowed when my children grew up, I'd live some day in Southern California, on this ocean that left me so breathless. But, we had two babies to raise and my husband's accounting career to return to, so the Midwest remained our home, for the next eighteen years. Windansea would have to wait.

Our annual trips to Grandma's, in Sarasota, Florida, nurtured my love of the water, as did Missouri's many scenic rivers. Sandwiched among garage sailing, dancing class, BMX racing, and cheerleading practice, most weekends would find our family traveling throughout Missouri, canoeing its many rivers. Even our annual family reunions were riverside, with all the cousins. Those child rearing years were magical. Camping in tents was a prerequisite, as was a tree swing over the water. Luggage was nonexistent; camping gear and a few, brown paper grocery sacks, with food, swimsuits, firewood, and black garbage bags for storm protection were all we needed.

And storm it did—unfortunately, right through my marriage. Like many complex, 1970s couples, we suffered through divorce. I was a full-time mom but somehow squeezed in a college degree in communications and business. I began my professional career at the "ancient" age of thirty-five at a terrific, St. Louis, public relations agency. As fate would have it, my work took me to California regularly on behalf of a banking client. I extended those trips to include reconnaissance missions for future career prospects and often got my fix of the ocean at Windansea while still raising my family. When I drove Andrea and Jason on a three-week road trip across the country to experience the Wild West and the mesmerizing Pacific Ocean, they caught the bug too. With Jason eager to become a scuba diver, the next summer we journeyed to Cozumel, Mexico, and experienced the wonders of snorkeling and scuba in the warm Caribbean.

The ocean remained my drug of choice. I've never kicked the habit.

Back in St. Louis, my children grown, I scoured southern California for a professional opportunity, exploring Malibu to San Diego. I begged my boss to open a West Coast office, but one California client does not a balance sheet make. It took a year, but my constant diligence paid off at just about the time Jason had forged his own trail to California and Andrea was attending St. Louis University. I landed my California dream at a major, San Diego, public relations firm, though with a 25 percent drop in salary (the "sun tax" they said).

I moved to San Diego, three blocks from Windansea Beach, and met Winston five months later.

Illusions plays a part

As I did every chance I had, I walked several blocks down from my new apartment to Windansea Beach. There the Pacific Ocean provided a fascinating show as it poured over huge boulders and shifted the sand into new formations along the coastline. It was one of the best surfing spots in southern Cal, with a constant, neighborhood crowd of sun worshipers playing in the sand, or surf.

On this May day, I was carrying my "bible," the book *Illusions: The Adventures of a Reluctant Messiah,* by Richard Bach. In *Illusions,* former mechanic and self-described messiah, Donald Shimoda, teaches a barnstorming pilot that people don't need airplanes to soar or wrenches to fix them, that dark clouds have meaning and messiahs can be found in the most unlikely of places. It's my bible because I can open it to any page and read a thought-provoking quote. A powerfully built, Hawaiian beach bum named Pete piped up that it was his favorite book too. When I responded, "Now that's a new pickup line," Pete quoted from *Illusions*. It was his favorite book. After a day of watching surfers, Pete asked me out dancing and gave me his company business card.

A week or two later, again at Windansea, Pete introduced me to his friend and partner, Winston, who almost immediately (and perhaps flippantly) invited me to go sailing in the British Virgin Islands that October. "You seem like the kind of girl who would like the Caribbean. Have you ever been sailing in a tropical paradise?" No, I hadn't, but, trying to imagine what paradise looked like, I smiled and said I'd think about it. But I secretly thought, *no chance am I passing this up. I have six months to get to know Winston and make sure he's a good guy.* Truth be told, he'd broken up with his girlfriend and needed to fill the spot to help pay for the charter.

Winston and I flirted on the beach several times after that. We joked occasionally about that British Virgin Islands trip but assumed, I guess, that we'd just run into each other on Windansea between smash-ball tournaments, or surfing wipeouts.

An avid snorkeler, even in that cold, Pacific water, with only five feet of visibility, I usually had my gear with me at the beach. One day, Pete borrowed my mask and snorkel to check out the bright orange garibaldi fish but returned with only my mask. The huge surf had ripped off the snorkel. Pete vowed to buy me a new one, but after a week, I was still swimming without it. My mask without its snorkel was like having lungs without a nose.

Aggravated, I dug out his business card and called. My goal was to get a new snorkel. The outcome: Winston answered the phone, told me that Pete wasn't there, and whisked away my heart, with his hour-long funny and captivating conversation. I don't recall everything we talked about. I just remember not wanting to hang up, ever, and him repeating, "You really do seem like someone who'd like the Caribbean."

I learned that Winston was the son of a prominent police officer who fought in World War II, in the Canadian Army. Winston grew up in the Maritime Provinces of Canada. His mother countered his dad's natural sternness, nurturing and influencing Winston's love of nature and adventure. She was his biggest supporter throughout his teens. His family home, with an older brother and younger sister, was in Fredericton, the capital city of New Brunswick.

"My childhood was filled with moose and bear adventures, in the woods around home, but I had even wilder fantasies," he told me. "One, as a preteen, I was dead set on going to California to find Haley Mills, the love of my life. I was sure she must live there because of her role in the movie *The Parent Trap!* My other, more grown-up dream was to join the U.S. Air Force." That he did.

After a stint at the University of New Brunswick, he took steps to become an airman. Winston emigrated to New Hampshire to live with his brother. When New Hampshire's air force recruiting office had met its quota for enlisted men, his girlfriend helped; she enlisted as well, which gave Winston his foot in the door. They married right after basic training. (Great reason for a marriage, right? Well, we all make mistakes.) Following initiation at Seymour Johnson Air Force Base, in North Carolina, Winston survived Vietnam as a combat engineer.

U.S. Air Force training in engineering helped Winston relocate to California, after the service. He and his wife settled in the Bay Area, close to the water, though most of it was 58 degrees. Ultimately, his marriage of convenience disintegrated, and he moved to Lake Tahoe. "That's when I figured out," Winston maintains, "that work and play can be synonymous. From being a full-time skier representing national brands on the pro circuit to managing ski lift operations at an Olympic resort, I played hard. Between skiing, I parlayed my engineering background into co-owning a construction management company in Tahoe, during the building boom of the early '70s."

When the boom stopped in the late '70s, Winston and his partner dropped out. They sold their company, moved to San Diego, and bought a forty-three-foot sailboat. With not one second of nautical training on ocean travel, they sailed this beauty down the Pacific Coast, through the Panama Canal, along the Windward and Leeward Islands, and up through the Bahamas to Florida.

After that year-long adventure, Winston returned to California a changed man. He settled in San Diego, right off La Jolla's spectacular Windansea Beach, and used his construction expertise—this time as an independent contractor. "Renovating historic buildings and finishing new, custom homes allowed me lots of time to go surfing and skiing," he said. The sailor inside him was thriving: Winston guided white water river trips, crewed on a sailing yacht based in Newport Beach and even one in the South Pacific for several months.

Then he found another lure—the warm turquoise waters of the Caribbean. Winston, with his friends, chartered sailboats, for a week at a time, in the British Virgin Islands. From Eastern Canada to California, to the South Pacific to the Caribbean, he was on his way to becoming the lead character in the movie *Captain Ron*.

Winston lived there at Windansea Beach, working and playing, for fifteen years. Waiting for me?

And then I called.

That phone call was the birth of the crazy couple we are today—and all because of a snorkel.

Our first sail together and more fate

That October, we chartered (boat-speak for "rented") a fifty-four-foot sailboat and sailed the British Virgin Islands, with some friends. We'd go sailing many more times, but this first trip introduced us to our future, watery life together.

The gleaming yacht was long and sleek, with five staterooms (bedrooms), four heads (bathrooms), a galley (kitchen with stove, fridge, and freezer that worked sometimes), and an inside U-shaped dining area. Outside, in what's called a cockpit, there were two long, nicely padded, emerald green benches and a huge wheel for steering, plus another table for eating, with the wind in our hair. Two large, white sails boasted green "Go Vacations" logos, as if to remind us we were on vacation. Dragging behind the sailboat was a dinghy (a small, inflatable boat) used to get us to and from shore when anchored in a bay. When underway, the most coveted seat in the house was the tip of the bow (pointy end of the boat), where our feet dangled over the edge and the waves splashed over us. I loved it!

During our seven-day charter, each British Virgin Island invited us to another new adventure: hiking the low, cactus-covered hills, swimming the warm crystal-clear water, snorkeling along the sea's surface eyeing tropical fish one hundred feet in any direction, and dancing barefoot into the night at crazy beach bars. Unhindered by the usual piles of "stuff" people acquire, islanders seemed genuinely happy with the simple life.

Sailing with Winston showed me several new sides of his personality. He liked running the show when we were sailing, as in ordering his "crew" to "throw your back into it!" when pulling up a sail, or grinding one in. And he loved showing off his mariner skills, as in sailing through an anchorage at full speed while flipping burgers on the grill simultaneously . . . not exactly appropriate or appreciated by the other boaters by the way. But hilarious to watch.

One highlight of our vacation was spending time at Pirates Pub, the quintessential "Jimmy Buffet style" bar on the tiny island of Saba Rock. Basically, a rocky point jutting out of the sea, with a rustic, wooden walkway around its front half, Pirates Pub had a substantial dock attached to it. Two floating platforms were chained together to house a multitude of dinghies arriving to party. Two picnic tables and a handful of barrel chairs (literally made from rum barrels and trimmed with dull-red leather padded seats) invited wet swimsuits and suntan lotion, as did a raggedy, hammock loveseat. The rocky path to the unisex bathroom labeled with a brass plaque, "La Pissoir," caught many a stumbling drunken visitor. Paper plates filled with "cheeseburgers in paradise" fare were shuffled out of the meager walk-up-and-order grill window without end. Signed dollar bills adorned every flat surface including the ceiling, and sailors could belly up to the big wooden bar or dance the night away to classic jukebox music.

We drank, swam around the island, and played with the talking, biting, singing, dancing parrots, Feather and Pita. We listened to weathered stories of treasure hunting on the sunken *SMS Rhone* from the iconic eighty-year-old pirate, Bert Kilbride, and his wife, Gayla, who owned the Rock, as it was locally known. Some of us even went scuba diving with the energetic old codger. (Gayla was half Bert's age and his fifth wife.) Bert and Gayla lived on the Rock with her seven-year-old grandson.

Returning home, I created a BVI memory by doctoring a postcard of Pirates Pub. It showed the owners arm in arm with friends in front of the Pirates Pub sign. I replaced the friends' faces with faces of Winston and me. That postcard, with our faces standing shoulder to shoulder with Bert and Gayla, hung framed on the kitchen wall in our home on Windansea. I didn't know it then, but our dream of an adventurous career unhindered by "stuff" had just been seeded.

Four years later, Winston and I would move to that very Rock, live with Bert and Gayla and run that pirate beach bar . . .

But first, that travel bug

During those four years, between many sixty-hour work weeks and visiting Andrea and Jason, Winston and I chiseled our travel legs. Amazingly, we were invited to sail across the Pacific from Hawaii to San Diego, in a fifty-four-foot sailboat. (Winston knew the owner.) Did we know what we were doing? Not exactly, but we couldn't pass up the chance and were quick learners. Our seven-man crew included two guys from New Zealand and a young woman just fresh from Antarctica.

In the middle of the Pacific crossing. Winston and Cynthia could go from swimsuits to foul weather gear in a matter of minutes.

That twenty-eight day sailing trip changed my psyche just as my road trip down the coast of California had in 1972. Feeling whales surfing alongside our sailboat and spying torpedo-like dolphins jetting under the sea illuminated with bioluminescence . . . how could I miss out on this magnificence? The Kiwis and "Antarctica" traveled the world, hitchhiking wherever they found a yacht needing delivery. Why couldn't I? They lived frugally, carried only a backpack, and enjoyed adventure after adventure. I came back home knowing I could live that way. Winston was still debating.

"I didn't know if I could live that way, but I must admit," he said, "when those guys drove off not knowing what was around the next corner, I was a little jealous."

Another winter, we trekked both islands of New Zealand with our new Kiwi buddies, almost getting annihilated by a virtual sea of sheep baaaaaa-baaaaa-baaaaaaing their way through a tiny village, herded by professional dogs that were intent on earning their living.

Our next vacation found us driving cross-country in our white-leathered, red, Mustang convertible to a family reunion, bungie jumping along the way, exploring the wonders of our national parks, including the Grand Canyon, Monument Valley and Mesa Verde. "Going through movie director John Ford's America in Monument Valley was a three hundred-mile side trip," Winston remembers, "but so worth it. I just sat there imagining John Wayne riding through that famous Navaho country. I'd seen nothing like it, not in real life anyway."

With us, it was never the destination . . . it was the journey. And that's been our mantra ever since.

After two years together, Winston and I moved into a condo overlooking Windansea Beach, a second-floor apartment with huge windows everywhere. I swear we could make love in every room gazing out at the sea. The glimmering Pacific seemed right at our feet, even inspiring our new phone number: 858-GLIMMER.

Every day we lived there was breathtaking: views of the ever-changing Pacific, whales migrating, rainbows that first appeared on the horizon and drove themselves right to our doorstep, and even just watching the traffic come to a standstill while passengers and drivers stood outside their cars to watch for a rare green flash on the horizon. Applause echoed down the street after each sunset. We were famous in the neighborhood for our large kite—a life-size osprey—flying off our rooftop, and regularly watched both man and seagull take second looks at it. Cyclers even fell off their bikes gazing up at our osprey. (That same kite would fly over our mega yachts years later, still with the same effect.)

The haunted Vulcan Hotel in Bathans, New Zealand, didn't scare the sheep one bit.

Sensational times were had at Windansea, with our party-loving next door neighbors, Ray and Kellie, and passionate Italian, Sandra, in the apartment below. Daughter, Andrea, moved to San Diego about that time, and she and her brother, Jason, visited often. My two sisters and I spent a rare, intimate week together there, and friends, Betty and Dan, from St. Louis, got engaged on our balcony. Life—with wine, lots of wine—was good. Together we'd all dream up new places to play, and our wise Italian would unceasingly put things in perfect perspective. "Only you have the power to make your dreams happen," she reminded us. Winston and I used to sit on the balcony, thinking, *where could we possibly go after this?*

A sneak preview of life to come

After four years of love and work intermingled with traveling and sailing, the summer of 1994 found us again in the Caribbean, this time with my sister and brother-in-law, Suzanne and Paul, plus our friends, Tim and Barb. This trip would change our lives.

Naturally, as with every sailing trip, we anchored off Saba Rock. (Anchoring entails dropping a heavy hook into the water and securing the boat to the sea bottom, rather than tying the boat to a dock.) I went scuba diving with a couple whose story intrigued me. They had taken a vacation in the Caribbean, gone back to Minneapolis, sold their home and bought a sailboat in Florida, even though they hadn't the vaguest idea how to sail. While they were taught sailing, they also took scuba diving courses and learned underwater photography. Their plan was to sail the world, making money by taking people scuba diving and photographing them. What guts! The wheels in my head started turning. Working and traveling the oceans simultaneously . . . hmmmm.

After the six of us rode our dinghy into Pirates Pub & Grill and drank a few Cruzan rum and tonics, owners, Bert and Gayla, asked us to help move a new hot tub up the hill to the top of the Rock. Payment would be rum and signed T-shirts. It wasn't a long way—the island was only three quarters of an acre at low tide—but the transport meant lifting the heavy tub out of a boat, onto a rickety dock, and up a rocky and winding dirt path, which was, beyond question, more like a ditch.

That good deed earned us all a chance to see the off limits back island and top of Saba Rock, Bert and Gayla's living quarters. "Cynthia and I maneuvered on a wobbling, makeshift dock past a disheveled palm frond hut. It had a corrugated metal roof and a foundation of debris, rocks, and driftwood. A sailboat mast, otherwise known as the tall stick that holds up the sails on a boat, laid sidewise and jutted out over the water, supporting one side of the hut. It was pretty cool.

"Down the way, a couple of small shacks housed generators and water makers. Right next to them on the water's edge was Pee Rock, as the locals called it. That's where they peed when the pub's sole *pissoir* was busy. Ha! A large, stone cistern holding the island's supply of water, and a wooden storage shed housing Bert's treasures from the sunken *Rhone,* accented the scene."

From what we could see, Gayla and Bert's living quarters were meager—a stone house, maybe two rooms, with a smattering of actual green grass and an eight-foot-tall palm tree—Gayla's pride and joy and the only tree on the island. A small, black cat named Gonja curled in residence in an inviting hammock stretched over the corner of the yard. Scattered about were relics of the *Rhone* and many, many pink and white, curled, conch shells. Most enticing (besides that new hot tub) was the outdoor shower. *What pleasure it must be to live on an island and shower with only nature as your curtain,* I thought.

This was our first look at our next home, but we were oblivious.

We should have been paying more attention.

As of November 1, 1994
Winston Hovey and Cynthia Zvanut

Have Moved To Paradise

Where...　　*The British Virgin Islands in the Caribbean*
　　　　　　　Longitude: 64°W Latitude: 18°N

Address...　*P.O. Box 40*
　　　　　　Virgin Gorda
　　　　　　British Virgin Islands

Phone...　　*809-495-9537*　　　　*Fax... 809-495-7549*

From...　　*Windansea Beach, 214 Rosemont Street*
　　　　　　La Jolla, California 92037 USA

We are charting an incredible new course, managing and maintaining the tiny island of Saba Rock (pictured here), a historic anchorage in the sailing and scuba mecca of the BVI, located just east of the island of Virgin Gorda.

Chapter 2
Work a Month, off a Month

*You are never given a wish without also being given
the power to make it come true.*

—Richard Bach

*Dubbed the last pirate of the Caribbean, the Keeper of the
Wrecks by the Queen of England, the Oldest SCUBA Diver
by Guinness Book of World Records and a national treasure
by the Governor of the British Virgin Islands, Bert Kilbride
welcomed Winston and Cynthia to his island, Saba Rock.*

San Diego to Saba Rock, British Virgin Islands
August 1994 - November 1994

We get the nudge

Only a few months after returning from our sailing trip in the
British Virgin Islands, with its tour of Saba Rock, my position as
vice president of my public relations firm suddenly disappeared. I
was laid off and devastated. To make matters worse, Winston's work

was stagnant, typical of the construction industry, which was either chicken or feathers.

In the normal panic most people go through when thrust into unemployment, I dove into searching for my next position, naturally in my expertise—PR and marketing. A driven, type-A personality, I could think of nothing else. My clients had been in high tech, dairy, banking, and, serendipitously, the tourism industries. By the grace of God and constant networking, I was offered a marketing position at one of the most prestigious resorts in Southern California. I breathed easy again.

As I was negotiating the employment contract for the next leg of my career, destiny intervened. Passionate Italian, Sandra, heard about my layoff and had witnessed the stress of my career over the years. One afternoon, she piped up with a bizarre request. "Hey," she said, "show me that photo album from your last Caribbean sailing vacation."

She zeroed in on the photo of me with a small, typed advertisement tacked on a rustic wall. (Winston had taken that photo on the day we moved the hot tub as a joke for me to show my boss.) The ad headlined, "Come and work in Paradise." The ad continued, "Must have good math skills, common sense, willing to work long hours in split shifts, patient with the public and willing to live on Saba Rock. Spanish language is a plus. See the manager."

"This is it. This is what you should do," Sandra prophesied. With the animation of a little child eyeing an amusement park for the first time, she blurted, "You've always talked about living in the Caribbean. Here's your chance. Just go."

"Cynthia and I both just stared at her, befuddled. We sat there in our glass condo, with that breathtaking view of the boulder-strewn, sandy beach, surrounded by our "life"—big screen TV and grand piano, antiques and original paintings, closets full of clothes, miles of Cynthia's shoes, (Got to sneak in a dig, whenever I can, about all those shoes!), king-size bed, the dresser I'd owned for thirty years, our glass dining table fingerprinted as usual and a kitchen stocked with every known gadget invented."

"And the best-looking dishes I'd ever owned," I piped in.

Sandra told us her story. She was raised in Northern Italy, a land she cherished. She left as a young professional and made a career in the United States, mostly in California. Several times she could have returned to Italy, but she'd continually postponed her trip. "Duty called," she said, "but I dreamed of the day when I would get back there again."

As life often does, it hindered living. Sandra never made it back to Italy. She had a friend beckoning her to come back to her beloved roots, but she let the invitation pass her by. When she retired and finally could take the time, "I had too much baggage to leave." Sandra was laden with personal challenges, bad health, lots of "stuff," a huge mortgage on a big house that wouldn't sell and meager financial options.

"I missed my chance, kids," she sadly warned us. "Don't miss yours." We let her message sink in.

People often say, "Maybe next year . . ." But they'll be older next year. "Someday . . ." But what if someday never comes? We never would have moved to the islands if it had not been for Sandra's kick in the butt. To this day, when people ask how we did it, she's the first person we credit.

Armed with Sandra's confidence and our own exuberance, we looked out at the ocean, took deep breaths, and dialed the island.

The interview

Gayla answered the phone—yes, the same Gayla whose picture stood shoulder to shoulder with ours in that doctored photo on our kitchen wall—and, yes, the Pirates Pub management job was still open. She had been advertising it in the local *Beacon*, as required by law, but had no qualified takers.

In more encouraging news, she had a place for Winston too. She needed someone to handle island operations such as cisterns that leaked, water makers that went awry, and generators that needed service in the middle of the night. There were bars to be built, stools to be hammered, and the whole top of the island to be cleared.

The icing on the cake was that Gayla informed us that the position managing the restaurant was work a month, be off a month. What more could we ask for? Gayla employed another woman, who would work opposite months. She said job sharing went very smoothly, plus, she said with a smile, "The island's problems sometime can be so intense (like employee drama, food shortages, or empty cisterns), you'll need thirty days to recover!" Hmmm, a red flag?

We told her we were part of that crew who'd helped install her hot tub, and she instantly knew us—or at least our muscles. She invited us to fly down for an interview (on our dime). We agreed.

We had just passed the first hurdle. One of many, it turned out.

Gayla's first advice to us over the phone was to read *Don't Stop the Carnival,* by Herman Wouk. She said if we still wanted the jobs after that, they were ours. That book is still required reading for anyone considering moving to the islands. We laughed our way through the entire thing, reading about a middle-aged, New York press agent who, on sudden impulse, leaves behind the rat-race and runs away to reinvent himself as a resort owner in the Caribbean. The jaw-dropping, poignant, and hilarious misadventures of his career change turned out to be the precursor for our life on Saba Rock, more realistically than we could imagine.

Reconnaissance

Since we were paying for this trip to the islands, we made it a reconnaissance mission, learning everything we could about working and living in the British Virgin Islands. We chartered a small sailboat out of Spanish Town, Virgin Gorda, and played detective. We sailed to North Sound, Virgin Gorda, and anchored off Bitter End Resort, across from Saba Rock. It was the off-season, with few tourists, which gave people time to talk to us.

We gingerly spoke to some Bitter End personnel about the good, bad, and ugly of working and living in the BVI. One particularly candid guy told us that interacting well with the islanders was the biggest key to working there. "Life here is a certain way," he said. "You can't bring your American hotshot business attitude and think it will work.

"The folks who work at these resorts are not motivated by money," he continued, "like Americans. They don't need fancy clothes and thirty pairs of shoes or have mortgages and car payments. Several families usually share a car and just park it on the street with the keys."

More advice: "You have to figure out other ways to get your employees to do what you want. If you can master the art of managing islanders here and earn their friendship," he said with emphasis, "you can work anywhere in the Caribbean." We took his advice to heart.

We also looked up the uncle of a friend who had lived for years in Leverick Bay, on the island of Virgin Gorda, right down the water from Saba Rock. (Leverick was a community of ex-patriots who settled in for the long term.) We sat in the cockpit of Tom's boat and listened to story after story of island life reality.

Tom suggested being discreet about research; islanders, understandably, didn't want outsiders taking their jobs. However, our computer and engineering skills set us apart from most of the available workforce applying to Saba Rock. That's why Gayla could justify hiring us.

Our "godfather," as we nicknamed him, encouraged our new adventure. He helped us create a list of things that would be completely unnecessary, what we needed to bring with us, and how to get it there. Godfather Tom would be giving us valuable clues to island living for many years to come.

Off we went to meet Gayla on Saba Rock. We tied our sailboat's ten-foot dinghy to the wobbling dock and walked through the bar.

Gayla greeted us with cigarette and sea breeze cocktail in hand. She took one look at us and could tell we were serious.

Next came the tour.

Previewing our new home

First, walking behind the Pirates Pub bar down a dock and up a flight of stairs, we toured the restaurant office and met my counterpart, a friendly and cheerful artist from St. Louis, like me. The businesslike computers, printers, and phones were matched with a colorful, Caribbean backdrop that Gayla had created herself. Beautifully faux painted walls, trimmed in yellow and aqua, showcased her collection of ceramic masks. Above the desk was a picture window that lived up to its name; its picture was the graduated shades of pale greens to deep aqua, crystal-clear Caribbean Sea, the reef, and neighboring islands framed by gently waving coconut palms. Also tucked into the lower corner of the picture was that tiny grass hut we'd sneak previewed on our hot tub delivery, just four months earlier.

Gayla gave us a choice of where to live. Weird that on this tiny island there would be more than one choice. We could choose the apartment below the office, a small, oddly shaped room similar to a crawlspace under a staircase but with a shower, toilet, and hot plate—not our romantic image of life in the Caribbean. "Dark and dingy," Winston labeled it under his breath.

Then the other choice—the hut.

We walked toward it, across some rather bouncy planks, trying to stay upright and not fall in the water. The tiny, wood-framed hut balanced itself half on a floating dock, half on that horizontal sailboat mast. Palm fronds nailed to the frame kept the wind out—or most of it. A gray, corrugated tin roof kept the rain out—or some of it. A Dutch door, a piece of unfinished plywood sliced in half and hanging on rusted hinges, announced the entry.

Even before we entered, we'd made it home.

Inside, the walls were made of colorful, cotton fabric stapled to two-by-fours. That's it for walls—no drywall, no paneling, no fiberboard, just 100 percent cotton fabric. It was like material for a summer dress. The windows were basically a sheet of plywood on a hinge you kept propped up with a stick when you wanted to see out and closed when it rained. There were high openings near the roofline for air and light.

The kitchen area was clothed in vibrant aqua and white floral cotton. It resembled a miniature kitchen, with a tiny sink, stove and fridge. A weathered driftwood shelf made a cabinet for a few plates. One pot and one skillet hung on hooks under the shelf—about as basic as you could get. The bedroom was another treat, a square room set off by bright, royal blue and white hibiscus fabric walls and graced by a gently curving, brown wicker headboard facing a double bed. That headboard was the only real furniture in the room, the focal point of the hut unless you counted the breathtaking view.

The hut had a closet, to my surprise, tucked right in front of the toilet—and I mean *right* in front. Speaking of toilets, our little shack included running water (from the cistern) plus a light bulb, or two, powered by the ever-humming generator that created the island's electricity.

I was in heaven. Winston was in shock.

"Well, maybe it had some potential, but, man, was it rough," he muttered. "Considering I came from a background of building beautiful, custom homes, in Southern California, this felt like a major setback. But what the hell, it was paradise."

Gayla got us back on track by outlining the next steps. She would apply for work permits allowing us to work on Saba Rock. We would have to leave the islands until those permits were approved, possibly sixty days from then. Meanwhile, we had to get physical exams, drug tests, AIDS tests, and police records saying we were good citizens, with no history of arrest.

Back to reality

We returned our chartered sailboat to Spanish Town, bid good-bye to Godfather Tom (after a few more million questions amid some rum and tonics), and boarded the plane back to San Diego. As we flew at thirty thousand feet, we made plans, to do lists, what-to-bring lists, and what-would-actually-fit lists.

Our minds seemed to fly way higher than we were.

The wait

We toasted Sandra with champagne as soon as we returned to Windansea. Telling the kids we were moving was easy; they saw it as their new holiday option. Prematurely, Ray and Kellie planned a farewell party, and we drafted our moving announcement.

Then we waited. And waited. And waited.

SABA ROCK

We passed our physical exams and drug and AIDS tests with no complications and applied for our police reports.

One day, Winston sheepishly mumbled that he was concerned he might have a bevy of unpaid parking tickets, from years gone by, that could keep him from having a clean police record.

Now he tells me! I read him quite the riot act. If his antics kept us from going to the Caribbean, I'd never get over it. A few days later, Winston got a call saying his report was fine and ready to be picked up. When Winston asked about my report, the policeman responded mysteriously, "Have her give us a call."

It seemed, after harassing Winston to no end about his lackadaisical responsibility to himself and his government, I was the one with a warrant out for my arrest. Turns out I had a taillight violation from two years before that I'd never reported fixed. (Note: when a cop tells you to report a repair, do it.)

You must know Winston to imagine his reaction at hearing this news. "Well, well, well, what do you know? Miss Goody Two-Shoes has a record! After all that crap about me being the villain around here. Soooo, the San Diego Police Department has been looking for you, eh? Boy, I'm going to remember this one for a long, long time. You'll be paying, girl, and paybacks are hell." He hasn't let me forget it to this day.

I appeared in court, loaded for bear. For Pete's sake, I'd never been notified about the outstanding warrant, even when I'd been stopped for a speeding ticket! I thought that a fair rebuttal. "This was so funny," Winston interrupts. "As she's sitting there waiting her turn and practicing all her arguments, the judge suddenly (and loudly) demands this gentle guy in front of Cynthia be carried away in handcuffs by the bailiff—for simply asking to go move his car. She was up next. 'Guilty, Judge,' she whimpered, and paid her fine. I loved the whole thing."

Meanwhile, I was still negotiating with the San Diego resort director who wanted to hire me. Feeling bad that I'd leave the resort stranded, if those work permits came through, I went to lunch with my potential boss and came clean. I explained the Saba Rock opportunity and that I was in limbo, having to wait sixty days for confirmation. I suggested he might want to hire another candidate rather than count on me. Thanking me for my candor, he said I'd be crazy to stay in

San Diego when the Caribbean beckoned so realistically. It was a risky conversation but worth it.

For forty-five days, we waited. Our emotions rode a roller coaster of anticipation and elation, trepidation and downright fear, eagerness to be gone, and then sadness to be leaving our family and friends. Could we do this or not? Should we, or shouldn't we? Would we be OK, or hate it? Did everybody think we were stupid, or did they wish they were us? How would we get along with only one bathroom? What was life with no TV news? Would we get island fever or never want to return to the States?

Then we got the call. Winston answered. "Your work permits have been approved." After a long silence, Gayla nervously questioned, "You *are* still coming, aren't you?"

She heard a quiet, unsteady "oh . . . yeah." Winston hung up, looked at me with that fifty-yard stare, and quivered. "Well, I guess we're moving to the Caribbean." After a few minutes of flat-out fear, we celebrated.

Dumping our stuff, cold turkey

We decided to store only our photographs, ski equipment, and a few pieces of artwork. Some people leaving the United States put everything they own in storage, thinking they would use it when they return, but we were not planning on returning.

We reviewed our "take with," "store at," "kids want," "give away to," "sell" lists and shed our belongings. Most people think this would be the hardest thing about moving to a remote place. But for us, it was relatively easy—probably because we were so ready to go.

First, we packed what we needed, fitting it into six UPS boxes. The only self-indulging thing I packed was a sampling of my prized, sunset-colored dishes. Most items were quite mundane: a few shorts and tops, swimsuits, flip flops, tennis shoes, boat shoes, snorkel gear and favorite tools. We collected some toiletries and medicines that might not be available and three hanging caddies with various-sized plastic pockets for storing clothes and such, since there were no drawers in the hut. After much deliberation, we each packed one pair of jeans (which were never worn again).

Then we distributed the rest of our "stuff."

My daughter, Andrea, the minimalist, chose to inherit little besides some photos. My son, Jason, was eager to fill his apartment and took everything he could cram inside and on top of our two hundred thousand-mile Honda station wagon, and off he went, happy as a musician with a new tune.

We shipped our antique Knabe grand piano (which wouldn't fit in Jason's digs) to friend, Betty, with the thought that if Jason wanted it someday, he could get it back. We shipped my parents' antique four-poster bedroom set to my brother in Texas and stored our family photos at my gracious sister's in St. Louis. Our clothes and probably sixty pairs of shoes got new owners, at battered women's centers and shelters. Our ski equipment took up residence, with our ski buddies, Ray and Kellie.

One of the toughest separations was selling our red, GT Mustang convertible. Watching it cruise away down Neptune Drive along the ocean and into the sunset with someone else in those white-leather seats was hard to take.

At a small garage sale, we sold many more things. Selling the old tarnished and broken trinkets from our traditional Christmas tree was the only thing that made me sad. The woman who bought them offered her phone number if I ever wanted them back. Though very comforting at the time, I never used it.

Last, we contracted with an estate sale company to take all that remained. We went to our old coffee hangout early one Saturday morning and came home that afternoon to an empty abode. Not even a paperclip in the junk drawer.

That night, our friends and kids threw a wild and wonderful farewell party, with lots of toasts and laughter and no tears. The next day, we flew off to our new life.

Winston and Cynthia's first Caribbean home on the tiny island of Saba Rock was situated in the North Sound of Virgin Gorda, in the British Virgin Islands, east of the U.S. Virgin Islands and south of Puerto Rico.

Winston and Cynthia eagerly adopted a permanent dress code of shorts, sarongs, t-shirts and flip flops as they learned the ropes of managing cheeseburger-in-paradise Pirates Pub and Grill.

Chapter 3
The Job Site

Argue for your limitations,
and sure enough, they're yours.

—Richard Bach

Proud as a pirate, Winston relaxes in his new Caribbean front yard.

Saba Rock, British Virgin Islands
November 1994 – December 1994

Getting there

Considering it was our transition from glass condo to grass hut, you'd think our airline flight would be traumatic. But, to the contrary, it was so without incident we could have been puddle jumping from San Diego to LA.

We traveled from San Diego through Miami and Puerto Rico to the U.S. Virgin Islands and St. Thomas's airport terminal, back then virtually a Quonset hut. A Volkswagen guided the plane to the one and only gate.

"Riding in our taxi from the airport through the neighborhoods of St. Thomas," Winston says, "I still remember the feeling in the pit of my stomach as I looked out at the ramshackle houses and the cows and goats wandering the gutted roads. Straight from pristine La Jolla, we saw our vision of paradise radically transforming to reality."

Oh my god, what had we done?

After spending the night in St. Thomas, we ferried to Tortola, in the British Virgin Islands, where we were to meet Gayla, our new boss. The forty-five-minute ride, on Smith's Ferry, was warm and windy— and late (as usual, we learned). We rode on the top level of the ferry, in the open air, so as not to miss a thing. Deckhands, with gallon jugs in hand, passed out endless cocktails of rum punch. Colorful West Indians overflowed the seats, and reggae encouraged everyone to jiggle and jive.

Gayla greeted us at the Village Cay Marina's bar in Roadtown, the BVI capital. Village Cay, the lively, familiar yachting center where we chartered our sailboats, helped ease our jitters. We piled into her thirty-foot boat, *Pelican*, Saba's official "truck," and unleashed the dock lines. Off we roared, jostling for forty-five minutes across Sir Francis Drake Channel and the North Sound toward our new home, the three-quarters-of-an-acre island of Saba Rock. We relaxed and then filled with excitement. Our next stop was Pirates Pub and our own little palm frond hut.

Our island mates

We lived with an icon.

Our eighty-year-old landlord, Bert, could swim before he could walk. His mom made him a makeshift snorkeling mask when he was the ripe, old age of eight, and that lit the fire for his lifelong scuba-diving adventures. Bert had been a treasure seeker in the islands over fifty years, charting one hundred thirty-eight shipwrecks. He was made Receiver of the Wrecks, by Queen Elizabeth in 1967.

Bert had purchased and developed two barren islands in the BVI, one as a scuba destination hotel. He owned Kilbride's Dive, a scuba diving tour business, for thirty years and had sold it just a few years before we arrived. He created the Resort Course for beginner divers, now taught worldwide, and earned a national award for diving education.

The governor of the BVI titled Bert a living legend, and, for his ninetieth birthday, the *Guinness Book of World Records* would proclaim him the oldest scuba diver in the world. A good friend of Jacques Cousteau, Bert had a date to go diving with Jean-Michel Cousteau for his hundredth birthday.

Bert and Gayla had been married for seven years. His age of eighty and her forty-six made for great island lore. Gayla opened Pirates Pub because people kept boating up to their island home, asking if it was a bar. Why not take advantage of the obvious opportunity? Gayla hated people, though, and she was the first to admit it. She rarely walked through Pirates Pub, and she'd wring your neck if you dared point her out as the owner. She was cynical and suspect of most people in general and employees in particular, daily expecting them to steal her profits away, bit by bit, toilet paper roll by bottle of beer.

I detected over time that our boss, Gayla, hailed from Idaho and had been married before but divorced early. Gayla raised two boys alone under tough circumstances with little money, but her ingenuity and persevering spirit carried her through. At one point, she was living in a car, and selling scrimshaw for a living. With her sons grown and independent, she moved to the islands to work as a diver. Tragically, both of Gayla's sons died in separate car accidents as young men. She had been planning a trip across the United States with her second son right before he perished. She inherited grandson, Tyrell, at that time.

There was nothing Gayla wouldn't conquer, and I respect her to this day for that trait. She taught herself everything about computers while living on the Rock. Then she figured out digital photography and video editing as well. "I just keep using the undo buttons till I get it right," she told me. Gayla taught me a freedom with computers I still use today.

Mischievous, seven-year-old Tyrell lived the life of a Robert Lewis Stephenson character. Lizards and fish were his playmates and the island his romping grounds. He was curious about the contents of our little house, with its palm frond sides and unfinished, plywood Dutch door, but only once came barging in. After that, he'd come knockin'.

Tim, the grill manager, didn't live on Saba Rock but was there probably ten hours almost every day. Hailing from Idaho, Tim was Gayla's nephew. A small, wiry guy, with a huge grin and a low, distinctive "He He" guttural laugh, Tim was one of the kindest and most goodhearted people we had ever met.

"Maybe Tim had his own private stash of something that kept him smiling," Winston slipped in with a smirk. "Tim had patience for everything—and that's saying something in the Caribbean!" His rough exterior hid a sincere kindheartedness. We could count on Tim to make any bad situation lighter, funnier and, consequently, easier to tackle. "He He," Winston reproduced quietly.

Polly want a rum drink

Our feathery friends, Feather and Pita, held court daily at the Rock. Their perch swung above a natural pond which tucked into the rocky island jutting through the bar. Sometimes a fish, or tiny octopus, magically would show up in the pond; no one knew how—or so they said.

"Feather was a beautiful, full-grown, blue and green macaw, my favorite," recalls Winston. "She'd lived at the bar since its beginning and thought she owned the place. Happily perched on the long rail of driftwood in the open area, above the rock fountain, Feather would chime in whenever Jimmy Buffet played. It was a riot! She'd rock back and forth, throwing her weight, until her perch was swinging and swaying to the island beat, all the time jabbering away. Feather would climb onto anyone's shoulder and sit for hours, if you let her. I loved that bird.

"Pita, the African Grey, was a pissed off pirate bird. Pita regularly took his anger out on people's fingers, even if they were just pointing at him. Maybe it was because Feather got most of the attention, or maybe because Feather was prettier. Possibly, it had to do with me antagonizing him so much. (I got in trouble for this on a regular basis.) I loved teasing Pita with a plastic cup. When he'd finally snatch it from me, he'd rip it to shreds. A tattered plastic cup in the claws of a parrot can make an amazing amount of clatter. Speaking of clatter, Pita could talk up a storm, but only between 8:00 a.m. to 10:00 a.m., before the bar doors opened. He'd croon melodiously and gossip away, chattering about Africa probably. Then he was mute the rest of the day—aggravating as hell."

My workweek

As Gayla explained it, managing the pub would be a piece of cake. Our job-share arrangement was thirty days on, thirty days off. During my month on, I'd officially be on duty from 10:00 a.m., when I picked up the crew, until 10:00 p.m., when, if lucky, I could sneak back to my bed in the hut.

Keeping in touch . . . 1994-95
Cynthia writing postcards to snail mail back to the U.S.

The pub had one little rule that made sailors really happy—but me, not so much. The bar doesn't close till the last person leaves. Some nights ended at four in the morning—hence, the month on/month off work schedule. Gayla maintained that no one could stand to do this "piece of cake" job without a thirty-day "weekend" to recuperate.

My basic work schedule, including driving the dinghy over to Bitter End's dock to pick up the cooks and bartenders every morning, rarely changed:

Monday meant inventory. Staff counted every hamburger bun, beer bottle, toilet paper roll, and so on and gave me reports. I had to double check almost everything. Tuesday was phone day. I'd telephone our myriad suppliers, in Roadtown and Spanish Town, and order all the foodstuff, booze, and supplies needed to bring our inventory back up to par.

Wednesday, the supply boats arrived at neighboring Bitter End to unload all our items onto the dock there. Winston and one of our crew would drive the bar's work boat, the *Pelican,* over to the Bitter End and load up supplies for the new week. Remember, we're talking about perhaps fifty cases of beer, twenty cases of liquor, and boxes upon boxes of groceries and paper products. As soon as the load was well-balanced and secure, Winston would drive across the water to Saba Rock and offload everything onto the pub's dock. I'd check the goods against my order and the invoice as Tim, the grill aficionado, carried them into storage.

All this would be going on while helping sailors dock their dinghies, greeting customers, serving drinks, cooking cheeseburgers, autographing T-shirts, answering tourists' questions, and stopping crew fights, often simultaneously. It could be a rather kinetic atmosphere.

Thursday, I went to Roadtown via a dinghy, ferry, and taxi to do the banking, plus shop for all the things the supply boats forgot to bring. Friday was payday, tallying employees' hours, recording social security tax payments, and writing paychecks. Once a month, I tallied and paid company taxes due the government, too. Saturday was catch up day, and for Sunday, no activities were scheduled.

All-Hell-Breaks-Loose Day, as we called it, was not a regularly scheduled event. It would appear without notice to wreak havoc on any day of the week and the disaster *du jour* always took precedence. By the end of thirty days straight without a break, ten in the morning to often midnight or later, I was practically frothing at the mouth for my month-long weekends.

Don't Stop the Carnival proves a primer for Winston's job

Winston's schedule was much less specific than mine due to the nature of the position. His hours were shorter than mine, but he didn't get those thirty days off either. He had daily and weekly scheduled maintenance on water makers, generators, cisterns, and plumbing, plus unloading the ferry's order of provisions each week. But, invariably, it was the unexpected projects cropping up that kept him swinging hammers and adjusting wrenches (and often his attitude), just like in Gayla's required reading, *Don't Stop the Carnival*.

Whether it was subbing as a bar back because some employee didn't show, assisting drunk customers into, or out of, their dinghies, planning pirate parties, or pulling some high jinx to torment the cooks, Winston was invariably interrupted for a more important task.

"Create a gate here, we're out of water, build a new bar there, the toilet's overflowing, repaint these fifty chairs, there's no electricity, repair these barrel tables, the dinghy is sinking, make Feather a new perch, bring a crowd over from Bitter End, Bert lost his gold coin under the dock, repack these cases of beer, the dogs are loose, the dock just broke . . . ," rattles off Winston. "These were the normal everyday honey-do projects.

"Thank God for Ralph, from nearby Necker Island, Mr. Fix-it in the flesh. Whenever I was stuck on something, here would come Ralph. I was amazed by the little tool he'd whip off his belt—the famous Leatherman, the go-to tool for anyone living in the Caribbean. He slipped that thing in and out of its black leather case, I bet, a hundred times a day. I was infatuated. To this day, I'm never without one—unless I've forgotten and left it attached to my belt when I go through an airport checkpoint. (I've lost a couple that way.)"

One of Winston's most colorful and long-running projects was Gayla's request to clear the junk off the top of the Rock. "That junk pile was made up of everything that had blown up on the Rock, or been abandoned there by any Tom, Dick, or Harry," Winston says, shaking his head. "It included every leftover piece of construction material ever brought to the island, every battered piece of furniture and rusty metal hinge that ever graced the restaurant, and every worn-out piece of equipment that had ever died there. It made for some great building materials. Mooring balls, line, netting, driftwood, old pieces of dock—if you needed to build something, you wouldn't find it there, but you'd probably find something that would do. *Don't Stop the Carnival* to a tee.

"Gayla wanted the pile burned, but I had some real concerns. The wind almost continually blew fifteen knots (about 17.2 mph) in the direction of the Bitter End Resort's hotel rooms and restaurant. To smother them with smoke from our junkyard would piss off some very powerful people. Bitter End's execs already labeled Saba Rock an eyesore that polluted its neighborhood with raucous music and drunken sailors. It's not good to add smoke to the fire.

"Timing was crucial. On just that day when the wind decided to die, I would need to burn debris. I'd have to drop everything else and start the fire. Inevitably, the project would be stopped abruptly by a ranting and raving Bert, a pack rat who didn't want a single thing destroyed. Bert cherished everything. Gayla hated all of it. I muddled about between the two of them."

On the Rock, Winston soon figured out that almost nothing worked, or what did was about to break, and that most things were held together with rusty safety pins—particularly the ice makers.

"God, I hated those ice makers," Winston says, rolling his eyes. "We had two ice-making machines, and at least one was usually on the blink.

When both died concurrently, which was often, I was elected to make the ice run. There I'd be, in a dinghy piled high with five dollar bags of melting ice, racing to get from the store back to the Rock, before having to wade through melted ice in the dinghy. Lugging ice was one of the most hated tasks at the pub. I swear, if you owned a shed full of ice makers, you'd be a rich man in North Sound."

Oddly, one of Winston's favorite jobs was loading up the dinghy with a dozen, yellow, five-gallon diesel fuel containers, hauling them across the Sound to the fuel dock, lining them up on the dock, filling each one, reloading the heavy tanks into the tender, driving back to the Rock, and then unloading them, helped by Tim, the grill maestro, because it got him off the Rock and out of earshot of those "I need you now" commands and honey-do projects, for at least a couple hours.

Town day

The best day of my week was town day, because I got to get off the Rock. Each Thursday, Winston would dinghy me over to Bitter End's dock, where I'd catch the 8:00 a.m. North Sound Express Ferry to Tortola. Forty-five minutes later, I'd arrive near the airport at the east end of the island to meet a taxi. The taxi would drive me the scenic thirty minutes to Roadtown, the BVI's capital, on the island of Tortola. We meandered along the coast over a windy, bumpy, semi-paved and mostly potholed road, the driver negotiating with stubborn goats and sheep and chickens and cattle all the way.

Once in town, I'd have eight to twelve stops to make on foot, all before catching the 3:15 p.m. ferry back to Virgin Gorda. First stop was always the bank. I'd be carrying around twenty thousand dollars in cash, in my purse. Depositing the pub's weekly revenue was my top priority. I continued on to Island Hardware, the marine store, the drugstore, Reese's and Tico's liquor stores, Bobby's Market, Bolo Department Store, Roadtown Wholesale, and Supa Value food market. Near Supa,

I often unwound a certain large, skinny, black and white cow from the tree where she was tethered. She had a habit of pacing in a circle.

My shopping list was quite specific. But if a store had something that was even remotely close to what I needed, I bought it. I never bothered asking if they had what I wanted in the back room, or would they be getting it in soon. I just bought what would do and crossed it off the list. I'd learned that if I tried to find *exactly* what I wanted at another store, when I came back for the one close, it would be gone. I adopted this lesson for life: Close is good enough.

Lugging all my packages while I shopped was impossible. So, I'd pick a corner in the drugstore and just stack my bags there. Then go to another store and return with more packages. Stack them and leave for more shopping. The owner didn't mind, and no one ever bothered a thing. If I was lucky and had the time, I'd reward myself at Capriccio's with a thin-crust pizza, something unheard of in North Sound, or maybe I'd choose a rum chocolate malt from the ice-cream stand near the ferry dock. Then I'd pay a taxi driver to help carry my load out to the ferry, which gave me a twenty-minute rest before landing in Spanish Town, Virgin Gorda—not home yet.

A personable taxi driver named Thomas dependably would be there, to pick up me and my treasures. He'd drive me across the glorious, mountainous spine of Virgin Gorda to Gun Creek, the end of the road, spewing the island's latest gossip all along the way. That ride highlighted my week. We'd unload the booty, and I'd buy Thomas a Carib beer while we waited for the next link. The Bitter End Ferry ran regularly to Gun Creek to accommodate commuting employees and on Thursdays, me. I'd load everything, take the short ride, and then unload it again for the sixth time, onto Bitter End's dock.

Winston would meet me at Bitter End with the dinghy, and together we'd load all my accomplishments of the day. (Sometimes, I'd be hauling four, fifty-pound car batteries, or two hundred feet of cabling, once even a palm tree.) Then we'd motor to the pub and, yes, unload one last time. Exhausted yet exhilarated, I loved these shopping days.

One of our best "town days," in Roadtown, Tortola, was the day we met Jane, an outspoken, brash scuba diver on her way to town to attain a newly required stamp on her papers, as were we. All of us were commiserating about the BVI government requiring at least one too many hoops, with their need for officially rubber-stamping every document we owned. Jane worked for the scuba company near the Rock. She hailed from England, by way of South Africa, and had such a crass, raucous personality, we were almost embarrassed to be seen with her. But her hilarious attitude and manner of speaking was so endearing, we became close friends on that first ferry ride. Since the government offices were closed (one of their many holidays), we purchased a generic rubber stamp and designed the thing ourselves. And to this day, we still laugh about keeping that secret.

Managing islanders

Though sincere and big-hearted souls, quite a few West Indian employees at the pub had never been taught customer service, or at least hadn't taken the lesson to heart. The pub's "order at window" style hid the staff's lack of service skills, as much as saved labor costs.

We kept the menu plain to facilitate speed. Our traditional bar food offered cheeseburgers, hamburgers, hot dogs, chicken sandwiches, chili, French fries, and the like. We had chicken wings, too, for a while, but that confused the cooks. My choice was a plate of poppers—fried jalapeños brimming not only with cheese but with sausage. Yummy. (No low-cholesterol choices here!)

Customers walked up to the grill's window, waited until they were noticed, and ordered food. They'd get a drink from the bar and put a dollar in the jukebox. Then they'd meander out on the dock that encircled the restaurant, pull up a barrel chair, and wait. And wait. And wait. A standard Caribbean rule: never go to an island restaurant hungry. The cooks would prepare the request and then, sometime later, shuffle out the paper-plated feast with the enthusiasm of a slug.

Delivery wasn't the only training issue. Food was definitely not made to order. I almost died the day I overheard Delia, a cook, indignantly telling a customer in sing-song Caribbean rhythm, with hands firmly planted on her ever-widening hips, "I ain't got no time to make it medium rare!" Yet, she sincerely questioned why her tip jar was empty.

We asked little of our crew. Winston pops in with "We tried to keep it simple, 'Just show up.'"

But we were continually pleased with their efforts. Slowly but surely, Winston and I brought them around. It took lots of joking and a few shock treatments like Winston mooning them once in a while to get them on our side. Eventually we shared mutual respect, and the tip jars started filling up.

Squeezing our personalities into the hut

After absorbing our Caribbean surroundings, plus our jobs, Winston and I were ready for the delightful task of organizing and decorating our tiny hut, spicing it up with our personalities. We'd asked permission, and Gayla had agreed.

Our six boxes from San Diego had finally been delivered—sort of. Winston was walking around Bitter End one day when he noticed two oversized boxes sitting by themselves out on the dock. He recognized the blue "Box #4" and "Box #2" lettering immediately. Sure enough, they were two of ours, sitting out there in the open, with no one around. He put them in the dinghy and went back to investigate. There, sitting by itself in another area of the resort, was Box #6. Hunting in earnest now, Winston discovered our other three boxes crammed here and there among the resort's storage. So much for security. He hijacked our shipment and brought it back to the hut.

With my obnoxious, type-A organizational skills haunting me, I utilized every nook and cranny of the hut. Thank goodness for those clear plastic, hanging shoe holders I bought in San Diego. They made invaluable hanging drawers for our swimsuits, shorts, T-shirts, underwear, and shoes. Yes, our clothes were jammed in, but, hey, no one cares about wrinkles in the islands. A couple skirts, one dress, and two collared shirts hung on hangers, in a zippered, clear plastic bag to hold off the inevitable musty smell.

Under the driftwood shelf in the kitchen, we stacked the indispensable, sturdy, red plastic Coke boxes we had used in shipping. They pulled in and out easily. One held a few plates, bowls, and cups, another, the most basic multiuse utensils. No room for a Martha Stewart spaghetti lifter, or extra-long zester in this abode. And imagine not having a junk drawer! I had no drawers at all.

Our windowsill, an eight-foot by four-inch board hammered under a big open space called a window, doubled as our "home office," where we had pens, a notepad, a tiny stapler, to-do lists, and so on. It's where we sat in early light, sipping coffee, writing postcards, and watching the eels swim by.

Our "medicine cabinet" was a shoebox under the bed.

Caribbean facelift

Winston painted the weatherworn two-by-fours bracing our floral cotton "walls" turquoise. And we didn't stop there. We trimmed every inch of brown wood with coral and yellow squiggles and dots just like in the Spanish Town restaurants, albeit not so professionally.

"We covered the ugly, plywood Dutch doors with natural bamboo stalks," Winston says proudly, "that I found in the junk pile. I sawed them in half and laminated them to the door. It looked really cool and matched our headboard, but Gayla was less than happy. She was saving that bamboo for something, she grumbled, though neither she nor anyone else on the Rock could think of what it might be."

Several of our silly trinkets from Windansea adorned the hut to where people would kayak by, asking if it was a gift shop. Two life-size, hand-painted, wooden birds hung in one corner of our window—a pelican and a parrot. Their wings moved in the wind. A multicolored fish mobile spun in the other. A three-dimensional star reflected the azure blue of our watery world.

We improved the hut structurally too. Winston found a sturdy pair of stairs in the "pile." He hauled them down to the hut and mounted them off the end of our small deck. Now we had our own staircase to the sea. Step down those stairs, slide on fins and mask, and snorkel our front yard—sure beats cutting grass!

Our front yard was an aquarium of tropical fish: yellow and black striped sergeant majors (Winston's pets), schools of electric blue tang, delicate yellow and white butterfly fish that swam in pairs, plus eels, and sea turtles, and—my preferred sea creature—huge, graceful, spotted eagle rays. We watched them from our windowsill, or underwater, right through our masks, eyeball to eyeball with our fabulous neighbors.

Becoming Gilligan

"When it rained, it usually poured," Winston remembers, "and, man, was it noisy. Our tin roof rattled and echoed to an almost deafening state. We couldn't even hear each other talk. Then I got a wild idea: cover the damn thing with palm fronds, just like Gilligan! When laughing about this with friends Blondie and Peter, a couple from nearby Eustatia Island, they offered us a gift."

"Come on over to our island and get some coconut palm fronds," Peter said. "Put them on your roof. There's a forest of them on our beach, and they just get in the way. Take all you want." This was yet another island exploit!

Winston continues, "We borrowed tools from Bert and boarded his old style, twelve-foot, flat-bottom boat, *Fugly* (which stood for "fucking ugly"). We motored ten minutes across the reef and pulled up onto Eustatia's sandy beach (no docks on that side of the island). Peter met us at the coconut grove with ladders and more tools, two we didn't even recognize. Then he hiked back up the steep hill to his house, with a peculiarly unusual smile on his face. Now we were on our own."

The first thing we ascertained, besides that we wore the wrong shoes, was that we needed gloves. It was hotter than hell and steamy under that forest. We tackled the easiest stuff first—the fronds on the ground. Did you know they have thorns?

Very choosey at first, we picked through all the dead and fallen fronds to find the best-shaped, greenest ones. We're talking palm fronds that had stems fifteen feet long with leaves spreading six feet across. Plus, they weighed a ton. By the end of the day, we were taking whatever was close.

"Schlepping the fronds to the boat was another matter," Winston grumbles. "Dragging those palm fronds across the beach through the sand and over the deep piles of other crap and rejected palms was backbreaking—especially when you're making fun of each other the whole time. When we finally attempted to actually cut some fresh fronds off the trees using the contraption Peter had provided, it was even more ridiculous. Never try this is my only advice."

Now, I had envisioned this project as a romantic, island escapade for me and Winston. I'd packed a yummy, little picnic lunch with a pretty, yellow sarong to spread under us. But by the time we were ready to enjoy it, we were filthy, sweaty, prickly messes. The romance was gone for sure. But we laughed our way through the meal, picturing ourselves more idiotic with each palm frond fiasco, and still made gentle, surfside love, in coconut grove seclusion.

"Cynthia and I dragged the fronds, one by one, down to the water's edge. Then we started loading. Fugly was so full, Cynthia had to spread eagle atop the pile to keep them from falling off or blowing away, while I, at the helm, carefully picked my way through the reef back to the hut.

"When we stacked up the palm fronds next to our tin roof, we couldn't believe it. We had maybe one fifth of what we needed! More trips, and more cuts, and more bruises. We were beginning to look the part.

"Eventually we were ready to build the roof. We didn't know exactly how to do this, but how hard could it be?

"First, I drilled holes into the tin sheets. Then I screwed one-inch by two-inch wooden cleats onto the holes, with rubber gasket roofing nails, so I could adhere the palm fronds. Next, we trimmed and shaped the fronds, trying to create shingles that would fit tightly together and lie smoothly and geometrically on top of each other. Naturally, I had one system, and Cynthia, being the type-A director that she is, kept wanting to rearrange my puzzle. I was sculpting a masterpiece and she didn't understand. You can almost still hear the arguing that ensued. Gayla and Bert just watched.

"After days of hauling, and cutting, and nailing, and arguing, picturesque palm fronds rustled gently in the wind atop our hut. Long palm frond leaves draped over the edges, framing our glassless windows. We'd created classic Caribbean ambiance—just like Gilligan. We celebrated in the privacy of our bedroom during the first rain."

New uses for black trash bags

Winston and I had built a substantial, classic roof and decorated our new home to our liking. We had running water, a little coffee pot, clothes tucked away, and a comfy bed to sleep in. Then it rained. Now we had a shower too—in fact, many of them.

Not that our roof was leaking. It was tighter than a drum (and quiet). The walls were good too—no leaks there. The walls just didn't meet the roof. A slight architectural error left a one-foot gap under the eaves in our bedroom. It was for air circulation, we were told.

We were sleeping when the first squall hit. Besides pouring in our windows, until we yanked out the sticks that propped the plywood open, the rain jutted straight under the eaves into the bedroom and down on us. *What the hell?* we wondered.

Then it dawned on us. That's why we found all those black, garbage bags stashed under the bed.

I dove to the floor and grabbed for bags. Winston bolted to our "office" and found the stapler and duct tape. The two of us, naked and dripping, laughing and muttering, clumsily tried to attach crappy, black trash bags across two widths of our freshly decorated bedroom's eaves. Not caring one iota what the place looked like, we went back to bed.

The next morning, we awoke in a sauna. In a flash, we ripped down our handiwork. But from then on, we'd be prepared to put it up in a flash, too.

Christening our baby

Now that our home was to our liking, we focused on buying our own boat. We wanted to get around, without borrowing one from the pub. We could drive over to Bitter End to catch the Thursday night movie,

View of Winston and Cynthia's dinghy from their grass hut on Saba Rock, 1994.
Gitana JK, Winston and Cynthia's newly christened dinghy, purchased for $400
plus a $1500 motor and $200 for paint, buzzed around North Sound with the
class of a Mercedes, at least according to them, or maybe a Volkswagen . . .

or putter off to Eustatia Reef to snorkel the Spanish cannons, or dinghy the short distance to Leverick Bay for a Pusser's dinner, or a local party. We needed some independence.

"For four hundred dollars, we took ownership of a beat-up, fiberglass, Tortola dinghy that our friend, Buddy, had used as a garbage trough," Winston tells it. "That was about as independent as we could afford.

"For two weeks, we improved her. We added fiberglass to her bottom to make her strong enough to hold a powerful engine. Then we whittled and swashed and sealed our new baby. We painted the inside gray to ease the sun's reflection on our eyes and the outside sparkling white. We trimmed her with deep turquoise bottom paint. That bottom paint cost half as much as the boat! I couldn't believe it!"

Ah, then the choice of a name. Our close friend, Judith, living in Houston, said she'd always wanted a boat named after her and that a dinghy seemed "most appropriate." A single woman of indiscriminate years who'd wandered alone through Europe and driven to the tip of Baja by herself, Judith was a true gypsy. So, we named our little boat *Gitana JK,* after our dinghy friend, Judith Keltner. *"Gitana"* is "gypsy" in Spanish.

Then we got fancy. We added sleek racing stripes and colorful *"Gitana JK"* nameplates to each side of our baby. We bought a fifteen-horsepower Yamaha engine to power *Gitana JK.* Most dinghies this size had only five or nine horsepower. But with our fifteen horses, we made a little hot rod out of her.

Winston bought a two-foot piece of plastic tubing to extend the handle of the engine, so I could drive standing up and see over the bow. We added a painter, the line used to tie her to a dock, and a v-shaped, little white bumper that fit her bow perfectly. Winston found it on an abandoned boat.

"To keep *Gitana JK* from banging herself on the dock," Winston explains, "we rigged a little mooring ball with a clothesline pulley system attached to the dock right next to the hut. We even painted the mooring ball white trimmed with turquoise. It was cool. The system ran like clockwork. We'd pull up to the dock, climb out, and then pulley the boat out to our mooring ball. It would spin around out there freely in the wind and waves, not get rocked and knocked under the dock like the dinghies tied up to the pub's dock."

Being nautical, we had to officially christen *Gitana JK* with a bottle of rum, right? One night, after many too many rum and tonics, we were up to the task. It would be the first party in our little home.

Judith wrote *Ode to Gitana JK* to be read at the ceremony. A crazy, self-professed orator and, I swear, half-pirate named Brian volunteered to do the honors. He dressed the part in pirate garb, even with a patch over one eye. Brian read the ode and then ceremoniously toasted our new baby, with raucous poetry, island lore, sputtering rum well into the night.

> *Simple, restless, and wild like its namesake*
> *The name will infuse every square millimeter of its fiberglass*
> *   being with imminent class*
> *No longer a boat, it will become a seaborne Corvette*
> *Its outboard a turbo jet of unbridled power*
> *Ready to surge forward to destinations yet unnamed*
> *Geared for speed beyond Man's wildest dreams*
> *On the horizon, its silhouette will strike envy in every man,*
> *   woman, and child*
> *It is the* Gitana JK, *the boat that could win the Indy 500, if*
> *   only it had wheels.*

The next morning, we carried *Gitana JK* to the edge of the dock and ceremoniously threw her in, again reciting *Ode to Gitana JK*. It wasn't until the ode was finished that we noticed she was floating away.

We'd forgotten to tie her new line to the dock.

This was the first of many of our *Captain Ron* moments. (If you haven't seen the movie *Captain Ron,* rent it.) Winston to the rescue—clothes and all. He jumped in, swam like hell and grabbed *Gitana JK,* to hoots and hollers and wild applause. More rum, that's what we needed!

Once correctly secured, we cracked a bottle of Saba Rock Cruzan Rum over her bow, slid her out to her matching new mooring ball, and then guzzled more Cruzan ourselves.

That evening, Winston and I had a flashback. We remembered that doctored photo hanging on our kitchen wall for four years, the one with Gayla and Bert and us standing together under the pub's sign. After shaking our heads in disbelief, a big hug, a wonderful kiss and warm smiles ruled.

We were not making much money, but certainly living a dream, with masks and snorkels hanging on a nail patiently awaiting their next assignment.

Chapter 4
Life on the Rock

Learning is finding out what you already know.

—Richard Bach

*Bar's open for thirsty sailors. Bushwackers
and painkillers specialties of the house.*

Saba Rock and Tortola, British Virgin Islands
December 1994 – August 1995

Keeping up with the world

Receiving U.S. news was impossible on the Rock. The Internet was barely user-friendly. We had no TV, and radio news was purely island-oriented. The national newspaper, the *BVI Beacon,* was only available in Tortola. An issue of *USA Today* cost four dollars. On the rare chance you could find one, it was usually a week old. Sometimes, we'd pose for a photograph with Feather, just to trade some guest for his newspaper.

Winston and I heard about the Oklahoma bombing in a bar in Roadtown. It had happened just a day before. We learned about the bombing of the Atlanta Olympics in another bar, the same week it had occurred. Luckily, we liked bars, or we'd never know the news.

The daily media barrage we'd been subject to in the states wasn't even remotely part of our lives, but we really didn't miss it. Only when some national, or international, crisis happened did we wish we were more in touch.

Communicating with friends and family was another matter. Emails were possible, but the internet was unreliable. Our first phone bill in the British Virgin Islands was four hundred dollars, which almost threw us into shock. Gayla had warned us that calls cost four dollars per minute, but we just didn't think we talked that long. Then we found a better way.

Phone cards we slid into payphones cost twenty-five dollars and gave us almost ten minutes of talk time. The hard part was finding a payphone with a dial tone. The one in Leverick was usually broken. Spanish Town had two, but it's a twenty-minute taxi ride away—a long way to travel for a phone call, especially if the person you wanted to call wasn't home.

If you got lucky and found a working phone *and* the person you were calling answered, at least you knew how much you were spending. The payphone counted down the dollars as you spoke. You talked, watching your twenty-five dollars tick away: twenty-three dollars, nineteen dollars, fifteen dollars, ten dollars, seven, two . . . You'd talk faster and faster and cut people off in the process. It didn't make for friendly conversation.

One time, I was talking to my friend in St. Louis and forgot to watch the meter. Suddenly, I was down to twenty-five cents and, in a panic, blurted out, "Oh my God, I'm running out of money," at which time the phone disconnected. Poor Betty, on the other end, thought I meant I was literally desperate for cash and was worried, until I was able to call her back days later.

The difficulty with communication was the hardest adjustment I had to make. Lonely I was not. Worried I was not. But missing my kids and even just the sound of their voices was absolutely a hardship. They were grown and busy with their own lives, but still . . . sometimes I'd waste a quick twenty-five dollars just to hear their message machines. What got me through? Knowing they'd come visit. Knowing I could open their world to this remarkable place.

Parties at the pub

Our full moon parties were crowned "Best in the BVI." Winston says proudly, "Sailors and tourists came from all over. Fifty sailboats would anchor in front of the pub, and people would pour in from the Bitter End Resort as well. I would dinghy out to every boat, with a flyer hawking the costume party and limbo contest. Who could miss a chance to win a bottle of Saba Rock Rum? A live band, albeit island-style scratch band, showed, or no-showed, depending on what else they might want to do. There were plenty of noisemakers at the pub and that jukebox, too, so music blared regardless. Painkillers and bushwackers, the famous drinks of the islands, were the order of the night. The bar didn't close till the last person left, sometimes at 4:00 a.m. Feather had a great time eating everyone's French fries and dancing up a storm when Buffet played. Pita hated the whole thing.

"One night, some people were still partying at Bitter End when resort management closed down their band. (After 9:00 p.m., most Bitter End guests expect quiet.) So, the partiers called the Rock, asking if they possibly could bring the band to the pub. The supervisor who answered the phone came to me for an answer. These people were having such a good time, they just didn't want to wind down. Could they come over and continue their party here? Though we were trying to wind down ourselves, I said what the hell, sure, and over they came. It looked like an armada of dinghies headed our way, bouncing the short distance over waves while trying not to spill their drinks. Within fifteen minutes, fifty people were dancing on the tables, jumping into the water, and, in some cases, getting naked. Our little, West Indian bartender was blown away. She even had me go back to our hut and get Cynthia just to see the sight. (She'd been sleeping. It was her month off.) What a night! We did get some noise complaints from Bitter End, but bar profits were way up that night, so I thought it was worth it. Gayla was out of town luckily. She'd have killed me!"

On Thanksgiving, Gayla became Santa Claus. Some thought of her as a penny-pinching slave driver, with an eagle eye for profits. But every Thanksgiving, since she'd opened in 1989, Gayla gave away Thanksgiving dinner to anyone who could float a boat over to Pirates Pub.

Bert would take center stage at the bar, welcome everyone, and thank Gayla and all the cooks. Then, laden with authentic gold chains and doubloons he'd found in the sea, he'd officially open Thanksgiving. Old Pirate Bert would lean back, fill his lungs, and blow the iconic conch shell (pronounced "konk"). There is nothing like watching an eighty-year-old pirate reenact one of his own legends. The trumpeting could be heard for miles. First come, first served until the food ran out. No cost. Just buy a drink. Happy Thanksgiving!

Gayla usually served Thanksgiving dinner to about three hundred fifty people. Our first year, we cooked seven turkeys, six hams, two hundred pounds of potatoes, and forty pumpkin pies.

Our Initiation

In December, Bert invited Winston and me to be his honorees on a boat ride to get a Christmas tree for Pirates Pub. We were looking forward to spending some personal time with this character.

I'd been to town earlier that week and saw a big sign on a fence announcing: "Xmas trees soon done." I wasn't sure whether that meant the trees were almost all sold out, or just about to arrive, but I knew

Bert wouldn't be taking us all the way to Tortola to get a tree. I was not sure where we were going.

We got into *Fugly* with Bert and Tim, the cook. Bert drove around to the far end of Mosquito Island and pulled ashore. "OK, you guys, this is it. Here are your tools. Hike to the top of that hill and cut down that tall, century plant, the really pretty one. Be careful not to crush it on the way down. We want the branches to be nice and symmetrical."

Tim just sat there, with a shit-eating grin blended almost perfectly with an empathetic look of mercy and watched us climb out. Then Bert backed the boat off the island and anchored.

Well, first, we didn't know we'd be hiking up a hill covered in cactus and thirty-foot-tall century plants. Consequently, the shoes were wrong. Our shorts made little sense either. And, we had no gloves. The tools Bert gave us were old, dilapidated, rusty tree shears and a hack saw that wouldn't even hack, much less saw.

Boldly we faced the hillside, tried to figure out which century plant Bert was talking about, and set our course. After forty-five minutes of hiking, tripping, and cursing—plus some yelling back to the boat and pointing about *which* tree we were supposed to cut down—we hacked away. It took forever and then some. All the while, Bert and Tim snickered away in *Fugly*, swigging icy-cold Carib beers.

We dragged the !!&#^@% "perfect" century plant down to the shore. It was more than a little worse for wear, but considering it was dried brown and dead, not that bad. We chiseled off most of the stem and transported the top back to the Rock, to be adorned with tinsel and ornaments.

The dead century plant was not the only thing adorned. Almost every inch of Pirates Pub was dressed in rusty tinsel and ornaments from days gone by. Little Christmas stockings for every employee hung across the bar. Good cheer and Santa hats were passed among all, as was a sugary-tasting, rather intoxicating rum liqueur.

Running Pirates Pub was an icebreaker for starting friendships. Almost from our first day, we were adopted by the community. Plus, everyone was eager to get to know us newcomers in order to glean fresh tidbits, for the coconut telegraph. Dan, from California, and Katie, from Toronto, ran the water sports rental business. They leased a large home as their personal party central, included us in every invitation, and were catalysts to our indoctrination. Jorge and Yani, from South America, lived with their seven-year-old daughter on an estate they managed. True sailors, they spent lots of time on their own sailboat and included us often. We weren't on Saba Rock a month when they offered us Christmas dinner at their home. Pam, from Colorado, and Presley, from the island of Bequia, danced the night away regularly at the bar—that is if they weren't sailboat racing the next morning. They kept our feet wet, literally, including us on racing teams religiously.

Never a dull moment

One favored pastime at the Rock was watching people get in and out of their dinghies. Winston grins with glee, "You'd think people who already had sailed to probably at least five or six BVI islands by the time they reached our neck of the woods would finally have accomplished disembarking a dinghy. But noooo. Docking a boat and climbing in and out maybe seems simple enough. But *lots* of little boats, *wavy* water, *crowded* docks, *butter-fingered* boaters, and *drinking* created a perfect recipe for never ending comedy. I swear there is nothing funnier than a woman trying to keep from falling into the water with one foot in a boat and the other on the dock while her purse flies through the air— except watching the face of a GQ-type guy, in nicely pressed pants, as he gets out of a dingy and realizes that he is brandishing legendary *dinghy butt*—the soggy seat of his pants circled with a large ring of white from the salt water he just sat in. Whether crashing into, riding up on, bouncing off, or falling from the Pirates Pub dock, the circus of vacationers never stopped entertaining us."

Snorkeling and diving were our recreations of choice. We swam off our little bungalow's patio, undisturbed for hours. Night scuba dives were a premium item, and we participated many times. Once, diving through the cave-like openings off Mountain Point, poor Tim got into some current and lost his two, fake front teeth. We dove and dove but never found those teeth. In the crystal-clear water, with masked and snorkeled swimmers peering high and low around every crevice, you'd think they'd show up easily but no such luck. I guess some things just don't want to leave the silence of the sea. Tim had to fly to Puerto Rico for new ones—the price of play.

The nice thing about being in North Sound, tiny Saba Rock has neighboring islands almost a swim away . . . Virgin Gorda, Eustacia, Prickly Pear, and Necker are all within a quarter-mile of us.

Fix-it Ralph, our engineering buddy, from nearby Necker Island (owned by billionaire Richard Branson), endlessly organized bonfires, on neighboring island Prickly Pear. Prickly Pear's only inhabitants were goats and they never objected to any of our antics. One time, they even led us to a full-size wooden door, just when we were searching for more firewood. Why a perfectly good door was stashed in the bushes of an uninhabited island was never questioned. However, the bonfire that night was as high as a house.

In Virgin Gorda's Leverick Bay—right around the corner from Saba Rock—Katie and Dan offered plenty of opportunities for us to waterski and parasail, on their rental boats. We were their human billboards used to drum up business. Fix-it Ralph and some of his staff from Necker sometimes would join Winston and Dan at Prickly Pear Island, to prepare for the small cruise ship that anchored in North Sound almost weekly. Our guys would arrive at Prickly's beach equipped with kayaks, dinghies, water skis, even small sailboats to rent to the crowd. A hundred, or more, people would descend on the island for six hours, eager to play in the water.

Sometimes, Prickly would suffer a no-show, no ship in sight, but those afternoons were never wasted. One dead calm "no-show" afternoon, the guys' combined brain power had a major short circuit. One of the islands had a high-speed helicopter to transport elite guests from Puerto Rico to it and, well, it was just sitting there doing nothing. Some weirdo suggested waterskiing behind the copter. And some other weirdo took him up on it. The toy of choice soon appeared overhead. Hotshot water-skiers grabbed the long ski rope dropped from the sky and waterskied behind the heli on a beautiful sea of glass, no wake to ripple the water. Talk about decadence. I was relieved Winston didn't have the nerve to potentially kill himself, but those other guys were nuts. If they didn't release the line at just the right moment they could find themselves flying instead of skiing. Luckily, they tired quickly. Then the cruise ship arrived, and the scene flashed back to normalcy.

Another day, Winston got a call from the manager of a scuba company who was short one crew member. She asked if Winston would drive the boat for a charter going on a shark dive that morning. After picking up six eager guests, Winston and the dive crew headed to Fallen Jerusalem, which was an uninhabited island not far away. But before they spied even one hint of a shark, they spotted something even more intriguing and ominous. A makeshift raft was floating just off the shore—a makeshift raft of cocaine bales. It obviously had been dropped the night before, because glow sticks still signaled its existence. The raft was a hazard to navigation, so it had to be picked up—good excuse, right? Janie, the diver in charge, directed the operation. The wide-eyed group heaved nine bales on board, all tightly wrapped in burlap coffee bags. Ironically, the guests were law enforcement officers from the States. They were a tad nervous, but not enough to miss a dive with sharks. They continued their scheduled dive, and left the contraband stacked neatly in the corner of the boat. Winston babysat.

After the dive, lots of jokes centered on what to do with the stash but eventually Janie decided: they'd return the guests to their hotel, sans any cocaine souvenirs, call the local authorities to pick up the cargo and dock the boat back at Leverick Bay. The cops didn't show up for three or four hours. Janie and Winston's imaginations ran wild meanwhile. Eventually, the cops appeared in full combat regalia and carried off nine bales of cocaine. Funny thing though, Janie and Winston later heard there had been only seven bales. That evening a patrol boat drove to the windward side of Virgin Gorda and found twenty-one more bales washed ashore. Soon a new trend appeared: *Save the Bales* T-shirts.

Presley and Pam, our friends who usually danced the nights away at Saba Rock, lassoed us often to go sailing, usually racing around the BVI. We and the rest of the crew would don red T-shirts flourishing a team crest and take off with Presley at the helm. The Around Tortola race ended with celebrations at a bar. The BVI Regatta and the Anegada Race were just as festive. To make it even more exciting, we usually won. It definitely helped that Presley had raced in the Olympics.

Super Bowl XXIX, in January, 1995, found the San Francisco 49ers pitted against our own San Diego Chargers, and almost the total North Sound community was pitted against Winston and me. Expectedly, Katie and Dan threw a party. They had 49er T-shirts, banners, paper cups, and hats. Winston and I bravely wore Charger paraphernalia sent to us by a buddy. The Chargers were demolished in the first quarter, and by halftime Winston had crashed from depression and drinking. Before he woke, the group faux-tattooed his face with "49ers." He wore that banner for the rest of the night, not even knowing.

"And speaking of Super Bowl," Winston joins in, "as soon as we'd heard our Chargers were in the Super Bowl, we had lowered our pirate flag over our hut and hoisted a five-by-seven-foot Charger flag. Waving in the fifteen-knot wind, it looked grand, and flying above our Caribbean palm frond hut, it looked bazaar. So, we showed someone. We took photos and mailed the whole roll of film (no digital available then) to the San Diego *Union-Tribune's* sports editor with the headline: 'Virgin Territory for Chargers.'

"To our amazement, not only did the *Union-Tribune* run the photo, but the Associated Press did too. For the next year, people were showing up at Saba Rock, with that news clip in hand, saying they came to the Rock just to meet us. One couple told us they saw the story on a CNN feature highlighting all the peculiar places Super Bowl flags flew. That was really great."

Those all-hell-breaks-loose days on the Rock

No hamburger buns in our "cheeseburger in paradise" kitchen.

Not one cook at the pub on a busy Thursday.

No water in the cistern—bone dry.

The pub's *pissoir* not working.

All these things happened, some many times. For example, one rainy morning, I drove the dinghy, as usual, over to Bitter End to pick up our cooks and bartenders, and the girls refused to get in the boat "'cause it rainin'." Now, they all had taken this job knowing they had to get to the island by boat—no correlation. And, they knew it rains regularly in the islands—no matter. They jist weren't gettin' in dat boat, and dat was dat. (Their manner of speaking always made me smile, no matter what their attitude.) Due to labor laws, there was very little I could do about it except wait until the rain stopped. I know what you're thinking but firing a local was practically out of the question in the islands, and challenging one was just as futile.

On another hell day, as I was driving the dinghy, from Bitter End to the Rock, my passengers, the cooks, were arguing so loudly, the seagulls were taking cover. I used the same technique I used when my kids were in the backseat of the car, fighting. Just pull over and wait. I turned the engine off and stopped the boat dead in the middle of a passage. I waited, engine off, rocking in a floating boat, until the fighting stopped.

It didn't take long to get their attention. And, I'm proud to say, they remembered the incident for a long time.

Another day, the morning after a downpour, there were no cooks, or bartenders, at the dock when I dinghied over to pick them up. Back at the bar, no phone was working in order to call in some substitutes (the rain drowned the phone), plus the toilet was stopped up. Talk about wanting to go back to bed. "Flexibility," I muttered continuously, as I slung burgers and made drinks.

A real doozy was the time our bartender tried to attack our supervisor, in front of the customers. We had the entire scene on video, thanks to the bar's surveillance camera, and she was wielding Winston's hammer. But we couldn't just fire her. It was mandatory to go through the labor board, and the board refused to accept our video as evidence. The bartender claimed we'd doctored it, and the board said they believed her, snickering all the while. The pub had to continue to pay her during the procedures, but the government wouldn't allow her to work. And we were prohibited from hiring anyone else to take her place. The rest of the crew did double time while the bartender vacationed with pay—island reality. The process took nine months to resolve, and we had to apologize to the bartender. Don't stop the carnival. The carnival never stops.

It's a small world

The fraternity of people who chuck it all and move to the islands is small. Winston and I were pleased to have made it through "freshman rush" and still loved our life and each other, after many weeks. We were "limin'"—that's "chilling" in local parlance—meeting new strangers every day.

Any given night, there were forty to fifty boats anchored off the Rock, averaging at least four people each. A constant breeze of a couple hundred sailors blew in to Pirates Pub for a "cheeseburger in paradise" and a Jimmy Buffet tune. They'd sign a one-dollar bill and staple it to the ceiling, proving to the world that they'd been there and conquered. Often, they'd want a pub T-shirt signed by Winston or me—we were the notorious pirates now!

Yet, as large as the world is, every once in a while, those two degrees of separation caught us off guard. During one full moon, Winston was hustling sailboats with flyers about our party when he noticed a sailboat flying the New Brunswick, Canada, colors. "Hey, you guys from New Brunswick? I'm from there too. Come to the party tonight, and I'll buy you a drink," he promised. They agreed, ready for some free rum.

"Later that afternoon, they dinghied over to the Rock," continues Winston. "One of the guys was playing darts with me when conversation centered on the group's hometowns. 'We're all from Fredericton,' he mentioned. I blurted out, "I'm from there too. I went to Fredericton High School."

"No shit?" the man said. "My wife went to school there. Hey, Judy, come over here and meet this guy."

"Over she came, smiling the smile synonymous with a few bushwackers."

"This is Winston. He's the guy that came by the boat today. He went to FHS."

"She grabbed my cheeks with both hands and stared. Then she started screaming, 'Winston, is that really you? Oh my God! Don't you know me? I'm Judy. We dated in high school. I still have a picture of you and me in the backseat of Bud's car. I can't believe it's you!' I was dumbfounded."

The camaraderie and reminiscing lasted well after midnight. Puberty stories were flying. I was eager to hear all about teenybopper, Winston, and they wanted to know how we ended up managing the pub. Before leaving for their next anchorage, Judy scribbled enthusiastically about Winston over four pages in the pub's guest book. I didn't know he was such a hunk way back then.

Three months later, Winston received a note from Judy. Enclosed was the photo, and it warmed our hearts. There was sweet sixteen Winston in the backseat of a '57 Ford, with his arm around Judy. We still have the photo.

Another time, in the office one day, up to my elbows in inventory, a bartender climbed the stairs. "Dere's some white guy here aksin' 'bout chu. Sure don't look yer type," she said with a wink.

Down I went, numbers still swarming my brain. The view as I rounded the corner cleared my head in an instant. Swinging on our precariously mounted macramé loveseat was my coworker from twelve years ago in St. Louis. He knew about me on the Rock because he'd seen that Associated Press article featuring the Charger Super Bowl flag, flying above our grass shack.

Talking with Rick reminded me so much of the creative world I'd left behind, to live in this world of pirates and rum-filled, painkiller drinks—coworkers, old friends, bosses. Eager for a taste of my past, I picked his brain about new promotions and old clients, industry updates, and office politics. It was a juicy buffet. I told him I didn't miss a thing about advertising and PR, and I meant it. Then I meandered back up to my office above the bar, in my shorts and tank top, gazed out at the gin-clear turquoise sea, smiled, and printed up more full moon party flyers advertising the next scratch band. Who said I wasn't still in the business?

Knowing your customer

Imagine arriving in a foreign country, knowing no one, and being recognized by a complete stranger, who then delivers you to your destination, with no questions asked?

Well, it happened in the BVI.

My daughter, Andrea, and her boyfriend ventured to Virgin Gorda on an island-hopping junket with no schedule. They were checking out Puerto Rico, St. Thomas, St. John, Tortola, and anywhere else they happened upon, before finding us at the Rock.

Cynthia's daughter, Andrea, braves the waves of the famous Baths granite formations at the south end of Virgin Gorda.

For weeks, I boasted to everyone that Andrea was coming. I was thrilled to show her our new life and proud to have my friends meet this bright, beautiful young, woman. No, I didn't know quite when she'd arrive, but . . .

One afternoon, Winston and I were savoring some chicken rotis in The Bath and Turtle restaurant in Spanish Town when, to my shock and amazement, in walked Andrea and her beau, guided by my Thursday taxi driver, Thomas.

"Mom, you must know *everybody* in the BVI. We were just leaving this overly crowded ferry, wondering where to go next and how on earth we were going to find you, when this guy, Thomas, comes straight up to me out of the blue. He says, 'I bet you're looking for Winston and Cyntya.'"

I was speechless.

Thomas just stood there with his usual big grin and boasted, "I *knew* she was your daughter, Cintya. Had to be. She looks jis' like you. You told me she comin' sometime, and I looked up and saw her, so here she is." I loved that guy even more.

Out of the hundred people who piled off that ferry, Thomas had noticed Andrea. He'd seen us earlier in the restaurant, so he brought her right over. Andrea and Erik were impressed. I was amazed. After that introduction to island living, showing them the BVI was fantastic, especially with my month off schedule.

The carrier pigeon

You know about Fed Ex and their impeccable reputation for fast delivery. Well, not so much in the islands. Winston and I had an opportunity to get off the island for a weekend, to attend our friends' wedding in St. Louis (Betty and Dan, who'd gotten engaged on our balcony at Windansea). We hadn't seen the mainland in six months and looked forward to the trip.

A stateside travel agent (remember those?) arranged for our tickets to be overnighted to us. This was way before electronic ticketing, by the way. And, you must understand that in the BVI, "overnight" did not mean tomorrow. It just meant maybe soon.

We waited and waited but still no tickets. We did our best to bolster each other into believing they would arrive in time for our trip. Winston would occasionally burst into a cursing stint about the problem, forcing me to act the optimist. It was times like these when we remembered either I could be mad, or he could be mad, but we never could be mad at the same time. We both sadly visualized our vacation, and money, going down the drain.

Then one day we happened to be at the Bitter End picking up a guest, when a complete stranger in shorts and flip flops sauntered up. "By any chance, do you know who Winston and Cynthia are? I have a package for them."

Turns out, this tourist was coming by ferry to the Bitter End. Some well-meaning mailman must have thought, *Ah, a carrier pigeon!* He handed over our valuable "overnight" Fed Ex package to this absolute stranger, and considered the delivery completed.

With a rather inappropriate burst of loud laughter, fueled no doubt by his sense of relief, Winston accepted the package, and we made our flights to St. Louis two days later. That's overnight in the islands!

The boys from the Hole

"Lots of sailors came and went on the Rock from all parts of the world," Winston reminisces, "usually for an afternoon or evening. Sometimes, they'd stay a couple of days. But two, silly sailors stayed three weeks. The two were waiting for a weather window, headed for the island of St. Maarten, ninety miles away. The wind had stranded them. They set sail one day but returned eight hours later, because the sea conditions were so ungodly rough. Sailboats need wind but not thirty knots (34.5 mph) of it. Pirates Pub and the Rock became their neighborhood. And if you were gonna get stuck, the pub wasn't a bad place to be.

"These two sailors, Country Lawyer Ben and Chef Butch, hailed from Jackson Hole. They were sailing a friend's yacht, and tenacious about cramming in as many island sights as possible. The wind had other ideas. It wanted them to get to know us.

"Ben and Butch ended up drinking bushwackers non-stop and entertaining us with stories of Jackson Hole. It seems Ben had recently only run for mayor because he hated all the people on the ballot. He lost but got quite a lot of votes in spite of himself. Butch explained that Ben was a lawyer, yes, but he didn't have an answering machine and refused to own a cell phone. He would not book appointments and was happy with his hit or miss practice—not quite politician material, though perfect for a sailor. It gave us confidence knowing he was living his career exactly how he wanted it. We were trying to do that ourselves."

Captain Ron lookalike

Our friend, Jorge, invited Winston and I to go to a world-renowned, six-day yacht race that took place every year in Antigua, two hundred nautical miles south of the Rock. Taking a break from his busy estate management job on Virgin Gorda, Jorge was sailing his forty-three-foot boat down to pick up a charter and knew we could help him sail. We'd be gone a week. It was my month off, but Gayla stubbornly told Winston he was needed at the Rock. He'd be fired, if he left.

During race week, Antigua was a mecca of world-class yachts, even Dennis Connor's America's Cup winner attended. True sailors just couldn't pass up the chance to witness one of the most celebrated international sailboat races in the world, even if it meant losing their jobs. Besides, Winston was now marketing for sailing crew jobs and what better place to network? After some cajoling, and with kindhearted chef Tim offering to cover for him, Gayla relented.

With barely a small duffel bag of clothing for our one week vacation, we sailed to St. Maarten, a half-French/half-Dutch island almost halfway to Antigua. St. Maarten is actually two separate countries and the smallest island in the world to house both, plus at least three hundred different restaurants on the Dutch side alone.

With a hilly geography of scattered valleys and a high point of one thousand three hundred feet, St. Maarten was known for its fusion cuisine, busy resort beaches, vibrant night-life and duty-free bargain prices on electronics, perfume and liquor. Winston and I had never experienced St. Maarten's allure, and were eager to take advantage of duty-free electronics. We sailed into Simpson Bay, all excited to snag a TV/VHS player for our little abode. But true to *Don't Stop the Carnival*, where nothing worked as planned, it was King's Day, a national holiday. Not one store was open.

So, basically, we toured the "Closed" signs.

In route to Antigua, we anchored next in ritzy St. Barth's, twenty miles to the south of St. Maarten. St. Barthelemey, its formal name, is eight square miles of arid volcanic rock housing about three thousand one hundred residents, with an eclectic mix of beaches, luxury yachts, iguanas and celebrities. We pretended to hobnob with the rich and famous, anchoring outside Gustavia Harbor's free port and enjoyed St. Bart's duty-free shopping. We ate at the bar where some claim Jimmy Buffet wrote "Cheeseburgers in Paradise," and I bought an awesome, yellow swimsuit at the fanciest, chic, French boutique I'd ever stepped foot in.

Then on to Antigua, a European destination and a much larger island of one hundred and five square miles and eight thousand people. Antigua, only five hundred forty-three miles in circumference, offered a phenomenal three hundred sixty-five beaches, several of which were along the race course. The protected English Harbor and restored national historic monument, Nelson's Dockyard, were our strongholds. We made love in the sand and slept on beach chairs before securing a terrific little villa front and center to horseshoe-shaped Falmouth Harbor, for the bargain price of fifty-five dollars per night.

We didn't get the opportunity to take part in any races, mostly because we were too shy to ask, but spent the week wandering through crowds of drunken sailors and docks of flashy, fast boats, marketing as we went. There had to be a full-time sailing job for us somewhere, but apparently this wasn't the place. On our return trip to Virgin Gorda, we stopped again at St. Maarten and snagged that TV.

By the time we returned to Saba Rock, word was out that Winston was an accomplished sailor. Charter companies started asking him (under the table) to deliver sailboats from one marina to another. After several, outstanding, day trips, more manna from heaven.

Yacht companies often chartered boats to people who really didn't know how to handle a sailboat. They knew how to sail but didn't know how to anchor, or knew how to anchor but didn't know how to navigate, or knew how to navigate but didn't know how to dock, without banging the heck out of the vessel. The companies didn't want to release highly valued yachts to people with weak sailing résumés.

A light bulb went on in Winston's head: he could make a living as a yacht captain, instead of making peanuts at the Rock. Winston's future was carved.

Charter companies contracted with Winston to instruct and oversee charterers, until they were competent enough to handle their yacht themselves. Sometimes that took a day or two, sometimes three. But, often, because of the fun Winston created spicing up the instruction, they'd request he stay the full week of the charter. And the charterers paid him for it.

Winston was now in demand as a yacht captain, proud as a seaman with a chest full of medals. Becoming known for his Jimmy Buffet style, he was lovingly dubbed Captain Ron, as

Captain Winston's first paycheck as a part-time yacht captain, more money than a month's salary at the Rock.

in the movie. His first charter netted him more money than he would have made in a month at the Rock.

Of course, there was that matter of having the proper work permit, but our friends came through there. They used their contacts with immigration and listed Winston as professional yacht crew. So, he was working legally, part-time as a yacht captain and part-time on Saba Rock, thanks to Gayla's generosity. We lived on the Rock in our little palm frond hut, me with my month on/month off schedule and Winston solving maintenance jobs between sailing gigs.

But after almost eleven months on the Rock, the winds were about to change.

Chapter 5
Blunder Bay Blunderings

*There is no such thing as a problem
without a gift for you in its hands.*

—Richard Bach

*With hurricanes threatening, Winston and Cynthia moved to this sturdy stone beach
house in Blunder Bay on Virgin Gorda, a fifteen-minute dinghy ride from Saba Rock.*

Virgin Gorda, British Virgin Islands
August 1995–January 1996

The bomb drops

We were adapted to island time now and getting the hang of living
on this tiny island where nothing worked and "tomorrow" just meant
"not today." Then Gayla dropped the bomb.

"Sorry, guys, but you're going to have to move. It's hurricane season,
and the worst months are September and October. Your shack will

67

never survive the storms, and I can't be responsible for your lives. You'll have to find somewhere else to hang your swimsuits."

The news hit me like a ton of bricks. I looked out at our front yard and my heart sank. Winston, however, was ready to go. "I liked the funkiness of the Rock and it was really cool living there," Winston admits, "but I'd been there, done that. Gayla was getting testy . . . she wanted thirty chairs painted in two days and I'm a contractor who believes in doing it right—one-stop job vs scraping and stripping and sanding first. We disagreed a lot. So, I was ready."

But where to go? We weren't paying any rent at Saba, so anywhere we moved would be a new, unplanned expense. We speculated about renting a house in Leverick Bay around the corner from the Rock, but it cost too much. One in Spanish Town, at the other end of Virgin Gorda, was too far away and would require a car to get to work, and the neat little community of Gun Creek, just on the other side of Bitter End, seemed reserved mainly for West Indians.

Peter and Blondie, the couple from nearby Eustatia Island, shared an idea with us. "You guys should move to Blunder Bay." Blunder Bay was an historic, little cove off Virgin Gorda along North Sound's coastline, just a little to the west of Leverick Bay, with only a fifteen-minute dinghy commute to Saba Rock.

We decided to investigate, though Winston was about as enthusiastic as a sloth.

Peter and Blondie ferried us to the property, building it up all the way. At the base of a steep hillside tucked into a small cove, the old, one-story stone house was ten times the size of our hut. It had a huge covered porch and a stone patio that disappeared into the bay, ten feet away.

"The place had a dilapidated, bi-level, half-leveled dock at one end of the cove," describes Winston. "A real eighteenth-century cannon anchored it. Sir Francis Drake's maybe? Nobody knew. It was cool, though, and created just the pirate atmosphere we were looking for. A long row of tall coconut palm trees lined the path to the house.

"There was no electricity, Peter told us, just a barnlike structure housing a huge, diesel-devouring generator that produced power upon feeding. White PVC piping, trailing down from a cistern on the hill, delivered rainwater to the sink," he continues.

"A plaque on the house boasted the lore of Blunder Bay: Around 1595 Sir Francis Drake had committed a fatal blunder there. The story goes his band of pirates was having such a good time in North Sound that Drake decided to extend his stay. In the meantime, the Spanish were building their own forces, in Puerto Rico. When Drake left Blunder Bay and arrived in Puerto Rico to fight, the Spanish far outnumbered him. He was wounded in the battle and died later of an illness in Panama. Hence, 'Blunder Bay.'

"And there's more. Blunder Bay backs up to haunted Blood Beach. In the 1700s, after the English had denounced slavery, a ship loaded with slaves anchored in Blunder Bay. A British warship approached from the east. The crew, fearing capture while carrying slaves, decided to kill their cargo. Lore has it they killed the slaves, cut up their bodies, and hid them in the underbrush on the hillside. The beach ran red with blood.

"Those slaves, though, decided to get even. Their spirits still live in the hills of Blunder Bay. Locals won't even approach the area. Haunted, they claim, by jumbies. Smell of blood, they claim. Ghosts, they've heard. 'Not goin' near dat Blunder Bay, no, sir.'"

That story made the bay even more intriguing to me. I love ghosts. (A friend of ours who had lived there was awakened from a dead sleep by the smell of fresh blood heavy in the air. He aborted Blunder Bay in the middle of the night! And never went back.)

Now the house . . .

What we saw excited me but discouraged the builder in Winston. His testament . . . "When I opened the door to the house, it fell off, literally, leaving nothing but hinges. I'm not kidding. That made me nervous. ('Flexibility—think flexibility,' Cynthia kept muttering at me under her breath.) The inside living area was large and sort of split-level, kind of neat really. You had to walk right through the bathroom to get to the bedroom—no doors at all. That was weird. And the bedroom offered that musty smell, so familiar to us by now. Plus, the whole place was dingy gray, inside and out."

"No worries." Blondie was encouraging, "Some bright-colored paint, and she'll be as cute as your hut. Whenever the floor gets dirty, just paint over it. I do it all the time! This place is definitely sturdier than your hut—not going to blow away any time soon. Bert knows the absentee owner too. Maybe he'll work a deal. Tell him, in lieu of rent, you'll repair the place. Just look at all this potential," she teased Winston.

There was certainly a lot to *fix*. Could that count as potential?

Blondie and I walked the grounds, spying wild purple orchids and fuchsia bougainvillea. Cute little lizards squiggled across our footsteps. "The place even has spotlights on the path along the water. Your palm trees will glitter at night."

We learned Bert from Saba Rock had originally built the house, along with another that sat vacant above it on the hill. Bert did know the present owner, who agreed to let us live there. Rent was three hundred dollars monthly, and we could spend the money on improvements. With rumblings churning in Winston's gut, we deliberated.

Our decision was made by the coconut telegraph . . . .

Katie and Dan came to the pub the next day to congratulate us. "We heard you're moving to Blunder Bay and we're so excited. We'll be neighbors now," Katie said. "Think of the great parties we can have." She wasn't the only one. It seemed the entire neighborhood was sure we were moving. So, we made everyone correct.

"Moving day was the following Saturday," Winston smiles. "We piled *Gitana* with our scanty belongings, started the Yamaha, and sped away. One trip from Saba to Blunder and we were moved. How's that for no stuff? Changes are simple when you have no stuff."

It was sad to leave our sweet little grass hut, but the prospect of Blunder Bay with its roomy privacy made it easier.

Nesting

All Winston needed to get excited about Blunder Bay was paint. He loves painting and is an expert at it. On my next going-to-town day, we both went. I took care of my Saba Rock shopping list, and he played in the paint store, the hardware store, and the building supply center.

He came home laden with gallons of paint, some lumber for trim, plus guttering. I hunted down the strongest, three-foot-wide push broom I'd ever seen. We had a *lot* of floor and a *lot* of dirt on it.

Remodeling had officially begun, three hundred dollars at a time.

We soon transformed Blunder Bay into a home as unique as our grass shack, with the stamp of our personality etched into every rotten piece of wood on site.

Surrounded by their Caribbean paint job of turquoise, peach and yellow, Winston and Cynthia enjoy their new digs at Blunder Bay.

A major purchase was a louvered door and some louvered windows to keep out the rain. Might as well be ready for the hurricanes, since they were the reason we were in this fix. For privacy in the bathroom, we found a hanging curtain of long chains. The chains were made of straw—not very private but very *islandy*.

Winston adds, "I accented the outside stone walls with turquoise eaves and coral trim. I framed our now coral door in bright, canary yellow to match a yellow hammock stretched in one corner of the porch. Our homestead was beginning to look like a Caribbean postcard. Pictures speak louder than words, but they hide a lot of secrets too."

He continues, "We scavenged furnishings from every place and everybody. There was hardly a person in "next door" Leverick Bay who didn't give us something. Hotel employees who played with us at the Rock knew when old furniture was being replaced. They appeared one evening with a pair of huge, designer, rattan chairs in elephant motif, another night, with a mattress and bedding. You never knew what they'd drop off.

"We scored white, wicker patio chairs, a dresser and mirror, an old piece of glass for an outdoor dining table, stumps of wood for stools, pots and pans, and buckets," Winston rattles on. "If we wished for it, it came, or at least something close. Lowering expectations certainly helped.

"In short, Blunder Bay was our own personal salvage yard," he concluded.

It took a while, but we learned to work the monster generator, and learned how much fuel it guzzled too. To ration our electrical power (and our fuel bill) we set a generator timer for two hours in the late evening. Our stove was gas, and we had no refrigeration, just a cooler with ice. We only needed electricity for lights and our St. Maarten TV, which wasn't really a TV, just a VCR player. Like clockwork, at the climax of a movie, the timer would go off and the power would shut down. No generator meant no electricity, meant no movie, and no lights. You haven't lived until you've read a book with a candle perched on your chest!

Sadly, we never met the ghosts from Blood Beach. But, in honor of them, we nicknamed our new home "Jumbie Junction."

"We hadn't lived there long when Cynthia and I started noticing that items kept floating up in our yard unannounced. Pieces of wood, old boat parts, waterlogged hats, inner tubes, oars, a water ski, a windsurfing mast, even a blow-up kayak. Tempted to begin our own version of Bert's junkyard, we opted to send most things back out to sea. But the stuff kept coming back! Seems our cove was the dead end of North Sound's current. Everybody knew that anything falling off a boat, sooner or later, could be found at Blunder Bay.

"We effectively made use of a wandering windsurfer mast, after our third go-round of sending it out to sea, only to have it return. It became Jumbie Junction's flag pole, with California, BVI, and skull and crossbones flying high. Our best prize was an inflatable dinghy with a fifteen-horsepower engine attached—no boat name, no numbers. We really thought we'd scored that time. But two weeks later, after we put the word out, sure enough somebody claimed her."

Our out-of-town relatives contributed to Jumbie Junction too, just like the locals. My brother, David, and his wife, Bettina, were our first callers from the mainland. They built us a cool fire pit, and a perch to hold the stranded, red kayak that showed up while they were visiting.

The best gift of all was the mural David painted dividing our living area from the bathroom and bedroom. An artist specializing in modern art, David used all our leftover paint. It was an abstract, Jackson Pollock-style splash of Caribbean color. He entitled the eight-foot, floor-to-ceiling masterpiece "Blender Bay," in honor of all the flotsam and jetsam in our seaside yard.

"David helped me create a neat, outdoor shower, too," grins Winston, "with a jungle of palm fronds for privacy. We used a sunken sailboat's teak grate for a floor, to keep the mud off your feet and the snakes under them. We painted the PVC water pipes black to attract the sun, so the water would be warmer when we showered—mid-day if possible. Early morning or late evening showers were a thing of the past. Come to think of it, hot water was a thing of the past.

"I got this harebrained idea thinking we'd be innovative and catch fresh rainwater. We dragged two discarded, three hundred gallon, black plastic barrels back from Tortola and let them fill with rain water.

According to island recipe, we added a drop of bleach and a floater of diesel fuel on top to ward off the mosquitoes. Well, it didn't work, and that's an understatement. The mosquitoes thought it was a luxury hotel just for them."

Winston built a wooden walkway from the house to the dock's long path and I transplanted wild orchids all along the way. It was perfect for long, naked walks. Then we replaced the path's spotlights with colored bulbs. They didn't shine more than two hours a night (because that's all the fuel we could afford), but they sure set the mood.

Our bedroom was festive indeed. I decorated one wall, with snapshots of our family and friends. I covered the collage with saranwrap, so rain couldn't hurt the photos. We balanced our mattress on six, huge, Styrofoam blocks we found stashed behind a shed. That way, if we flooded in a storm, the bed would remain dry. To protect from mosquitoes, we hung sheer white netting over the bed, from the bedroom ceiling—so romantic. It draped dramatically over each corner of the bed and reached the floor just like pictures in *Island Living* magazines. The only hitch was when we rolled over, our bodies were up against the netting. We soon learned mosquitoes bite *through* netting, whether it's pretty or not.

Now in tune with island mentality, we devised a method to outthink the bastards. We'd climb into bed, arrange pillows all along the edges of the bed, and tuck the netting outside and under those pillows. Then we'd gently nudge each pillow over the edges of the bed, so they were almost like hanging bumpers. That way the pillows kept the netting off our bodies.

Ingenious. We still could hear their angry buzzing and feel the rivers of sweat rolling off our bodies because it was so bloody hot under that damn net. But they couldn't bite us . . . until we had to go to the bathroom in the middle of the night. Climbing out of our beautiful contraption took some serious maneuvering. The mosquitoes, needless to say, took full advantage. They feasted as we sat on the pot grimly recounting the mosquitoes in *Don't Stop the Carnival.* By the time we got ourselves tucked back into our "fort," we'd be wide awake.

Our next purchase was going to be outdoor carpeting to put inside. Quickly, we had become weary of grimy, concrete floors, under our bare feet. Sure, one solution was wearing shoes, but who wants to wear shoes when you can walk around naked? So, we checked out the carpet store. Yes, they had a carpet store in Tortola, and, yes, it was on another Thursday. "What color are you looking for?" we were asked.

"The color of dirt," panned Winston.

We hauled a fifteen-foot roll of carpet to the ferry, then into a taxi to drive across Virgin Gorda to Gun Creek, then to another ferry to Bitter End where *Gitana* waited. Then that dirt-colored carpet rode all the way to Blunder Bay, in little old *Gitana,* without ever getting wet. Unrolling it in our living room gave us power. We christened it with sex and rum.

Plumbing, like I said, was challenging at Blunder Bay. Besides the hillside plumbing system, which we conquered, there was the toilet, which we never did. The water drained out of the toilet, the toilet handle flipped up and down, and the commode held the correct amount of water. But it wouldn't flush. No amount of messing with it would make it flush.

We figured it out, though, and boy, were we becoming die hard islanders. You just walked to the edge of the patio carrying a drywall bucket, swooped up a bucketful of seawater, and lugged it back to the toilet. When you did number two, you poured the bucket of water into the water closet and—ta dah—it flushed. Every time. Perfect. It was easy, and possibly the most unique exercise I'd ever get.

There's an island saying: "If it's yellow, let it mellow. If it's brown, flush it down." We added, "If it's big and brown and serious, climb up to the house on the hill." Gravity is very beneficial.

To Florida for business

Just in time for us to master that technical, flushing process, we were off to Florida and the land of toilet handles. Winston had decided to become an official yacht captain by U.S. Coast Guard standards, to improve his chances for a full-time, sailboat job. The best place to do that was Fort Lauderdale. For two weeks, he took classes and crammed.

I, on the other hand, played. I rendezvoused with friend Judith (*Gitana's* namesake) for a road trip. I had hired her some fifteen years before at my PR agency in St. Louis, and with our history, we could talk for miles. She was my mentor in life, my Dear Abby in love, and my Dr. Spock in child rearing. Not having driven a car for months, I was ready to drive the highways. We took her Mustang convertible from Houston to Key West, Florida, scripting our own version of *Thelma and Louise* all the while. We met my proud and victorious Winston in Fort Lauderdale, U.S. Coast Guard captain's license in hand. He had spent two weeks almost overwhelmed with studying (something he hadn't done in twenty years) reviewing navigation, chart plotting, tidal calculations, safety regulations, anchoring, mooring, docking, basic weather, basic stability, passage planning, seamanship and rules of the road, and then was tested for several hours. He was proud indeed.

Back to Blunder the two of us went, with his newly minted credentials. We felt proud of ourselves for paying attention to opportunity and preparing for our next dream.

Going to and from

Commuting to work from our new home was a feat in itself. Driving our dinghy, *Gitana JK,* was a treat, and now I got to take her on a long trip every day, well, fifteen minutes maybe—long by my standards anyway. My highway to work was across Blunder Bay, through Leverick Bay, and out into the crosswinds and currents of the North Sound. It was a wet and rough ride at times, at least until I arrived in the lee of Prickly Pear Island and then reached Saba Rock. This was my daily commute, about nine in the morning and who knows when after dark, whenever my day ended.

How pleasant it was, when compared to my old daily commute of jammed highways and crabby drivers. Not missing that corporate life one bit.

My dinghy driving was perfected during those road trips. I'd stand in the stern with my knees slightly bent and my body leaning backward (kind of the water-skiing position). I held *Gitana's* painter (the line attached to the front of the boat used to tie her to the dock) in one hand and the Yamaha's handle extension in the other. Rev the extension and off I'd go, riding the waves as if I were on a bucking bronco. I loved that commute, even in wet weather. I was conquering the raging sea.

However, coming home in the pitch black was another story. With no lights in the house, I couldn't see the entry, let alone the dock. I tried memorizing the silhouette of the mountainside. Our house was directly below that dark, third hump from the right. Failsafe, right? Many times, I found myself motoring back and forth in the channel, trying to decide which hump was third, or it was so pitch black I couldn't even see the humps. More than once, Winston heard my dinghy engine crisscrossing back and forth and came outside waving a flashlight and yelling from the dock. My love grew every time my handsome, personal lighthouse came to my rescue.

Compared to the wavy commute, our private little bay was peaceful. A baby-eyed puffer fish that lived under Blunder's dock seemed to welcome our petting. When we'd snorkel, the resident nurse shark played hide-and-seek with us, tucking himself under a big boulder. Half his torso stuck out from the rock, but he never caught on. It was his habitual hiding place. The same little boxfish greeted us each morning, and spotted eagle rays glided their way across our front yard every night.

Land crabs were another story, living in holes under the ground. They were huge. They were fast. They were erratic, and they crawled sideways. They'd stand up high on all their legs and charge right at you, accidentally, of course, but still. They gave me the creeps outdoors. Inside, what a nightmare.

"We had rats and snakes too," echoes Winston. "The snakes came compliments of good old Frank Drake. The sailing ships kept little rosy boas mixed in with the ballast (heavy stones in the bottom of the boat for stability) to keep the rat population down aboard ship. When the ships arrived at their anchorage, the sailors would throw the ballast to the shore, so they could maneuver more easily and make room for the heavy bounty they hoped to collect. Out with the ballast went the snakes. And there they stayed."

One must learn to cohabitate with all these creatures, if one wants to live in the islands. For someone like me, who shivered squashing even a roach, this was a big step. I persevered because of Thelma and Louise and Jane.

Some British friends of ours had recently sailed across the Atlantic with their pregnant cat, who gave birth at sea. We adopted two little sisters. Cuddly, gray-striped tabbies, the two kitties took to Blunder Bay like lions to the jungle. They were jungle kings, or, rather, queens. Not a predator around. No barking, pain-in-the-ass dogs chasing them, no other cats trying to mark their territory. They ate lizards for breakfast, rats for lunch, snakes for dinner. They were the official park rangers of our cove.

One liked to stick close to us and approach things cautiously. She was christened Louise. The other ran up to everyone and flirted. I swear, she'd sleep with anybody too. That's why we baptized her Thelma.

Cats, Thelma and Louise, scampered down the path every day to greet us when they heard Gitana's motor whining across the water. They purred us to sleep every night. They generously brought us presents, too: a rat on our doorstep or a dead snake, laid ever so gently on the shower floor. The mouse population reduced quickly. Those crabs, not so much. Thelma and Louis were not particularly fond of crab claws.

Winston loves this story. "One night we were awakened by eerie, unexplainable sounds coming from the living room. In the black of night (no electricity), I climbed out of the web that was our bed, grabbed my trustiest tool, a flashlight, and went prowling. Naked and on my tiptoes, I heard more noises—lots of loud clawing and scratching, accented by banging. Thelma and Louise were in plain sight.

"Thelma's back stood hunched. She was curious and petrified at the same time. Louise was at full alert, ears rotating like radar, eyes wide as pies, frozen in place. Clearly, they would not be a bit of help.

"More banging and clanging and that strange, eerie clawing again. All of a sudden, I yelled, "What the hell?" which got Cynthia through our bed web in a flash. We stood there together, naked, beating off mosquitoes and staring at the cabinet under the sink. What in God's name was making all that racket? What the hell was in there?

"Shining my flashlight at the door, I stretched out over the cabinet and threw it open. God knows what we expected: a werewolf, a mountain lion, or at least a small goat to come careening out and mutilate us? Maybe it was a haunted jumbie.

"What came out at us? Nothing. The flashlight searched for the noise. Low and behold, sliding around in our oversized metal salad bowl, donated by a well-wishing restaurant owner, was a huge land crab. Unable to get traction on the slippery metal sides of the bowl and desperate to escape his prison, the tortured but hair-raising thing struggled with all its might.

"Finally in sight, the monster wasn't so monstrous to us now, but Thelma and Louise were still frozen in place. Massively relieved and doubled over with laughter, I threw the bowl out onto the kitchen floor. It was like a scene from *Alien*. The clatter on the concrete scared the shit out of our poor pussies. The crab scrambled every which way it could, trying to get the hell away from us while not being nailed by the flying salad bowl. The cats, however, were not his worry. They now cowered in the corner, hissing ferociously, but cowering just the same.

"Armed with the trusty broom, bravely I chased/guided/coerced the unwanted, midnight alien back into his own territory in the yard, and together Cynthia and I climbed back into bed, tucking in the mosquito netting as we climbed. However, the night was young.

"About an hour later, we heard another scratching noise, this time coming from our closet. Pissed, I jumped up, sure that Thelma was prepping to take a leak on our very limited wardrobe. I grabbed my flashlight. No, not again. Yes, again. Another monster land crab, only this one even bigger, grinned up at me. Maybe it was the full moon . . ."

Me Jane, rat killer

Remember our outspoken, English friend, Diver Jane? Well, she ended up living with us at Blunder Bay. Our couch, really a single bed disguised as a day bed and doubling as a couch, became her cot. Jane had her own dinghy to tie up in our "garage," and the kitties ran to her just as they'd run to us every evening. Jane won the prize for being the first and only of us to fall into the drink while boarding her boat, which was often a major negotiation. There is nothing like taking a salt water bath right before work. She still holds that record.

Jane had extraordinary ways of solving critter issues. A rat-trap *aficionado,* Jane even caught rats in our oven. Every time she'd hear the scurrying of tiny, rat feet in the rafters, her eight-foot boat hook was put to the test. "You bloody bostards," she'd scream at the top of her lungs, with her fine English accent, pounding the boat hook into the ceiling to the beat of the Minute Waltz. "Get the f@#$ out of here!" She was especially pissed off at the ceiling dwellers one night; they'd eaten an entire bag of pot stashed there.

Between the cats, traps and boat hook, our rats were well-traumatized. Jane had no solutions for the goats, however.

Just after we had decorated the path with orchids and transformed the vibrant bougainvillea into foundation planting around the house, there came the goats. In the heat of the night, with nary a sound, they sneaked in. Not that we had any fences, mind you. It *was* their territory,

I suppose, if you must get legal about it, but, still, should they gobble up every one of the lush plants?

"We woke up the next morning to a completely stripped and naked yard," says Winston, and he's not exaggerating. " Not a flower fluttering. Not a leaf left. Those damn goats devoured every last petal we had except the cactus. I was ready to force-feed them cactus!"

The incident brought to mind a story our godfather, Tom, had spoken of back on his boat. He and most residents of Leverick Bay had become tired of the goats devouring their lavish landscaping. The men wanted to shoot them and be done with it, but the wives just wouldn't have it . . . too gruesome. The men's other option was to gather up the goats and ship them off to Prickly Pear Island. Prickly had no inhabitants, plenty of plants, and the buggers could eat all they wanted.

So, on a certain evening, Tom and his cohorts in crime started catching goats. As soon as they got a boatload, off they motored to Prickly Pear. With no dock available, the boat just slowed to a stop a short distance offshore. Tom picked up the first victim, an innocent-looking, little baby goat who could probably eat his weight in flowers in two minutes. Tom leaned over the side and dropped him in the water, expecting him to swim to shore.

Well, this baby goat was not like a baby turtle. He didn't know how to find the shoreline. He didn't even know how to swim yet!

All those macho men watched mournfully as the little bastard's tiny, baby face disappeared. "Ye gads!" yelled Tom as he and everyone else jumped in to rescue the drowning goat. After that, they hand delivered each goat to shore. These guys had been dying to shoot the buggers on site just a few days before yet jumped in to save a drowning one.

And the summer rains cometh

Our next stateside visitor was my friend, Judith, from St. Louis. True to form, she just showed up one day, unannounced, at Leverick Bay.

Standing on the dock, with suitcase in hand, she'd asked, "Anybody know Winston and Cynthia?" to anyone she saw. Of course, everyone knew us. We lived around the corner. We ran Saba Rock. Winston was a yacht captain. I ran the pub. Who was this weirdo, and what did she want?

"I need to get a message to them so badly. It's urgent." (Everything was, with Judith.) "Could you please radio them that Judith is on the dock?" And so they did, across channel 16 on the VHF radio, for all to hear: "Hey, Winston, some tall, blond woman named Judith is here to see you."

Winston and I were flabbergasted, and not surprised at all, to see our gypsy friend. Desperate to relieve her curiosity and experience our island life firsthand, she'd hopped a plane one day and was there, ready to inspect her namesake, *Gitana JK*. At sixty-five-plus, she was still making hay, traveling like a gypsy whenever she could.

I was at work at the pub, but Winston zipped over to meet her. He introduced her to Blunder Bay and stashed her bag. Then off to Saba they came, to my waiting arms. Judith met Gayla and Bert and Tyrell and Tim and Feather and Pita, plus our unabridged gang of misfits. We celebrated with rum and tonics well into the night.

Exactly as expected, Judith adapted rapidly to her surroundings. This is a woman who drove the length of Baja Mexico alone in her convertible, who tramped across miles of ground at low tide to reach Mont St. Michel in France, who signed up for classes at Oxford knowing not a soul there. She was an adventurer, and we were her latest throw of the dice.

Tropical Storm Iris arrived about the same time as Judith.

As I came home from the pub one day, she met me at the doorstep of our porch standing in rivers of pouring rain, with buckets in each hand and a look of despair on her face. Winston was gone on a one-day sailing charter.

"Cynthia," she lamented, "I kept trying to catch all the leaks, but they just kept coming. Your living room is awash and floating away. I'm so sorry," she apologized as if it were her fault. Anyone else would have lambasted me for leaving them in this predicament.

With Iris dumping seven inches of rain in just a few hours, our bottom-of-the-mountain, Blunder Bay homestead was flooding fast. JK, as I'd nicknamed her back in our PR days, and I tried to salvage what we could. I feverishly but futilely marked the stone walls in the living room where streams of water were seeping through the mortar, hoping to repair them later. What a joke. There were dozens of leaks. We frantically captured water pouring from ceiling cracks, in the few pans we had, dumped them outside and ran back for more waterfalls. There just weren't enough pans.

After the storm passed, as she and I lugged our sopping wet, dirt-colored carpet into the sun for drying, I joked, "Well, welcome to our world." Tropical Storm Iris had rudely awakened her to an undisputed fact: actual life in the islands doesn't always look like the one in the brochures.

Summer, the hurricane season, could be long and slow in the Virgins. Tourists didn't come, and ex-pats revisited their stateside lives of traffic and grandchildren. Population dwindled the way ice melts in the sun. It was lonely.

Winston helped friends, Dan and Katie, by managing their watersports business while they paid a call to Canada. He'd sit in the company shed on that dock, waiting to rent a dinghy, take someone waterskiing, or collect mooring fees, only to fall asleep due to boredom. If suddenly he glimpsed something moving in the distance, all senses would go on high alert. Was it a person? Did he know him? Where was he going? Might he drop by for a chat? Oh, please, drop by for a chat, or just to borrow some money, or to ask when the next ferry was arriving.

Those were some long, hot days in the summer doldrums of vacationland.

Luis storms in

Not long after Judith flew back home to St. Louis, we had another out-of-towner blow in, Monster Luis.

Hurricane Luis was seven hundred miles wide with sustained winds of one hundred fifty mph and gusts to two hundred mph. The weather bureau didn't even have categories that high. I labeled Luis an 11. He was the size of Texas.

Hurricane Luis gave notice a good two weeks before showing his ugly head. All of us islanders were prepared for all our belongings to drown. Updates would clamor across VHF radios hour by tense hour. It was nerve-racking. Luis would prove to be Winston's and my primer on how to prepare for hurricanes; we were to weather twelve more over the years.

Pirates Pub on Saba Rock was virtually shut down, as was every business on the surrounding islands. We ceremoniously kissed our little, abandoned grass shack, with its soft, tropical palm frond roof, goodbye. We battened down the pub's inventory, piled the outside tables and barrel chairs into the bar, lashed the shutters, and sent the crew home. Winston and I rode *Gitana* back to Blunder Bay, and Gayla waited out the storm with Bert and Tyrell in their sturdy, stone home atop the Rock.

Dead serious now, Winston and I teamed with Jane, to secure our belongings. First, we bagged everything we had in the house in black, plastic garbage sacks. Then we dragged our dinghies up onto the land and tied them to trees. We filled the boats with water to weigh them down, hoping they wouldn't blow away. We removed the heavy engines and humped them inside the house, protecting them from salt spray, which would ruin them. We lashed down everything that could be a threat if airborne—like the fire pit grate, tables, chairs, brooms, rakes, shower floor, and empty barrels. Luis was our first hurricane, but we'd seen the pictures.

Then we climbed away from the sea and up the hill to the vacant house, waited, and listened to the VHF.

Luis wreaked havoc on Virgin Gorda. The eye of the storm went right over our beloved North Sound.

We couldn't trust the house to stand up to the wind (even though the house had heavy metal chains securing each corner of its roof to the ground, for just such an occasion), so we three musketeers endured the brunt of the storm in the empty, concrete, windowless cistern, under the house on the hill. We played with Thelma and Louise and ate lots of fattening foods that didn't require energy to cook. We drank and told stories of past lives, good, bad, and ugly and we tortured the cats with tinfoil balls bouncing five feet high off the end of fishing poles.

As the eye passed over us, we literally felt the deafening silence and, unable to resist the temptation, went outside against all counsel. How could we pass up the chance to look into the eye of a hurricane? Sound was nonexistent. Even the kitties were in awe. The world around us looked in frozen turmoil, trees stripped naked and ripped from the ground. Nothing moved. As quickly as it had approached, the eye passed beyond us, and all the noise returned. We darted back to the cistern. Pounding torrents of rain and mighty gusts of unstoppable wind drove us back inside.

Holed up for several days, Winston and I took full advantage and completed courses in CPR and first aid. Jane was a documented instructor, so why not? There was no better way to pass the time and practicing on each other was a riot. Indeed, again please, what part of this sumptuous, erotic chest do I compress? We graduated despite ourselves.

After many hours of ripping our paradise to shreds, Luis at last blew north, and we emerged to see the damage. Our fine, wooden walkway was gone, replaced by soggy rivers of deep mud. There wasn't an orchid to be found. It was heartbreaking. Every dock was missing, pushed up and de-nailed, by the violent storm surge. In this land only negotiated by boat, docks were crucial to the infrastructure. Now they were gone. Saba Rock lost our tiny hut with all its cute painted wood—not a palm frond to be found—just as Gayla had predicted. And the prized singular palm tree she had nurtured for ten years had flown who knows where? The pub survived but lost part of its kitchen—no more French fries in paradise for a while. Bert, Gayla, and Tyrell were fine, miraculously. Feather and Pita sulked.

There was no communication about the rest of the islands. Our VHF radios only transmitted within the North Sound area. No one knew how badly Tortola or St. Thomas, or any other islands had been hit. We could only imagine, looking at the huge piles of uprooted docks strewn everywhere along the shorelines.

Thankfully, no lives were reported lost in the Virgin Islands. However, hundreds of boats were battered, some piled up against each other in one corner of the Sound. Many boats sank, and the powerful wind relocated many others, miles away, on a jagged coral reef. Winston and a friend helped raise a sunken, luxury catamaran by inflating lift bags under its pontoons. The owners had returned to the States and never knew who had saved their yacht. (Eighteen years later, we oddly happened upon the owners on a beach in Baja, Mexico. Idle chat led to boats and the BVI, and as soon as they named their yacht, we told them how Winston had helped save her. We all were amazed at the coincidence.)

The island after the hurricane was dismal. Any existing foliage was burned from the saltwater, which blew as high as three hundred feet in the air. Cisterns were contaminated with salt. No one could get anywhere, and everyone was needed to help rebuild the docks. It took a week to assess the damage, get organized, put private households back together, and then tackle the public devastation. Everyone chipped in. At Blunder, we became ground zero for scavenging any semblance of reusable items. Like a mask and snorkel, we helped islanders see through the debris and breathe again.

Ten days later, along comes Marilyn

"And then, only ten days after Luis ripped apart North Sound, another, even more vicious hurricane attacked," Winston still feels the shock as he tells the story. "The worse part, no one had any advance warning. Hurricane Marilyn turned on a dime and headed our way. The region's population was still wiped out from Luis. People could barely believe that now they faced another onslaught.

"Hurricane Marilyn followed Luis's footsteps, again gusting to two hundred mph and spreading thousands of miles. This time, the eye went right over St. Thomas in the U.S. Virgin Islands, thirty miles away from us. Unlike Luis's powerful water surge, Marilyn's weapon was her wind.

"I was away on a weeklong charter, with a pair of honeymooners. Jane and Cynthia held down the fort at Blunder. At least we had practiced just ten days before. They made a good team, going about securing everything, almost by remote. Hauling our two dinghies up onto land and dragging their engines into the house were their worst difficulties. Together, they conquered them, nonetheless, and again climbed up the hill and into the cistern.

"I had no way to reach Cynthia, nor her, me. Phones were down, and VHF radios didn't transmit to the other side of the BVI, where I was sailing. We could only imagine each other's fate.

"When I got back to Blunder, almost a week later, I told Cynthia and Jane my story. Hearing the weather warnings and noticing all the other sailboats heading for shelter, I had notified the charter company's owner that I'd be bringing the guests back to shore. 'No, don't be a chicken. Stay out there. And don't alarm the guests,' was the response. There are all kinds of words to describe what I thought about this guy, but I can't say them here.

"An hour later, I again called headquarters, this time announcing, "I'm on my way in, so make room. These people need a place to stay. Find it." I made it into Nanny Cay on Tortola without incident, but the winds were picking up drastically. I settled the charterers in a hotel and then dedicated myself to helping secure all the other sailboats for the storm. It wasn't until the end of the day, with Hurricane Marilyn due to reach land in ten hours, that the charter company noticed my plight—I was homeless. 'We've got to take care of our captain,' demanded a very kind office worker to her asshole boss. When no response came from above, she invited me to her own home for safety, and served me several wonderful meals to boot. I never worked for that guy again.

"North Sound withstood Marilyn's winds fairly well, but our good friend lost the roof of her hilltop home, ruining most of her belongings, including a grand piano. Hardest hit was St. Thomas. Eighty percent of the homes there lost their roofs. The airport was annihilated. Most roads were impassable, and the waterways jammed with sunken yachts and debris. An official U.S. Coast Guard vessel was blown out of the water and up onto the roadway in downtown Charlotte Amalie. 'The pile' referred to the dozens of luxury sailboats smashed together at one end of the island.

"Two-by-four boards had impaled telephone poles as if they were Styrofoam. Foliage looked scorched from the ravages of saltwater spray. The world, as we knew it, had stopped.

"Now thoroughly disheartened, islanders began their second massive clean up in two weeks. Adrenalin wasn't flowing as fast as it had after Luis, but eventually it started pumping again. It would take months to salvage all the boats, but slowly and surely, it would happen."

With chagrin, Winston added, "The foliage, on the other hand, bloomed tiny green buds almost immediately and die hard Pirates Pub opened for business. Can't go on without cheeseburgers in paradise and cold beer. With each pour of another painkiller, heavy on the rum, things got back to normal."

Nourishing the mosquitoes

My son, Jason, and his girlfriend, Lisa, spent a week at Blunder Bay, right after the hurricanes. His broad smile and great laugh were even better than I had imagined. I was proud to introduce him to our friends, and have him experience our island lifestyle.

It wasn't the best time to stay with us, though. Fresh water was pooling everywhere from the storms, and mosquitoes were having sex nonstop. All those new babies were only too happy to drink some fresh blood. Red-headed, fair-skinned Lisa was like luscious French pastry to those beasts. They ate her alive, even under her mosquito netting.

Jason, an avid scuba diver, mined the sea with rat killer/scuba expert Jane. She guided him on his first BVI night dive—the bottom of the sound looked like the moon, he said. Another night, he and I swam through bioluminescence in the water that lit up our bodies like glow worms. He and a friend tried to snag some lobster that lived under our dock, creating makeshift snares from my various kitchen utensils, PVC pipe, twist ties and rubber bands. No luck, unfortunately, but lots of funny memories.

Just as my brother, David, had built a fire pit and painted a mural, Jason contributed to improving our little haven. He helped Winston rebuild the washed out shower and refastened the floundering gutters. The best improvement, as far as I was concerned, was the dive light he gave me. He could hear me cruising back and forth in the dark,

On Blunder Bay's dock in the dead of night, Cynthia's son, Jason, holds the megawatt underwater flashlight that becomes his mom's beacon for finding her home after midnight.

trying to find my way to our dock. So, he stapled reflector tape on the palm trees in front of our house, and gave me his megawatt dive light. It weighed a ton but shot a beam of light that reached the stars, I swear. Never again did I wonder "Where in the hell is our house?"

Our San Diego neighbors, Kellie and Ray, popped in to Blunder that fall, as did Andrea again, this time with a new boyfriend. Between sailing trips, ski boats, Mexican fiestas, Blunder Bay bonfires, swimming naked and showering in the wild, we showed them the best of island living—so did the mosquitoes.

Winston's lifelong friend from Hawaii, Janet, got to see a different side of island life: the sick side. Shortly before she arrived for a BVI sabbatical, Winston contracted Dengue fever, a gift from the thriving mosquito colonies. A virus similar to malaria, the debilitating ailment causes 104 degree fevers and excruciating joint aches.

Winston winces as he reminisces, "Goddam, I couldn't eat, I couldn't sleep, I couldn't even sit up. Friends came over to check on me, and I just wanted them to go away. Talking was too painful. Even opening my eyelids hurt. I laid in bed while Cynthia played tour guide for Janet. Luckily, it was her month off.

"According to a doctor we knew on Virgin Gorda, there was no medicine to ease the pain. I had to just wait it out. Cynthia and Janet gallivanted all over the BVI, and I lost fifteen pounds. When I did recover, it took forever to gain my strength back. Even after three weeks, walking up a hill still required a nap. Thank God that's over."

The charter from hell

Winston's position as yacht captain was gaining ground. The charter companies teased him, "We bow to you and your new license, *O Captain! My Captain.*" Winston would just grin, knowing he was preparing for opportunities down the road. I quarterbacked the Rock; he took people sailing. It was such a deal—until the charter with Antonio and Maria.

From the country that looks like a boot, Winston had two charter guests he wanted to *give* the boot. The man was fifty-seven, his new wife twenty-six. They'd eloped in Las Vegas, after knowing each other for thirty days. He spoke only Italian, she a fair smattering of heavily-accented English. They'd been evicted from their honeymoon hotel in Virgin Gorda for disturbing the peace. Now they were on a sailboat charter with Captain Winston.

Antonio would wake Winston at 3.00 a.m., pointing to his watch and whispering desperately in the most basic of English, "Me airport now!"

Winston had no intention of moving a sailboat in the middle of the night. (Reefs are invisible in the dark, and they eat boat bottoms.) But here was this new husband shaking Winston, begging to go to the airport. What the hell was up?

When Winston asked Maria about it, she retorted, "Oh, we don't need Antonio anyway. You, me, we do the charter." Oh shit! Winston high-tailed it to Blunder Bay. With topless, longhaired Maria crawling around the bow of the sailboat on all fours, Winston pleaded with me to join him in his misery. It was my month off, so what the hell. I was game.

Now how do I put into words the anguish that was Maria and Antonio? Let's see . . .

"We *don't* have to stop to fill the water tanks!" she'd scream. "I don't *want* to stop for water. We need no water. I will just wash my hair in Perrier." She showered three times a day.

"*Why* on earth are we *here?*" was another tantrum. "This place is disgusting. I want to leave *now*. We *must* go to White Bay. *That's* where my friends said we must go. Take us there *right* this minute!" We were in White Bay.

"*Why* can't we go to Anegada right now? It's *just* this far on the map," she'd spout off irrationally, showing an inch with her fingers. Never mind that an inch equals three hours of sailing and it was almost dark already.

Table slapping, book throwing, door slamming, and Italian screaming, screaming, screaming below deck and above always gnawing at our nerves. Lovely charter.

"Antonio! Antonio!" she'd scream at the top of her lungs. "Get me this. Do that. What's wrong with you? I'm in a hurry!" Then she'd rant in Italian. And he'd rant right back. The charter got very old, very fast.

We'd both seen Antonio sitting midship on the sailboat with his feet dangling in the water, his face dejected and his head shaking. "Big mistake," he'd mutter to Winston, pointing to his wedding ring. "Big mistake."

At our wit's end with this difficult couple, Winston and I made a plan. He'd take Antonio ashore and find an interpreter. That way, at least Winston could get the straight scoop on what was bothering the man. I'd keep Maria busy—sunning, cocktailing, showing off her Barbie body topless on the bow. Lucky me.

"Through the interpreter," Winston laughs, "I figured out that Antonio was sick to death of his new bride and afraid he'd be ruined financially by her. Duh. According to this guy, if Maria could get a witness to sign a paper saying Antonio was a bad husband, she could be entitled to much of his estate. Antonio was afraid I would sign that document and ruin his life forever. I told him to relax, no worries. I preferred him a hundred times over her *(the dreaded, deafening, longhaired vixen brat, I thought)*. 'There's no way I'll sign anything, Antonio. Let's just go back to the yacht and try to have a good time.'

"Off we sailed to Anegada, an island only twenty feet tall, known for its spectacular coral reefs, everlasting beaches, and heavenly lobster dinners. It is designated a BVI national park, and people are prohibited from removing anything natural such as shells, or coral. Of course, that didn't apply to Maria. After prancing around waving a purple fan coral for all to see, she was stopped by a park ranger. She proceeded to argue with him so incessantly that he ultimately gave in. Throwing his hands in the air he shrugged, 'OK, lady, just take the darn thing,' to which she abruptly responded, 'No, I don't want it now,' and threw it on the ground.

"Salivating to cook some lobsters onboard, Maria batted her eyes and wiggled her ass at the owner of a restaurant, renowned for its lobster dinners. At first, he flatly refused; he didn't sell raw what he made money cooking. Five more minutes of Maria's badgering and he was already beginning to cave. 'Well, how much do you need?' After another several minutes, exhausted from her obnoxious bullying, he agreed to sell. Then she asked, 'How much?' 'For you, madam, I'll charge only twenty-five dollars.' Like clockwork, another tantrum. 'What do you think I am, stupid? You're ripping me off! I know it. I wouldn't pay that price for gold!' And out she stomped."

This charter was my first long-term charter with Winston. It would hold the record as our worst charter for literally ten years.

O Tannenbaum, O Tannenbaum

After hurricane season, we "settled in," me at the Rock and Winston on charters. Christmas at Pirates Pub was again the usual festive conglomeration of rusty tinsel and tiny staff stockings, rum toasts, and century plant tree.

Our holiday at Blunder Bay called for a different kind of tree. Rat Killer Jane found a rather distinguished branch that sort of resembled a Christmas tree, if you leaned to the left and squinted your right eye. It had been ripped from its mother during Marilyn. It would have to do, 'cause we sure weren't going on another century plant expedition.

Ornaments were easy: bits of paper, sea shells, red ribbons, even paperclips if they were shiny. We handmade snowflakes and hung them with silver twist ties from the buns at the pub. To accessorize, Jane bought me a small, brown Rudolph made out of wire with moving legs and long antlers. (He still sits on our tree every Christmas.)

I splurged on generator fuel and shined our colored lights on our palm tree path well into the night. It seemed that everyone in North Sound dropped by our house to share a holiday drink. Our rickety old dock was full of boats, and the kitties were spoiled rotten. The place brimmed with good cheer. The only thing missing was Winston. He'd gone to St. Thomas to help rebuild the airport.

With his construction expertise and the St. Thomas airport's devastation from the hurricanes, Winston's skills were in high demand. Maria and Antonio had taken their toll, and he was ready for a break from sailing. Besides, construction pay was great, and replenishing our bank account would be smart. He moved to St. Thomas to help rebuild and was sleeping on a dock in Charlotte Amalie, like many people from all walks of life who'd lost their homes to Marilyn. Hundreds of houses were covered in blue FEMA tarps, and would remain so for months. There was plenty of work for Winston.

Because I was working at Saba 24-7 the month of December, it wasn't practical for Winston to come home to celebrate Christmas at Blunder. But, I was off work by New Year's Eve, so that was a different story. Separated for the Christmas holiday, we didn't want to be apart on New Year's Eve, too.

"My trip back to Blunder was a fiasco right off the pages of *Don't Stop the Carnival*," Winston loves retelling this story. "First, my twenty-dollar cab ride took the wrong turn, and then the thirty-dollar ferry left without me. There wasn't another ferry until morning. And it started pouring rain. I ended up crawling under an overturned dinghy for shelter. Then an earthquake—that's right, that's what I said, an earthquake—shook the wet, muddy, lumpy ground where I slept. In the morning, now thoroughly stiff, crusty and crabby, I caught the ferry to Bitter End and Cynthia's arms. Happy New Year. She really let me know how much she appreciated my return, too!" he grins.

In January, back in St. Thomas, Winston was asked to babysit a thirty-two-foot Pearson sailboat, named *Sea Breeze,* that had been one of Marilyn's many victims. She had washed up on the Frenchtown beach in St. Thomas during the hurricane. *Sea Breeze* could float, so she had been tied to a mooring ball, in front of Frenchtown near the Hook Line and Sinker restaurant. Her hull was in perfect shape, but she had a bent rudder, a broken mast, and no canvas bimini for shade. Plus, water had to be brought onboard in gallon milk jugs, because she couldn't be moved to the dock to refill her tanks. In return for babysitting, Winston could live aboard *Sea Breeze* for free. She was luxury compared to the dock.

During my month off, I joined him in St. Thomas for a visit. *Sea Breeze* was nice and cozy inside, and it was the smallest space we'd ever lived in together. If we could survive that situation, we kept telling each other, we must really be in love. Commuting to shore was hit or miss. The rubber dinghy that came with *Sea Breeze* had a flat bottom and a fast air leak. Plus, it had only one oar. A swift current ran strongly out to sea between *Sea Breeze* and the shore at Frenchtown, so picture the two of us, in a rapidly deflating rubber boat, weaving through the current in a circle, Winston paddling frantically toward shore while I shouted directions to land this sucker. There was no dock to master, thank God. We'd just row the wad of rubber as close to the beach as we could, then take a deep breath and wade ashore.

Winston was determined to live full-time in St. Thomas making serious money using his construction skills between his sailing gigs, and I liked the intriguing, energetic vibe that permeated the island. With all the businesses in town, I realized I could easily find work there. So . . .

The wheels in my head shifted gears.

Newfound friends

Our Virgin Gorda friends Buddy and Susie, who ran the red sailboat and sold us our dinghy, had moved to St. Thomas after the storms. They lived on their boat in rundown Yacht Haven Marina, better known to the locals as Rat Haven. Buddy was salvaging sunken boats for insurance companies. Susie waited tables at Tickles, a pub in upscale Crown Bay Marina.

Winston and I bumped into Susie at Tickles, and in nothing flat

Cynthia and four other women sailed this racing yacht from St. Thomas, U.S. Virgin Islands, to Isla Calebra, 12 miles west of St. Thomas and 17 miles east of Puerto Rico.

our network of friends expanded. Susie knew some cool and interesting women living in the area. Carla was a world-class, America's Cup, yacht architect in St. Thomas running her boss's sleek, custom sailboat. Its high tech, carbon fiber mast dwarfed everything in the harbor. She'd brought the yacht down from Newport, Rhode Island, to compete in the international Caribbean regatta circuit. Blond, buxom Helen and her attached-at-the-hip, show-stopping friend, Mary, had a house painting company on Water Island. (That's the small Virgin Island a half-mile from St. Thomas, famous for its Honeymoon Beach.) Heavy smoking, quick-to-laugh Ginger bartended at Tickles, with Susie.

After only a few rum and tonics, I was invited to a weekend girls' trip to Culebra, Puerto Rico, on Carla's sailboat. Five chicks sailing a red-hot racing yacht without a man in sight! We were the talk of the island even before we arrived. Refusing to be intimidated by my own incompetence, I sucked up every tidbit of sailing knowledge Carla spat out, and got more highs from driving the boat and adjusting sails than I had from drinking the rum.

By the time we returned to St. Thomas, Captain Carla and I were fast friends. Now enticed by living in St. Thomas and starting yet another chapter in our eclectic lives, I let her know I was looking for work. Carla introduced me to premier restaurateurs, Craig and Sally, owners of the five-star establishment of the same name. Craig needed an evening bartender, and, with Carla's recommendation, I got an interview.

Now I'd never been even a waitress in a diner, much less a bartender in a fine establishment, and I didn't know fine wines at all. "But you can talk with strangers," Craig said. "That's all you need. Customers know which wines they're going to choose. All they want is someone to talk to." With that, I was hired. I was apprehensive, but opportunity knocked. Trained to pay attention to opportunities, by Italian Sandra back in San Diego, I jumped.

This could be perfect. Craig and Sally's was located right in the heart of Frenchtown, only a rowboat's ride from *Sea Breeze's* mooring and this was no Jimmy Buffet "cheeseburgers in paradise" dive either. The creative menu was different every night. My domain was a large, sumptuous, walnut bar with candlelight accents and roomy, comfortably padded chairs. Walls of fine wine spread floor to ceiling. I could serve sixteen, mouth-watering dinners at a time and offer twenty different wines by the glass—a far cry from Pirates Pub. It put me smack dab in the midst of the island's movers and shakers and the pay was lucrative.

I bought *Bartender's Guide to Success* and at the end of the month ferried back home to Blunder.

Blowing out of town

As soon as I returned, I gave Gayla notice. Sad as I was to leave the pub, I explained, I wanted to be with Winston. What's a life in paradise without your lover?

Winston and I put our hearts and souls into finding a good home for Thelma and Louise. We just couldn't stand the thought of them living on the street, dealing with dogs and cars in noisy St. Thomas. Some locals we knew adopted both in an instant, and they were off to new lives of their own.

We did one last project for our landlord at Blunder. We unpacked the screens that had come with those louvered windows we'd bought when we first moved in. We hadn't used them because we wanted a clear view of our paradise (plus the mosquitoes got through them anyway). Installing them now, at least, might keep the screens from getting lost. Unwrapping the first one, we got the laugh of our life. The screen didn't fit. No matter how we tried, it just didn't fit. None fit, in any of the windows. We tried them all. The store had sold us screens for the wrong windows. Live and learn. Don't stop the carnival. We packed the screens back up and stored them in the generator shed, both of us grinning the whole time. NGP—next guy's problem.

Packing didn't take long. Most everything we had was borrowed or 'leave-behinds.' Ahhh, the delicious ease of no "stuff." We were finished almost before we started. Good-byes to our home and our friends were poignant. My heart broke a little. I was melancholy because yet another incomparable sliver of our life together was ending, yet simultaneously anticipated our brand-new adventure. We'd left our old life. Now we were leaving our new life.

But at least we left it in style. Carla graciously offered use of her sailboat as a classy moving van. *Gitana JK* lurched along behind.

Many times, Winston and I had stood seaside at Blunder Bay, watching the ferry boat drive away, taking our friends back to their motherland or off to a new life. Watching them disappear perpetually made us sad, knowing our friendships were as transient as the people who offered them. And now, we were the ones saying good-bye.

Full circle, I thought, with a new circle right around the corner.

Chapter 6
Life in the Other Virgin Islands

Rarely do members of one family grow up under the same roof.
—Richard Bach

Moving day finds Winston ferrying the few belongings he and Cynthia own to their new home on Hassel Island, U.S. Virgin Islands.

St. Thomas to Hassel Island to Antigua to California to Hassel
January 1996 – August 1996

Frenchtown Frenchies

After Hurricane Marilyn, St. Thomas in the U.S. Virgin Islands was in terrible shape. Those two Category 4 hurricanes had devastated not only the island, but the islanders' moral. Marilyn and her twin, Luis, had stolen the life out of hundreds of private homes, hotels, shopping centers, and schools. Many people were striving to rebuild. Roads were

99

barely cleared. Stores demolished. Crushed dreams lay everywhere—gutted million-dollar homes here, a kid's baseball cap with nothing left but the bill and seams there.

But, despite the devastation, crispy brown plant life, burned beyond repair from that saltwater sandblasting, suddenly burst forth with budding greenery. Life was refusing to be drowned out and our own life was budding anew just like the greenery.

Winston and I were now official residents of Frenchtown, a small community of fishermen adjacent to the main city of Charlotte Amalie, on St. Thomas. We were Frenchies, living on thirty-two-foot *Sea Breeze*.

After completing his work on the airport, Winston ran a drywall finishing crew that rebuilt custom homes for people now forced to camp. His skills were in demand because there were few journeymen-level tradesmen available. Carpenters were being flown in from New York and New Jersey. Utility workers came from Tennessee. They crowded into barely standing hotel rooms and put their talents to work.

I covered the bar at Craig and Sally's from 4:00 p.m. until usually 1:00 a.m. Winston toiled from 6:30 a.m. to 4:00 p.m. We had our little *Gitana* for transportation now, but still felt like Gilligan's crew twice removed. I'd take Winston to shore in the morning, where he'd catch his own personal cab to the worksite, always driven by George, the cabbie. Then at 3:30, usually after going to the beach with a friend, or reading a book curled up in the V-birth of *Sea Breeze*, I'd maneuver *Gitana* to shore in my new uniform from K-Mart: black slacks, one of three flowered shirts, and black tennis shoes. A quick spit bath in the restroom at Hook Line and Sinker and I was good to go. (For real showers, at least once a week, we both used the hotel up the hill. It had a pool and a generous manager.)

Winston would finish his shift, ride back to Frenchtown with George, retrieve *Gitana* and drive back to our "house" for the evening. Then, at midnight, he'd jump back in the dinghy and come pick me up at the restaurant. Funny but schlepping back and forth in the wind and rain and dark of night brought us that much closer to each other. We had a system and it worked.

"About once a month, when we were really feeling flush," adds Winston, "we'd splurge and ditch *Sea Breeze* for a night at the Marriott. 'No,' we'd tell the front desk clerk, we didn't want an ocean view. 'No', we shook our heads, we didn't care about a view of the bay. We lived on water all day. We didn't care a thing about seeing it from a hotel! All we wanted was a working TV, a working remote control, and lots of hot water, preferably in a Jacuzzi, for Cynthia."

For fun, we wanted to hike nearby Hassel Island, a large, beautiful island situated directly across the channel from Frenchtown and basically an arm's length from our boat. At night, it looked across at the twinkling lights of downtown Charlotte Amalie, and during the day, invited explorers for sure, or so we thought. We explored it only once.

It was a Sunday, and the place was deserted. Walking along the photogenic, stone breakwater, we passed by a small, yellow, two-story cottage. A much larger, sky-blue home sat right next to it—no people anywhere. Then we came to what appeared to be a field, but actually, after spreading our way through it, we found an overgrown stone patio. Behind the patio, hidden in jungle debris, stood a picturesque, stone building. Continuing to wander, we discovered a group of stone cottages alongside it, all jammed with what looked like someone's long-forgotten junk pile. Further on, a huge swimming pool was just barely detectable, buried under debris, overgrown foliage and uprooted full-grown trees. Stretching out on the far side of the old buildings was a big open clearing with a modern, single-story mansion in the far distance. We started toward it. We never made it to that mansion.

Winston frowns, "As we got closer to that cool home sitting like an icon on the waterline, I eyed something strange on the mansion's porch. At first, I couldn't tell what it was. Then I murmured low and slow, with all the breath I could muster, 'My God.' There were two, gigantic, stainless-steel dog dishes on the mansion's porch. At that same moment—as if by telepathy—these two huge, black Rottweilers bounded toward us, announcing with their teeth that they intended to eat the crap out of us. Apparently, we'd crossed some imaginary line and were now on their menu. Trying to express urgency without scaring the shit out of Cynthia I whispered lowly through gritted teeth, 'Stop! Dogs! Slowly, carefully, back up! Keep backing up 'til we've crossed whatever imaginary line those goddam bastards respect.' We didn't stop till we were safely in the yellow cottage's front yard. (Still no people.) That's when we finally breathed."

The back of the island was much safer. Besides lots of conch shells and sea glass on the beaches, we discovered the ruins of a railway and pulley for big boats and equipment that was part of a coal loading station for early 1900s steam ships. Several tall stone structures sat in ruins, a marine repair facility, an apparent residence, even a cast iron cistern, each inviting us in for a tour. We felt like conquistadors (as long as we weren't being chased by the "bastards").

Winston and I lived in that thirty-two-foot boat for eight months. For a while, we even had roommates. Rat Killer Jane from our Blunder Bay days came over from the BVI just for fun. One day, Jane and I were riding to the grocery store with Winston's cabbie, George, when Jane piped up, "Hey, George, you look so familiar to us. Have you ever lived in the BVI?"

George answered, "No, never have. Not even ever bin dere. But my bruder lives on Virgin Gorda. Hid name William." Turns out that William drove the garbage barge for Saba Rock. I'd written a paycheck to William for picking up the pub's garbage every week for almost two years. And now his brother was driving us around St. Thomas. We loved these twists of fate.

One of Jane's lasting impacts on our lives involved permission. Winston had always been a Harley-Davidson guy. He'd built an award-winning custom chopper that graced the cover of a magazine many years before, and the love still festered. Any chance he could, he'd window shop in the Harley store in St. Thomas, or check online at the local Internet Café.

We were lounging on *Sea Breeze* one day shooting the bull when Jane said "Come on, Cynthia, why don't you just tell Winston to go buy a Harley? So what that you live in the islands and only drive around the U.S. a few months a year. Who cares? You know he bloody well deserves it." With that bit of permission to do something rash, Winston and I were off and running. Delivery time for Harleys would take up to a year, so we had time to save the cash. We vowed on Jumbie Junction to take a trip back to San Diego that summer and search for the perfect bike. Thanks, Jane.

Interesting how it took the nudging of friends to help us make life-changing decisions: Sandra, Peter and Blondie, and now Jane. We were learning to listen for cues.

Got into the rhythm

"In St. Thomas, we had a basic but regular social calendar that kept expanding our network of friends," Winston points out. "Friday night meant Tickles for happy hour and roving dinners with alternating menus of KFC, Pizza Hut, or Chinese food. I loved that. I'm a junk food junkie.

"Sunday was swim/drink/tan day at Honeymoon Beach on Water Island. Honeymoon brought us two of our best friends ever, Glenn and Barbara of Hassel Island—Hassel, that island we'd hiked with those damn Rottweilers."

Tall, lean, blond Barbara managed a boat rigging company. She'd been a swimming athlete in college, and it showed, even at fifty. Deeply tanned Glenn had the smoothest skin I'd ever seen. As a young man, he had designed restaurant kitchens for an international hotel chain. Then he dropped out of life and made his living chartering sailboats and teaching islanders how to harvest conch in the Bahamas. His side company silkscreened T-shirts and marketed them throughout the islands. He figured out how to live in the islands and make money. Glenn was retired now and a homebody except for those Friday night roving dinners and Sundays at Honeymoon Beach. We envied his spirit.

Glenn and Barb had been married for thirty years. Ten years before we met, they'd rented a small cottage left over from the defunct and mostly destroyed hotel on Hassel Island. Only seven inhabitants were on Hassel, plus three dogs and four cats. Eventually, Hassel Island was designated Virgin Islands National Park, but not before Glenn and Barb purchased their little piece of paradise there. (Their house was the little, yellow one we saw before we met the Rottweilers from hell. The defunct hotel was the abandoned stone building with the swimming pool/junk yard/jungle we previewed when we first hiked Hassel.)

Glenn milked his scotch and Barbara her vodka. They both smoked liked fiends, and Glenn indulged in the devil's lettuce every afternoon. Each Sunday without fail, they'd drive their boat to Honeymoon Beach, beach chairs and cooler piled in. (That's why they weren't home the day we found the dogs, or the dogs found us.)

Glenn could usually be found either plopped on his side of the couch near his pipe, on his bed reading/napping/reading/napping, or on the cane patio chair outside with a drink. Ever appreciative of the island's beauty, he would say with a cheeky smile and a sincerely deep sigh, "It just doesn't get any better than this."

Likened spirits, we adopted each other immediately. Our little *Sea Breeze* was moored directly in the path to Honeymoon from Barb and Glenn's home. Glenn offered to be my taxi to the beach on weekdays when I was off work. We spent hours sharing our histories and his myriad stories of early St. Thomas. We talked of chartering boats and Bahamian cultures, dreams yet to be realized and dreams run afoul, our running the pub and life at Blunder Bay, sailing the seas and weathering hurricanes. Speaking of hurricanes, only five months before, Barb and Glenn had lost almost everything in Hurricane

Marilyn. Their home sat only six feet above the water and ten feet from it. Even their refrigerator had been washed out to sea in the storm.

One day on the beach, we received an invitation of a lifetime. Glenn and Barb invited us to live in the apartment above their home. "There aren't too many people who can fit into our lifestyle on Hassel," Glenn had said. "We know, for sure, that you guys can."

We were thrilled and agreed to move in within a few months, after Glenn and Barb's vacation to St. Bart's and after all their household repairs were completed.

Winston and Cynthia's presence brought the island population to a whopping nine. They made this sign to commemorate the occasion and carry it around to this day.

Any sail maker, any sail maker, come in, please

Meanwhile, Sailor Carla invited Winston and me to be part of her team in the upcoming Antigua Race Week, the race we'd originally attended with Jorge and one of the most prestigious sailboat races in the Caribbean series. She would be racing on a classic yacht for a week and then on her boss's state-of-the-art, forty-five footer the second week.

Earning the time off from Craig and Sally's, we boarded the racer with Carla and sailed away. Jane hitched a ride, too. She figured once there, she'd find a team needing a good, strong sailor. She was right, too. Three hundred sailboats filled the docks and the harbors. Lots needed crews.

Just hours from rounding the corner to our destination, we snagged the long line of a crab pot. It tangled itself around our prop, stopping us cold. "Prop" is slang for propeller, the bladed wheel under the boat that spins and propels the boat through the water. Jane was skippering; therefore, she got credit/blame/good-humored teasing for the mistake. Diver Jane to the rescue, though. Down she dove under the sailboat, knife in hand, to cut through the wrapped line and free the prop. (So glad it was her and not me.) Within thirty minutes and a whole lot of deep breaths, we were sailing again, overcoming one of many, many mishaps encountered on the water.

For "Classic Race Week," we crewed a fully-restored, classic Sparkman and Stephens seventy-two-foot sailboat, originally built by Carla's boss's family. It would be racing a fleet of historic, show-stopping, world-renowned yachts, every day for five days. Winston and I were part of her fourteen-man crew. (Murphy, and all of his laws, came aboard as well.) Winds screamed thirty-five knots all week, overpowering most of the yachts. Everyone was hell-bent for the finish line, barely hanging on. Then, as if in answer to our prayers, during the second-last leg of the last race, the wind died. Suddenly— dead calm. Not a breath of air—anywhere. Every yacht flopped in place, going nowhere.

After some serious deliberations, our yacht's owner, a cheerful Austrian in a tall, green top-hat, who had supervised restoring this beautiful yacht, shouted, "To hell with it" and popped the celebratory champagne originally meant for the end of the race. "When you can't sail, might as well drink," he grinned.

Just as we were finishing our premature reward, the wind decisively picked up and we were flying again. We were first at the finish that day but, alas, got beat by a thirty-four footer with a better handicap. Then it was time to race Big Red.

For the second week's races, winds had grown to thirty knots again. The start was the most critical and dangerous part of the race, and the most exciting: human timers shouting out seconds to the get away, skippers yelling, "Starboard!" as they demanded right of way, and muscle-bound grinders wildly adjusting sails and booms, as yachts flew from one point to the next.

We saw more than one collision during these races, but the worst was a direct smash-up right through the middle of an eighty-foot maxi sled (pure race boat) by another maxi. The bow of one yacht sliced a raw, open, V-shaped gash into the other's side, just aft of the helm station. The skipper was propelled into the water, right in our direction. We rescued him before he could be trounced by another boat. No one was seriously injured, but it shook everybody to the core.

By the third day of thirty-knot hard racing, we were exhausted. We'd lost one thousand dollars' worth of line to the wind right after it spun loose and knocked the GPS off its pinnacle and right into the sea. Our huge, balloon-like spinnaker sail that flew in front of the boat was ripped to shreds. Other sailors were facing the same agony. Voices on the VHF incessantly begged, "Any sail maker, any sail maker, any sail maker, *please, please* come in."

The power of the wind destroyed the top of our mast—not once, but three times. It happened so often that a professional photographer even caught the event on film. Nothing is more humiliating than seeing a full-color glossy posted on the bulletin board showcasing your yacht with its massive mainsail falling to the deck. Even worse, the photo captured three quarters of the crew straddling the rail, staring up in disbelief.

We didn't win that race but what a time we had trying. Jane's luck was no better. Her boat T-boned another yacht and was disqualified.

Winston's favorite part about that Antigua Race Week: "Our crew, plus Jane, opted to skip the awards ceremony in search of booze. You had to wear long pants to the ceremony and have a tie—I had neither. And you had to have a car to get there—again, none. But our night was burned into our memories forever. We ended up at a deserted, dockside bar that was being dismantled. Its Brit owners were closing it down and moving back to England. Eager to get rid of all their stock, they invited us in and basically opened the bar to us. We'd discovered the mother lode! The scene surpassed *Animal House* on all counts.

"We took over the place, downing shooters, throwing back rum drinks, and essentially trying every way we could to shake off losing the race. The party really disintegrated when the owners started groping each other behind the bar. Out came the soda guns. We sprayed everything and everybody, even a poor, attorney-looking gent who had wandered in unwittingly. Soon after Jane started to relieve him of his coat and tie, he was taking part like the rest of us. It was one wild night of revelry.

"A hell of a lot better than an awards ceremony."

Bertha bites

Back in St. Thomas after the race, we were able to give Hassel Island a test run: would we really want to live there? Glenn and Barb asked us to babysit their house while they vacationed down island in St. Bart's. We jumped at the chance.

As they walked us through the property, outlining how the cistern functioned and where breakers were located, Winston calmly asked, "So what do we do if there's a hurricane?" "Oh." Glenn chuckled. "No worries there. I have storm shutters but it's only July. Storms never show up until late August and September. But just in case," he added, "only one rule: get yourselves off the island. It can take care of itself."

Next thing we knew, sure enough, Hurricane Bertha, of July, was spinning its ugly eye our way. Babysitting had suddenly become a lot more complicated. Bertha was packing winds of only one hundred mph, but still. Barb and Glenn had just made brand-new, plywood, custom-sized panels to fit every opening in their home, with custom-made hardware to secure them. Thank God. The installation was relatively easy, considering we'd never done it before. The perfunctory black trash bags were easy to find so, with synchronized teamwork, we got everything bagged, off the floor, and away from the windows. We boarded up the house and then prepared to dinghy our way off the island, to wait out the storm in a substantial hotel in Charlotte Amalie, right across the Harbor from the house but much further away from the threatening sea.

But not before Winston and a construction coworker named Rich drove Barb and Glenn's boats the half-mile to Honeymoon Beach on Water Island. Well-practiced in the art of hurricane survival, some of the Water Island residents had a tractor ready to pull the boats up on the beach. That done, we pulled our own *Gitana JK* out of the water and stored her in Frenchtown, on St. Thomas. Then we walked ten blocks to a hotel in Charlotte Amalie.

Just hours before the storm hit, we had booked a ringside hotel room, with big windows overlooking the main street and the vast white-capped Harbor to Hassel Island and beyond. We could see Glenn and Barb's little, yellow cottage being pummeled, in a blur of wind and water. We watched streetlights go flying and cars being blown off the road. A large commercial ship paced back and forth in the harbor, determined not to be washed ashore. The roar was deafening. We wondered about our judgment, renting a hotel room full of glass panels . . .

Then the hurricane was gone.

Bertha was comparatively gentle to St. Thomas, and sidestepped St. Bart's completely, to Barb and Glenn's relief. There was some water and sand to clean up, but, all things considered, the house on Hassel faired quite well. (The Rottweiler's house wasn't damaged at all.) When the vacationers returned, Winston and Rich had already started bringing the island back to norm. Glenn took advantage of his captured manpower and made an offer the guys couldn't resist: lay a new tile patio and get paid in the process. Deal.

Stateside to Harley hunt

By the time our leave rolled around, we were ready. The first time stateside in ages (except for the Betty and Dan wedding weekend in St. Louis), we planned a good, long road trip.

Winston and I went straight to San Diego and stayed with old neighbors, Ray and Kellie, at Windansea. They filled their inflatable mattress and lent us a Subaru station wagon for wheels. (Ray was in the car business.)

After some great times with Andrea, Jason, and our friends, Winston was hell-bent on searching for the best Harley deal he could find. Filling a backpack with clothes and the Subaru with gas, our route was dictated by Harley-Davidson locations. Each dealer had only a limited supply of motorcycles for sale. We shopped Los Angeles, the San Francisco Bay area, and then Yosemite Valley. We crossed the Sierra Nevada mountain range to Tahoe and then Reno, visiting an old construction partner of Winston's as a bonus. Between the Harley stores, the scenery was splendid. We relished the smells of the redwoods and aspens, so different than the palm trees of the tropics.

The travel bugs in us were elated.

Fix A Flat (make that plural)

"Then we headed down Highway 95 to Las Vegas," Winston sees the journey played out in his head. "That's when the real comedy began—if you call two flat tires in the emptiness of Death Valley a laughing matter.

"Coming down the straightaway of Highway 95—boom—a blowout. Off to the side of the road we went. Our tire was shot. I went to the trunk to retrieve tools and the spare. Well . . . no tools. Plus, the spare donut tire was as flat as a pancake. Oh, shit!

"We spent the next two hours in the heat of the deserted desert, hoofing it back to a little oasis we had noticed, a typical middle-of-the-desert junk pile with a couple of crusty, old codgers hangin' out by the swamp cooler. We passed several off-road brothels on the way but found them deserted. We scrounged behind those vacant structures looking for tools that might help, with no luck and no hookers either. By then, those crusty, old folks by the swamp cooler were looking good.

"After guzzling about two gallons of water and having quite a conversation with a huge lady behind the counter, we borrowed some

*After a stint at sea, a nice long road trip through Death Valley
dried out Winston and Cynthia.*

rusty tire tools and bought her last can of Fix A Flat. Generously, she offered to drive us back to our car. She said it's kind of an unwritten rule that you don't leave anyone stranded in the desert. They could die. Good to know. With that thought burned into our brains, we piled into a beat-up junker, with six, yappy mongrels in the back, and off we went to our crippled car. Things were lookin' good, right? Wrong.

"As our good Samaritan/rule-follower drove away, I put the tools to work. I removed the blown tire, installed the donut, and stuck that Fix A Flat nozzle in the valve stem. It fit perfectly. Unfortunately, a little too perfectly—like forever.

"Even after the donut was inflated, that can refused to come off, no matter how we yanked, twisted and pulled on it. Desperate to get back to civilization before our tire ran out of air again, I made a decision. Screw the can! Let's drive. Down the street we rolled, back to the swamp coolers. Stubborn ol' Mr. Fix A Flat came right along with us, spinning and banging all the way. Talk about looking like damn, old codgers.

"By the time we reached our 'oasis' to return the tools, the donut was again flat and worthless. The nearest town, Beatty, was fifty miles away—our only choice—a little, desert casino town just off the entry to Death Valley on the way to Las Vegas. I called ahead to see if the tire store there for sure had our size tire, which, by the grace of God, they did. Then I had to beg them to stay open, until we could get there.

"The next step was actually getting there. We started hitchhiking, carrying the dirty, dusty, blown tire under my arm. Sweat rolled off me, over the tire, and down my legs, carrying with it lovely, blackened road grime. Not one car in sight. Not one ride. Finally, we hoofed it to a gas station and got the attention of a couple in an RV, basically begging for help. They were at a crossroad in their holiday, to go east through Death Valley (away from Beatty), or south to Las Vegas (toward Beatty). We didn't stop fast-talking about the wonders of Las Vegas, until we were snugly tucked in their cab, heading south.

"When we arrived in Beatty, everybody in town was expecting us. News travels fast, just like in Leverick Bay back in the BVI. Everyone knew we were the *stupidos* who went to Death Valley without a spare. Several people came to greet us—just to see us, I'm sure—and walked us over to the tire shed. Lo and behold, it was still open. After exchanging the tire, we paid the incredibly fair price of forty-five dollars. (We would have paid hundreds.) 'So how you gettin' back to your car?' we were asked. Hadn't thought of that yet. The couple in the RV were long gone, heading to Las Vegas.

"'Why don't you call the police?' someone suggested, pointing to the payphone across the lot. 'They'll take you.' Brilliant idea!

"No 911 at the payphone. In fact, no numbers at all. It was one of those dial 0 phones. After chatting with the operator about our state of affairs (she'd already heard), she put us through to the police. Sure, they'd come pick us up and drive us back to our car. No problem.

'Well, only one problem, sort of,' said the policeman. 'We're a canine unit, so we'll have to drive the dogs back to the kennel before we get you guys.'

"Only too glad to wait, now that we had dependable transportation, Cynthia settled in on top of the Coke cooler. I, as usual, was jawing with every Tom, Dick, and Harry around. Later rather than sooner, after maybe an hour, the cop car approached and opened a welcoming door. I sat in the front, deputy style, and Cynthia was anointed the criminal in the backseat, penned in by the now empty dog cage and a sound screen."

I interrupt. Off we went. Stuck in the back, I could see Winston and the police officer talking but couldn't hear a word. Then the siren blared. We spun around in a U-turn and careened down the highway at top speed, in the opposite direction of our car and our happiness.

"What's happening?" I yelled, but no one could hear. Winston just looked at me with that "can't tell you now" posture. Not ten minutes later, we spun around again, another U-turn, but this time in the correct direction at least. The siren stopped. Speed dropped back to normal. *Ah*, I thought, though still confused as to what had just happened.

When we finally arrived at our deserted, lopsided car, I got the scoop. Right in the middle of our delivery, the cop had received an urgent call to respond straightaway. Drama! Just after he did, the urgency was canceled, and another officer was on the case. Cancelled drama! Consequently, the multiple U-eeees!

Breathing easier now that we were back at our car, Winston removed our flat donut and put on the new tire. Our policeman/savior didn't drive off, until we'd started the Subaru and were back on the road, but not before reminding us, "It's the law to help anyone stranded in the desert around here." Thank God.

Undaunted, we continued our quest for the perfect motorcycle, seeing the sites but now nervous that we had no spare. We succumbed to fear, and bought a tire in another little township. Then we headed back to San Diego. We'd driven thirty-five hundred miles, through the Wild West.

Every Harley dealer we toured had a waiting list of more than a year, just like we'd heard. Ironically, Winston chose our own San Diego dealer and ordered a 1997 Softail Custom in Caribbean turquoise and white trim with chromed forks. Down went his money, and up went his spirits. "You have to have a carrot," he smiled, "something to look forward to." He was a happy bunny now—seeing a big, luscious, juicy carrot dangling in the future.

Hello again, Hassel, and the last "cheeseburger in paradise"

We flew back to the Virgin Islands renewed and excited. It was great to be back and great to have a Harley on the books.

Winston fell right back into his building career, but I'd lost my barstool at Craig and Sally's. I freelanced as a bartender for busy nights and private events but got nothing dependable. As luck would have it, it was better that I wasn't working full-time.

My sister and her husband wanted to go sailing with us again and brought along her daughter and boyfriend. They offered to pay for the charter, if we'd sail the boat. Gladly, we grinned. We chartered a sailboat and spent a week in our old digs in the BVI. Throughout the trip, we presented our résumé and talked to charter companies about hiring us as crew, always watching for opportunities to land our next dream. All we wanted was a long-term position as captain and chef. We needed a seaworthy yacht that included a nice owner, good pay, and tropical surroundings. Were we ever going to get that yacht job?

We sailed to Cooper Island for a roti, Anegada for lobster, Norman for the caves, and Saba Rock. After a warm homecoming, we realized this was the very last day of Pirates Pub as we knew it. Gayla had sold Saba Rock to a Hawaiian restaurateur who was closing the place for extensive remodeling.

With mixed emotions, Winston and I hung around the Rock, so we could eat the *last* "cheeseburger in paradise" and have the *last* pile of greasy, hot French fries from our legendary Pirates Pub. We felt displaced.

Gayla presented me with the last Pirates Pub shirt on the rack, a deep-blue T-shirt silkscreened with old Pirate Bert and Feather. It was a child's size small, but that didn't matter. I insisted that both Bert and Gayla sign it, and I treasure it to this day.

When the charter was over, Winston and I moved to Hassel Island as permanent residents and became neighbors of Barb and Glenn. We created a long and lasting friendship with those two and brought the population to a whopping nine.

Chapter 7
Hassle-free Hassel

A farewell is necessary before you can meet again. And meeting again,
after moments, or lifetimes, is certain for those who are friends.

—Richard Bach

In early 1996, Winston and Cynthia moved to Hassel Island
in the U.S. Virgin Islands, into one of the little bungalows
featured in their favorite book, Don't Stop the Carnival.

Hassel Island to the Wild West to Hassel Island
August 1996 – February 1997

Don't Stop the Carnival—Living the book

Winston and I had moved up. We'd advanced from Saba Rock's grass hut to Blunder Bay's crab house to Marilyn-battered sailboat, *Sea Breeze*, to two solid rooms, with light switches and a working bathroom, in a national park, no less.

We were now living in that small, yellow, two-story cottage we'd passed when we were living on *Sea Breeze,* moored off St. Thomas. This was the house next door to those threatening Rottweilers. How weird. But it gets even weirder.

We discovered that Glenn and Barb's home was actually part of the original hotel featured in *Don't Stop the Carnival.* How's that for irony? Gayla had warned us so long ago that everything in that book was true. Over time, we became believers. Now, we literally were living in the place it memorialized.

Most of the hotel had been demolished, years before, in a hurricane. Tall, naked, rusted pilings from the now-absent hotel dock still stood at attention in the bay. Two cottages were saved, and Barb and Glenn were living in the yellow one. The sky-blue place next door was the other, though the owners had expanded it. Both cottages still used the same cistern described in the book. Best of all, they shared the sea, just footsteps away.

Was this fate?

The landlords, Barb and Glenn, lived downstairs. Our place upstairs mirrored theirs. Our balcony looked over a shared patio and a six-foot-deep front yard, fenced by a short, stone wall perfect for sitting. Behind the wall, right along the sea, a cement walkway stretched the length of the property. Barb's gracefully curved, coconut palm tree leaned toward the sea, a rope holding it steady. A colossal philodendron wound up its trunk.

Our little home on the second floor had a living room/kitchen separated by a counter with bar stools. It came furnished, thank goodness, because we arrived with everything we owned which was almost nothing. We inherited a three-cushion, green couch, white wicker table and lamp. A trunk did double duty as a coffee table and storage, and a few shelves invited knickknacks. The kitchen offered no dishwasher or disposal, but it was the grandest kitchen I'd seen in some time. My Caribbean colored dishes fit right in.

Our bedroom showcased a cane headboard almost like the one in our grass hut, with a queen-sized bed attached. The closet was almost as big as the bathroom, and the shower divine. A built-in desk ran the length of the back wall.

The windows were island-style, louvered glass slats, and there were no screens—just like at Blunder. Curtains invited privacy, but we never shut them; there was no one to look in. The most movement those curtains ever got was when wind blew them straight up to the ceiling. In a twenty-five-knot wind, they'd stay there for days.

We inherited a pet—sort of, anyway. Winston became fast friends with Buckwheat, Barb's black, short-haired kitty who drank water only from a martini glass and talked a good streak. Winston would have long conversations with his new pal, and Buckwheat would come and go through our screen door (and I mean *through*) repeatedly.

Our cottage had its own built-in alarm clock. Religiously at 6:00 a.m., a blue and yellow seaplane revved its loud engines, sped across the harbor right in front of our bungalow, and lifted off for St. Croix. The roar jarred even the resident iguanas out of a dead sleep. Then our alarm clock would rise and gently disappear over the hilltop, leaving behind a hazy mist of saltwater and some people ready for coffee.

Our garage, as we called it, was a series of mooring balls floating in front of the island for everyone's boats. There was no easy pulley system like the one Winston had built at Saba, but the moorings were spring-loaded which helped. Each boat hung between a cleat on the concrete walkway and a mooring ball floating thirty feet away. Parking was always a challenge. I'd have to carefully steer *Gitana* near the ball, without snagging the prop (first challenge), hook a line from my boat to the ball while still moving (second feat), then drive forward to the wall, bounce off the wall while grabbing a line and hooking it to the boat (final success). But wait, not home yet . . . Climbing out of the boat onto the three-foot-high wall was the real art, especially on a windy day with choppy seas bobbing everything up and down. De-boating required forethought, timing, dexterity, nerve, and guts. And when I was carrying groceries, it was even worse. Either I'd almost fall in the drink, or my packages would.

Life on Hassel was good. Neighbors Jack and Tina (of the blue cottage) welcomed us with wine in delicate crystal stemware, the opposite of our plastic glasses from the Pub. Jack had lived on the island as long as Glenn and Barb, but Tina was a new addition. A tall, good-looking guy with a quick smile and a deep chuckle, Jack was Barb's boss. He owned the main rigging company on St. Thomas where she worked. Tina was tall and slim, worked at one of the elite jewelry stores in town, and looked impeccable no matter the circumstance, even piling into her dinghy. She wore simple but elegant clothing, matched and ironed, and often even heels. Heels and irons—where were we again?

Almost daily, Glenn entertained us with the history of the island. He took us to its far end, where the remains of an incredible stone fortress guarded the entrance to Charlotte Amalie's harbor. Pirates had stretched a huge chain under the water from this fort to a twin fort on the other side. When enemy ships tried to enter the harbor, the chain would foul their plans.

Hassel was the perfect place for treasure hunting, whether in the sea, or in the hillsides atop the island. Bottles from olden days were a prize, though Glenn and others had already discovered most. Torpedo-shaped bottles, square gin bottles, and ones with two-inch thick bottoms remained hidden in the brush and under the mud in the sea. Bits of pottery, an old spoon, a few beads . . . our imaginations ran away with the stories they could tell.

Back to the briefcase

While Winston labored steadily, now rebuilding St. Thomas's jewelry stores, I looked for a permanent position. My search ended at Cellular Connection. The owner of the only cell company in the Virgins hired me as marketing manager. Overriding my misgivings about returning to a marketing job, I focused on the solid salary and the good brain exercise. Besides, I reasoned, refitting my marketing hat would keep me in the loop, just in case I ever needed to go back to the real world.

The assignment required a briefcase (ugh), but my office was on a dock, in Crown Bay Marina. I wore shorts and T-shirts and drove to my watery work world in my trusty dinghy, *Gitana*. Sometimes, neighbor Barb and I even rideshared. Her office was in the next bay over. I'd meet Barb on her porch for tea, or coffee, at around 6:00 a.m. Then we'd boat over to Frenchtown and take an energetic walk down Charlotte Amalie's waterfront for exercise. When we had the time, we'd climb the picturesque hundred steps in the middle of town, those same steps featured in *Don't Stop the Carnival*. Then back to Hassel for a shower and off again by dinghy to our offices.

I couldn't have picked a better business to market. The hurricanes had downed most communications, and people needed phones. Even those who'd never dreamed of buying a cell phone, now were almost desperate for one. Marketing wasn't the issue. Creating ways for folks to pay was. Many islanders didn't have bank accounts. Many didn't even have a trustworthy address. We introduced Pre-Pay phone contracts and sales soared.

I traveled to St. Croix and Puerto Rico twice monthly to confer with other Cellular Connection offices. Sometimes I took a seaplane. Sometimes a hydrofoil, a boat that actually lifts above the water to gain speed, but I don't recommend it—impossible if you intend to do any writing during the trip. Those big waves jostled me erratically, even if the boat was air born. Still, it was commuting, island-style.

I was employed by Cellular Connection, for eighteen months. During that time, I worked from home on Hassel Island a day or two a week. I even took a three-month motorcycle trip while working for Cellular Connection via computer. It was an ideal job, except for the fact that it wasn't on a sailboat.

Harley homecoming

"With our second year of island living under our belts, Cynthia and I were ready for a taste of wide open spaces," Winston salivates with the thought. "Not the open ocean kind. The hard kind. Dirt. Blacktop. Real highways again. Plus, it was time to pick up my new baby. My carrot was about to be eaten.

"Cynthia arranged to work for Cellular Connection via email, and I put my construction life on hold. Away we went, back to California.

"My new Harley-Davidson, a 1997 Softtail Custom, had arrived two months earlier. It was supposed to sit on the showroom floor until we arrived, but the dealer asked us to move it 'because everyone wants to buy that beautiful aqua and white show-stopper.' With the help of our Harley salesman, our good friends, Rick and Tammy, moved it back to their garage, and there it sat, simmering. We had barely landed in San Diego when we hot-footed it to Rick's doorstep.

Winston brakes in his new baby, a 1997 Harley Davidson Softtail Custom, in the mountains of Utah.

"When Rick raised the garage door, I was just like a new papa ready to hand out cigars.

"Dying to personalize my new toy, our first stop was the Harley store or the jewelry shop, as I call it. We needed helmets, leather jackets, boots, gloves, goggles and, of course, a tool kit and luggage bag. I bought wax and oil and metal polish, too. Plus, a cover for the bike and a cable to lock it safely. Probably our most useful purchase was the map of scenic motorcycle roads. Now we were ready. What a far cry from our life in the islands.

"We christened the Harley, with a four thousand-mile road trip through the western United States. And Cynthia worked for Cellular Connection in every motel, earning the title 'Email Queen' from her boss. (A computer and printer took up a hell of lot of room in those days, too. We didn't have saddlebags, just a pack on the back.)

"Our first hook up, after visiting Jason and Andrea, was with Cynthia's lifelong friend, Otto. They'd lived across the street from each other back in St. Charles, Missouri, and raised their kids together. His wife and Cynthia's dear friend, Winn, had died several years before in a car accident. Otto now lived in Prescott, Arizona, and knew every back road in Arizona and Utah. We were the only two vehicles on the road for miles and miles on end.

"We rode the wide open panoramas of California, Arizona, Utah, Colorado, and New Mexico, mostly on back roads. We checked out Yosemite and Lake Tahoe. We cruised the 49er Trail through gold rush country and Lonely Highway 50 across Nevada. We drove through Arizona on classic Route 66, cycled the north and south rims of the Grand Canyon and wound through Bryce Canyon, Zion National Park, Red Rock country, Escalante, and Capital Reef. With our 360 degree view of the world on the Harley, we didn't miss a thing along the way.

"Even the characters we met on the road were scenic. We came across a funny district attorney whose license plate read "Hang em" and visited with two, crazy ladies who had just bought a fixer-upper hotel on their credit card! I told them to read *Don't Stop the Carnival*."

Fresh from family visits and our Harley pilgrimage, we felt happy and renewed. It does the soul good to go after dreams.

From vast land to azure sea

After putting the Harley to bed in our friend's garage, Caribbean waters and Hassel's hassles welcomed us home—Sundays at the beach, Friday nights at Tickles. Sailing squeezed in here and there, working in between. Life was a beach again.

We got back just in time for St. Thomas's Carnival, an annual celebration that brightened the streets for two weeks. Steel drum bands, reggae contests, costume parades, and midnight junkanoo culminated in a night of colorful fireworks, from a barge in the middle of the harbor.

We had our own carnival on Hassel, with Barb and Glenn, neighbors, and the Sunday Beach crowd from Water Island. Barbecues smelled of juicy hamburgers. Rice and beans, salads and desserts covered the table. Rum flowed freely, as did scotch, vodka, gin, and beer.

Winston and Cynthia enjoy one of the never-ending parties on Hassel Island. Whether it be sailboat races or Carnival parades, their Hassel Island home was party central.

The group sprawled across the patio and down the wall. People hung their feet in the water and listened to the backdrop of carnival music from across the harbor. Everyone watched with glee as one guy fell in the water for the third time. Entertainment was cheap and plentiful.

As soon as dusk fell, the fireworks barge lumbered out to its position in the harbor. The government hosted a dazzling display of snap, crackle, and pop. The reflection of fireworks on the water made the view even more stunning. The world shimmered in colored lights. Don't stop the carnival. But then it did. Suddenly the fireworks stopped, without the usual finale. Odd, we thought.

Just then, Glenn got a phone call from a friend in the States. "Glenn, your island is on fire!"

While we were gawking from our patio at the fireworks in the sky, the rest of St. Thomas was gawking at us. We all inched out to the water's edge, so we could see back up the hill, over the cistern, to the top of our mountain. Searching the sky, we could just barely make out the orange of glowing embers. Our island was indeed on fire, embers floating down on the island and flames spiraling up.

The blaze grew, now unmistakable. As our friends loaded their boats, we got busy inside packing our important papers and photos just in case we had to evacuate. Our guys tried to work their way up the mountain to check things out, but the cactus and brush were so thick that passage was impossible. All we could do was wait and get reports via Glenn's friend and CNN.

Now we witnessed firefighting without fire hydrants, and without firefighting roads. Hassel Island had no roads. St. Thomas firefighting helicopters, with huge water buckets dangling from long cables, appeared out of nowhere. They dipped the buckets into the sea and hauled the salt water up to the fire. Dumping the load, they'd fly back for another dip. These guys not only labored through the night getting the blaze under control, they continued through the next week. Their system was intriguing to watch.

The fire never got to us, but it scarred a huge area on the back and top of Hassel Island. Barb and I would stare in disbelief at the barren, charred hillside on our way home from work for a long time to come. It was like searching a beautiful reef in a mask and snorkel and suddenly finding dead, broken coral bits and no fish at all.

So much for carnival.

Chapter 8
The Long Way 'Round

Your conscience is the measure of the honesty of your selfishness.
Listen to it carefully.

—Richard Bach

From Key West, FL, to San Diego, CA, by way of
New Brunswick, Canada, Winston and Cynthia
never took a direct route.

Hassel Island to Key West to New Brunswick, Canada, to St. Louis to San Diego to Tonga to San Diego
February 1997— October 1998

Joining the sludge

Not long after our fire, I received disappointing news from Cellular Connection. Our parent company in Puerto Rico was restructuring. My boss was retiring, and my function as marketing manager would disappear. Crap. He urged me to go for his position, take the leap to head honcho.

But once again, faced with choosing career, or lifestyle, I chose lifestyle. After my freedom at Saba Rock and the exhilaration of sailing, I just couldn't set myself up for the pressure of general manager. I reasoned that wireless was exploding, and maybe I should keep my fingers in the industry—but not my entire being!

Winston and I decided to make a change. Either we would pursue our dream of crewing sailboats full-time, or go back to San Diego for a dose of reality.

Sailing was our first choice. We put the word out in earnest. We were available as a couple—captain and chef/first mate. We had the license, lots of sailing under our belts and lots of island lore, too. We made the rounds incessantly, with companies and individual owners. We had resumés and photos and references and sample menus. Not a job to be had. Not even an interview. Was our dream hopeless?

Dejected, we were forced to reconsider. In San Diego, we could catch up on technology, not to mention money. Now that I had cellular marketing expertise, I could expand on that industry. Might be a nice fallback later, I told myself. I could freelance for an agency or work directly for a cellular client no matter where I lived. Construction was on the move in Southern Cal, so Winston could slip right into his old career, too.

Determined to continue pounding the pavement for our dream job crewing sailboats fulltime—via phone and internet rather than in person—we reluctantly pointed ourselves north, for a dose of reality.

Rather than go directly from Hassel Island, population nine, to one of the largest cities in the United States, we thought of a good place to cushion the blow: Key West—a natural bridge between island life and reality. We weren't sure how long we'd stay but at least until the weather warmed and we acclimated our psyches. Our friend Jorge was living there.

I'll forevermore remember my eighty-eight-year-old dad kidding when he heard we were considering Key West. "That's an awful place,

Cynthia. My friend told me it's rumored the gods tipped the states and all the *sludge* rolled into Key West. You want to live there, with the dregs of society? And there's that saying in Key West, 'We're all here because we're not all there.'" Dad thought we were nuts.

Key West was a good place to wait out the winter. We joined the sludge.

Winston loved Key West. "How could you not love it? Key West had a neat, little boating center. The weather was relatively warm, and there were lots crazy people, with lots of bars. Everyone either rode bicycles or walked almost everywhere. Wealthy conchs (that's what they call the locals) were remodeling their homes constantly, so there was lots of work for me. And we figured Cynthia could find temp work, between the boats and the bars. Key West Yacht Race Week was about to start, too, and Jorge enticed us, saying he'd get us crew jobs on a race boat. That did it for me.

"The reality of leaving Hassle was tough. Here we go again . . . Sadly, we told Barb and Glenn we were on the move. To safe-keep our little home above theirs, we advanced them six hundred dollars (our rent) to retain the first right of refusal (whenever our spot was available in the future). It was hard giving up another sweet place. We knew we'd miss it, just like the Rock and Blunder Bay. Barb and Glenn stored a few things for us: two Adirondack chairs, some scuba gear, and our three-foot-tall flamingo. There wasn't much, but storing them seemed to signify we'd be back.

"When Cynthia gave notice to Cellular Connection, they asked her to stay an extra week to help with the transition. She'd have to miss the yacht race in Key West, but felt committed to helping her boss, so she and I bought plane tickets, leaving one week apart.

The pilot will come get you

"My plane left at 8:00 a.m. on a Saturday," Winston continues, "I was flying from St. Thomas to Puerto Rico, taking another plane from there to Miami, and then a puddle jumper to Key West. We got my usual cabbie, George, to take us to the airport at 6:00 a.m. to be sure we'd get there in time. (The airport was only fifteen minutes away, but you never know what will go wrong in St. Thomas.) Cynthia came along just for fun.

"When we got to the airport, it was closed—totally closed. Not a damn person in sight.

"George dropped us off at the taxi stand across from the airport, thinking maybe we could bum a cup of coffee, at least, while we waited. But the only guy who knew how to work the coffeemaker wasn't there yet, so no dice. We waited, and waited, then walked back over to the terminal. Still no activity at the airline counter, and no coffee either. I was pissed. Cynthia tried the airline's help phone, but no one answered.

"Back again to the taxi stand, where at least there were places to sit. At 7:30 a.m., we saw some humans in the distance. Grabbing my bag, we ran back to the airport. Sure enough, there was an agent behind the American Airlines counter now but at Caribbean Air, my airline, not a soul. The plane was supposed to be there in thirty minutes! A couple other passengers were milling around now, too, looking lost.

"When I asked the American agent to please check for us, he spoke in singsong, 'No problem. Der's still time. He be here soon.' He didn't blink an eye and was as relaxed as I was anxious.

"Cynthia called the helpline again and turned on her charm. This time, the nicest woman in the world confirmed in a very soft-spoken voice that yes, indeed, der was a plane scheduled at 8:00 a.m., and, no, she don't know why it don't come. At 7:50 a.m., I again approached the AA agent. She looked me straight in the eye without the least bit of sarcasm and calmly stated, 'No worries. When de plane come, de pilot, he come inside and get you.'

"Well, surprise, surprise, the pilot didn't come inside to get me. In fact, the plane didn't come at all!

"As I griped over my inevitable fiasco of missed flights in Puerto Rico and Miami, Cynthia ran back to American and bought the first ticket available. I took off an hour later, a very unhappy guy going to a very happy place, by way of whatever expensive flight I could find."

Winston and I still shake our heads and laugh at that fiasco. That plane never showed up, and we never found out why. Expecting the abnormal was normal for us now. I had booked that same airline for my trip the next week. I switched to American, trying to head off the jumbies.

Becoming a conch

By the time I arrived in Key West, Winston had already raced a sailboat and was building houses. He'd walked into a construction company and was hired almost before he spoke. The boss told him, "I knew I was going to hire you the minute you showed up. You were wearing real shoes, not flip-flops." Winston had all the work he could handle. He offered inventive designs for remodeled conch houses and new condos and helped refurbish the historic Customs House.

We shared the upper half of a house with friend Jorge. At Mile Marker 1, on Highway 1, it was a furnished place hidden behind huge, beautiful trees. We enjoyed a big porch and a large loft.

I took full advantage of my life as a conch. Four to five mornings a week, I rolled out of bed and almost directly into the aerobics studio across the street. I was in the best shape of my life—abs even—because exercise was so convenient. Afternoons, I crewed as a mate on two historic schooners, taking vacationers on day trips and sunset cruises.

My boss on the schooners was a Key West legend, just as Bert had been on the Rock. Finbar was an ancient-looking sailor and one of the most illustrious citizens of the Conch Republic, as Key West was dubbed. As admiral and first sea lord of the Republic, Finbar presided over tongue-in-cheek Conch Independence Day and the sea battle that was re-enacted each April. Winston and I were mates for the battle.

The story goes that back in the 1970s, the U.S. government embargoed the Keys, trying to limit the rampant drug trade. With its daily supplies of general goods cut off, Key West was crippled, and conch citizens were enraged. They 1) organized, 2) formally seceded from the union, and 3) declared war on the United States. Then 4) they immediately surrendered and requested financial aid.

Celebrating Conch Independence Day involves what the Discovery Channel labels one of the biggest, baddest battles of the sea. Tall ships and tiny sailboats and everything between are pitted against U.S. Coast Guard cutters, all with good humor. The weapons: USCG fire hoses against rotten tomatoes, stale Cuban bread, and anything soft that will fill a sling shot. And we're talking some really big sling shots!

Winston and I bravely defended our ship wearing yellow, foul-weather gear, dripping in bright-red tomato guts. We really had become the sludge.

Tiny Key West offers lots to take in. Many historic, Queen Ann style homes, built when the first railroad linked New England with the Keys, accent the main streets. Tucked up the alleys and sandwiched down the small streets are rows and rows of small, one-story cottages (conch houses), each looking cuter than the next.

We bicycled everywhere, checking out fascinating aboveground cemeteries, President Truman's Little White House, and Hemingway's home. We fell in love with Key West's wild, six-toed cats. You see them tucked under cars, stretching out in eaves, hidden under bushes, and lounging on porch swings like they own the place. Many are purported to be direct descendants of the white, six-toed cat Snowball, given to Earnest Hemingway by a ship's captain. Hemingway's home had forty to fifty cats right on the premises.

There was an exquisite, butterfly sanctuary at one end of town and a noisy, wild sunset party nightly at the other. The southernmost point of the United States drew a lot of attention, and so did the "Duval crawl," crawling from bar to bar along the promenade, for a drink and a stamp (the "sludge of the earth," no doubt, Dad, but amusing to watch).

Hopping a fast ferry, we traveled seventy miles west to investigate Dry Tortugas National Park and historic Fort Jefferson, built with over 16 million bricks. A highlight for me was seeing a large spotted eagle ray swimming by the fort, reminding me of my underwater neighbors back at Saba Rock and Blunder.

We rented a car and took a road trip to Daytona for Bike Week, the second-largest, motorcycle rally in the country after Sturgis. By now, Winston was salivating for his bike back in storage in San Diego, but we'd get there soon enough.

Another weekend, we donned our professional sailor look and went hustling. We travelled to the acclaimed Miami Boat Show and soaked in the energy of sailors and yacht brokers. We walked miles through the show distributing our resumés nonstop, securing face time with anyone who would listen. "Need sailboat crew? Know anyone who does?" No. No. NO NO NO. Everyone had warned us networking was a long-term endeavor. No kidding. Long, long, long-term, it seemed.

We reconnected every time we'd spot someone from our island days. But all the rejection pierced even my enthusiasm. We didn't want to appear begging for a job, but we wanted to break in to the industry so badly.

The weather was turning warmer. Maybe it was time to go north.

Never a straight line

"We knew the quickest route from Key West to San Diego runs straight across the south, but how necessary was that?" questions Winston. "There was an entire country to see. We found this great deal, with a company needing rental cars delivered to California. It would charge us only ten dollars a day for forty-five days. So, of course, we took the longest way possible to Southern California—by way of New York City and New Brunswick, Canada. It's the journey, not the destination, right?

"We tied up our loose ends in Key West, packed what we had in the rental, and bid our friends farewell. We headed up the highway, with anticipation in our guts. We checked out the stately, moss-laden trees in old Savannah, Georgia, and Myrtle Beach, South Carolina, where I'd been stationed in the Air Force. Carolina BBQ was a must-stop in Goldsboro, North Carolina, as were the monuments of Washington, DC. As a veteran, I experienced the honored Wall for the first time on that trip. Being a survivor of Vietnam, I was deeply moved. I searched for names, and remembered my long-lost friends.

"We continued up the coast to New York, and took in every tourist attraction we could find. Actually, we saw much more than we'd planned, since we were lost half the time. We could navigate a yacht really well," Winston laughs, "but this road stuff was a nightmare."

In New Jersey, we searched out the home of my eighty-six-year-old mother's childhood best friend and had a memorable time. I'd heard of Nina all my life but had never met her. Chatting with Nina left me with a warm, loving feeling, knowing my mother just a little bit better and feeling closer to her, too.

We drove the coast of Maine but were disappointed with the dense fog that kept much of the beauty hidden. We took advantage of the seafood dinners, though, and stopped in Bangor to meet Winston's Aunt Virginia and cousin David.

Crossing the border into Canada was moving for Winston. He hadn't been back to his home in Fredericton, New Brunswick, since his dad had died ten years before. We stayed with his sister, Kim, and her family. Catching up took days. There were photos to pour over, memories to clear up, and stories to laugh at.

Winston's mother was thrilled to see her long-lost wanderer. It was my first meeting with her, so I had lots of questions. Every subject was fair game with Queenie. When I asked if Winston had any traits similar to his dad's, Queenie quickly piped up, "Well, Holly always loved a good fart." (So, Winston came by his talent naturally.)

Queenie told many heartwarming stories about Winston as a little tyke: How she always knew how to find him, because she could hear him singing. And about the day he brought home a bear cub. And the time she saw him running out of the woods as fast as his little legs would carry him, with a bucket of bouncing blueberries and a big black bear lumbering behind. He was adventurous even back then.

Winston visits his mother, Queenie Hovey, in Fredericton, New Brunswick.

Winston rekindled friendships with old schoolmates, Bud and Jim. Over beers and burgers, they created a completely different atmosphere than the one his loving homestead had projected, more like a gang of hyped-up high school buddies out on Friday night. I tried to soak in every word, learning new things about this wonderful, crazy guy I'd been with for almost ten years. (I've spent more time with them over the years, and they still belly laugh over the same stories.) We tried to find Winston's old girlfriend, the one who'd shown up with her husband at Pirates Pub on Saba Rock and was so gaga over him, but she had moved away.

We didn't know it then, but it was the last time Winston would see his mother. She died that year.

Back in the United States, we headed for Lakewood, Ohio, the Cleveland suburb on Lake Erie. My childhood home looked exactly the same, no kidding. I gave Winston a tour of the grade school and the ice skating rink and city swimming pool where I'd spent so much time. My parents had moved from Lakewood to Missouri when I was in sixth grade, but I was still sentimental about my first home.

Next stop was St. Louis. We stayed a few days with my sister and brother-in-law. Then we crossed the city and spent more time, with my close friend, Betty, my coworker in PR, and her husband, ex-ATF agent Dan (that couple who got engaged on our balcony). We hooked up with my old boss, too. We enjoyed a dinner with sailors, Ron and Sheila, who'd we met in the BVI, and blabbed about motorcycles with all their friends. Ron and Sheila were avid Harley riders. We planned to rendezvous at Sturgis someday.

I took Winston to his first baseball game at Busch Stadium, where the St. Louis Cardinals were playing their arch rivals, the Chicago Cubs. I'd lived in St. Louis for thirty years, was an avid baseball fan, and didn't see one person I knew in the stadium. Yet, suddenly, we heard someone yell from the crowd, "Hey, Winston!" I was floored. I swear he knows someone *everywhere*.

In Kansas City, we caught up with our old Pirates Pub supervisor, Kendra. We reminisced about how she and her scuba diver boyfriend had married, under the blue moon on Prickly Pear Island, arriving in two separate dinghies and walking up a sandy conch shell path, to an arch of fuchsia bougainvillea. It was a fairy tale wedding. But their bliss sank, literally, after the wedding, when their overloaded boat sunk in the middle of the bay, wedding dress and all! It was hilarious since no one was hurt and rescues were spot on. Eventually, after having a baby, they moved back to civilization. He resumed his regular life as a computer geek, and she became a full-time mom. Their little baby, born on Tortola with the middle name, "Islands," now toddled everywhere. We chowed down on Kansas City barbecue, talked all night, and left the next day full of happy memories.

On our cross-country trek, we were now entering the wild, Wild West. We drove the green highways of Colorado and stayed in historic Durango. From there, we headed to Otto's, in the high country of Prescott, AZ, another of our designated homes away from home. After a good rest and a lot of time at the coffee shops, we high-tailed it across the desert and picked our way to San Diego, trying to avoid traffic. No dice. Still, we rolled into San Diego not wanting the journey to end.

We moved in with our friend, Tim, temporarily—both us and our motorcycle. Winston was so happy when he cozied up to his long-lost, aqua and white, laden-with-chrome bike again. I swear it was like he was looking at a new baby. Tim teased Winston about how much the Harley had missed him, too.

Tim and his wife had just invested in a big, new home in a suburb of San Diego and wanted our company. We had some really silly times trying to be suburbanites with our roomies, decorating the double car garage, with lights and island posters, wiring it for sound, and adding a few folding chairs. Bingo—an outdoor living room. (OK, so maybe we didn't adapt to suburbia that well.) Our stored motorcycle inspired Tim to buy one, so we became riding buddies, too. Whether it was a day's run to the beach, or an overnighter to the desert, we put plenty of miles on our butts.

Winston fell right back into construction, but I had a hard time finding a marketing position. To pass the time, and maybe ignite the gods to do something, I enrolled in a U.S. Coast Guard captain's license course. Winston had his license. If I had one, too, maybe we'd be more valuable—a sailing couple with two captain's licenses. That just might move us up the crew employment ladder.

The two-week sea school was incredibly tough. Every one of my classmates was a U.S. Navy guy, but I stuck it out anyway, the only girl in the class of twenty-five. The second week I spent holed up in a motel room across the street from the school, overloading my brain with nautical facts. It paid off, and I earned my hundred-ton ticket. I had to log more time at sea, to be fully credentialed, but I was good to go. Now if only a yacht company would hire us.

I eventually landed an account supervisor position at a marketing agency that specialized in wireless technologies. Just what I'd had in mind: keeping my feet wet in the cellular industry. The price was sitting in an office, for forty to fifty hours a week. The people were nice and clients interesting, but something was missing. Could it be the Caribbean?

Sailing the South Pacific

Never going long without exploration of some kind, Winston and I were searching for a location to spend the upcoming millennium. Tonga sits on the international dateline, and is the first place to see the sun, and it was only five thousand three hundred thirty-seven miles away from San Diego, so why not? Maybe that would be a good place to begin a new century. Just to be sure, we scouted it out months in advance. With our four sailing friends, Tim and Barb and Rick and Tammy, we chartered a sailboat in the Polynesian archipelago, Tonga, flying to Fiji on the way.

Treasures from the sea on the south Pacific islands of Tonga.

We spent two weeks in Vava'u, a very remote area much different than the Caribbean—very few resorts, or restaurants. And the grocery stores offered only unrecognizable food—"Oh my God, there's only food from *scratch*," as Tammy had put it. (We ate a lot of canned spaghetti, the only thing we recognized.)

We dove with sharks and poisonous sea snakes. We raced packs of spinner dolphin. We experienced the awe and mystery of swimming up to the edge of a drop off and staring out into the deep blue abyss. When we anchored off the island of Ofu, we couldn't see a soul onshore. But suddenly, the beach came alive with a dozen little children antsy to meet us. They were hoping we could give them some paper for school, they said. They needed paper. Imagine. We obliged and threw in a bunch of Harley-Davidson pens to boot.

The chief of one of the many Tongan islands invited us to his village dinner, where we felt like royalty. Dancers performed a pre-dinner show while the foliage-wrapped dinner smoldered in underground fire pits. We sat on the ground before a long, narrow table covered with banana leaves, our plates. Silverware was nonexistent. Soon we were being served delectable but unrecognizable tidbits of juicy this and crispy that. I tried my flashlight as if to read my food, but it didn't help. No one knew what we were eating, but we had seconds and thirds of almost everything.

From vendors displaying their wares at the dinner, we bought several, intricately woven bread baskets and a carved wooden mask, the God of the Sea. (We didn't know it then, but eventually both would live in our crew quarters on yachts.)

It was an unusual time in the Kingdom of Tonga. The king's nephew had died, and the country was in mourning. All the men were wrapped in floor-length *tapas,* which doubled as mourning blankets used at the grave. The churches were alive with harmonious singing that echoed through the island.

Our friends were speaking about extending their trip since it was so enjoyable. But then . . .

The palm trees grow too tall

"Our trip was ending," Winston continues. "We called the airlines to confirm that everything was in order and sadly packed our bags. At the small, airport office we checked our baggage and readied our boarding passes. Then turmoil appeared out of nowhere. People were rushing about. Pilots were stomping. The agent was fretting and looking at us frantically but saying not a word.

"The girls were sure there had just been a coup on the island, a takeover of some sort. The explanation, it turned out, was simple. Off the wall and unbelievable, but true. The palm trees at the end of the runway had grown too tall. The plane with our luggage had taken off fine. But a plane heavy with passengers was grounded.

"The pilots had gone on strike. The palm trees were too tall.

"You'd think this could be fairly easily remedied with a saw. And, yes, it could. However, there was a slight problem: these trees were the king's palm trees, and he was out of the country. No one could cut his trees without permission. So, there we sat. You can imagine how Cynthia's boss reacted when she gave him the news. I tried to buy a weekly newspaper to prove the story, but it wasn't printed, by the time we left two days later.

"Cynthia and I took the news with laughter. Island life had trained us in flexibility and in lowering our expectations as well, I guess. The others, who only days before had yearned to extend their trip, suddenly were bursting with urgency to get home. Weird what that word 'can't' does to some people.

"We ended up staying two extra days (sans luggage), compliments of the airlines. To us, it was icing on the cake.

"By the way, nobody in Tonga seemed to know anything about the Millennium, or what events might be planned. We got the distinct feeling that none would be. We crossed Tonga off our list of places to be for the birth of the new century. But we loved our trip just the same.

"Back in San Diego, it didn't take long to realize we were submerging ourselves in our old routines again, albeit minus the stuff. Cynthia was doing the daily nine to five, (or six, or seven) thing. I was commuting to Tahoe and even Seattle to help friends with construction projects. Even when we had the good fortune to land an apartment in the same building as our former Windansea castle, we didn't feel settled.

"As poet Rachel Field wrote, "If once you have slept on an island, you'll never be quite the same." (1926, *Taxis and Toadstools*) The Carib had spoiled us. We were sure there had to be more out of life after forty."

Then the telephone rang.

Chapter 9
The Ups and Downs of Going on Everyone's Vacation

You teach best what you most need to learn.

—Richard Bach

*Winston's and Cynthia's first
full-time crew job, living and
working on the fifty-foot Orion.*

San Diego to Tortola, British Virgin Islands
November 1998 – December 1998

Term charters, here we come

Winston took the call from Lucy, head of the crewed yachts division at The Windwards, in the British Virgin Islands. The Windwards was the largest sailboat charter company in the world. Lucy wanted to hire us as full-time captain and chef. Finally! I was in San Francisco for the weekend, with son, Jason, and his girlfriend. Winston called from San Diego and, somewhat apprehensively, announced, "Well, looks like we have a new adventure."

It was happening. It was actually happening. Our dream was coming true. We'd persevered and landed our dream job!

We would live aboard a fifty-foot, luxurious sailboat based in Tortola, in the British Virgin Islands, taking people on sailing vacations, for seven to ten days at a time. It would be the first time in paradise for many of our charter guests. We'd feed them breakfast, lunch, appetizers, dinner, and dessert each day, with unique table settings, five-star presentation and, in between, take them snorkeling, diving, beachcombing, island hiking, picnicking, shopping, dancing, and, usually, drinking. For parties, we'd offer Caribbean noisemakers, colorful costumes, and even Rasta wigs.

Our living expenses were covered, and we'd get paid, too. We would live on a yacht! As a curly-headed, bright-eyed, seven-year-old charter guest would sum up our job years later, "You guys are so lucky. You get to go on *everybody's* vacation." Not a bad job description.

I was a tiny bit hesitant to leave Windansea, again, but ready to be a yacht chef, especially since it included swimming and snorkeling every

Winston and Cynthia proudly show off their first official uniforms as full time sailboat Captain and Chef.

day. What a dream come true. I gave notice and bought a mandolin (not the musical instrument, the slicing tool), a set of knives, and some exceptional stackable cookware. If I was going to cook seven days a week, at least I'd have the right tools. Then I collected recipes and Winston gathered navigation instruments.

We knew the drill from our preparations for Saba Rock. Lucy would get the work permits. We'd get the physicals, police reports, and drug and AIDS tests. In the blink of an eye, we were back in Tortola, looking at our new floating home and receiving our uniforms of shorts and polo shirts.

The Windwards was in Roadtown, on Tortola, in the British Virgin Islands. It had its own marina and one hundred fifty-plus sailboats ready for charter. But only fifteen had crew like us. The rest were bare boats, without crew, rented to people who could sail themselves (or *thought* they could, as Winston had discovered).

Our sailboat's name, *Orion,* bore the Windwards colors, white hull with royal-blue-trimmed sail bags, and blue and red logo. The cockpit (the outside sitting area on a boat) was roomy. Besides two bench seats, it had a fold-up table in the center and a built-in cooler for easy access to cold beer. There were two, oversized, steering wheels, one on each side, with navigational equipment centered above them. Two wheels allowed Winston to have control of the yacht even while letting a guest "steer." A bright blue kayak graced the foredeck, and *Orion* came with a twelve-foot dinghy.

Lucy showed us the yacht, said the other crews would help us when we had questions, and was gone.

Orion was in hurricane status, wrapped up tighter than a drum with all her cushions and loose items stored inside. Winston unlocked the companionway, and we climbed down. If we ignored the pile of outdoor cushions and kayak paddles, we could kind of see the place. The whole interior of the yacht was golden wood. There was a tiny L-shaped galley (kitchen, remember?), with fridge, stove, oven, sink and freezer, around a two-foot-by-three-foot floor space. You could reach everything without even moving your feet. An aqua settee (nautical term for couch) stretched along one side of the yacht and a table with matching bench seats along the other. A few small cabinets perched above the settee. We excitedly set about "unstoring" all the items and making *Orion* charter ready.

Four matching staterooms (bedrooms) were spread forward and aft (rear) on *Orion.* Each stateroom had its own head (bathroom), with shower. Three staterooms were for charterers. The fourth was ours: a bed, two small drawers under the bed and a triangle-shaped closet too narrow for hangers.

The main cabinet space for food and drink was the salon floor. Well, to be specific, *under* the salon floor. At least eight panels on the floor lifted up to expose large areas to store food, booze, and whatever else might fit.

In what seemed like a New York minute, the other crews invited us into their inner circle. It was a tight-knit group, and we soon found out why. There was almost no support from the main office. Everyone depended on each other. Anything that needed fixing, we had to do ourselves. Crews were quick to help, because they'd probably need help themselves soon enough.

South Africans, Greer and Brenda, had been promoted from *Orion* to a catamaran. They explained the basics to us:

- We'd get credit cards and petty cash from the office.
- We'd maintain our own sailboat, wash it, fuel it, and repair it, inside and out.
- When notified of a charter, we'd receive the guests' food and drink preferences.
- The budget for provisions for a charter was twenty-five dollars per person per day.
- Purveyors delivered provisions (food and booze) to the boat if ordered by phone.
- Any provisions left over from charters were ours to eat and drink.
- We'd keep a record of our expenditures and turn it in after every charter.
- In the event of a twenty-four-hour turnaround (one charter immediately following another), we could hire Veronica and her husband to clean the interior of the boat at Windwards' expense.

- Charters started at noon and ended at noon.
- After every charter, we'd bag all linens and our uniforms and drop them at the Windwards laundry for pick up the next day.
- On charters, the captain rules (but guests tip well, so, if at all possible, give them their way).

Greer reviewed the engine and generator with Winston, explaining little idiosyncrasies about each that we might need to know later. He reviewed all the safety equipment and systems that ran the sailboat. Brenda showed me how she organized the boat and what she kept where. They showed us a chart of the usual route captains take on charter, including Saba Rock. That would be weird.

Pamela, the other half of the British couple, Charles and Pamela, was my first tour guide. I had done lots of shopping for Saba Rock, so I knew most vendors, but I bought in bulk, not small doses.

Pamela was an encyclopedia of provisioning. She dragged me all over Roadtown. "We all buy our breads here, because they give us a discount. We buy our canned goods there but never our cereals; they have bugs. We get wine from Tico's, liquor and beer from Reese, except if you want Bud. Then you have to go to Roadtown Wholesale. Ms. Penguins' undoubtedly has the

Staterooms made up, wood polished and dusted, produce displayed and flowers fresh, Cynthia checks on some homemade local rotis for lunch.

best fish and conch. And for the best hamburgers, go to Supa Value. You have to buy two dozen, and there's no room in your freezer, so crews usually split the box." I already knew the most important rule, "If they don't have what you want, just buy something close."

"Where can I buy those savory rotis?" I asked, already hungry for the Caribbean staple similar to a curried burrito. Veronica, the West

Indian who cleaned the yachts' interiors, made them with a native touch. I learned she'd deliver them right to the yacht, made to order and steaming hot.

Besides the English and South Africans, crews hailed from Australia, New Zealand, New York City, Canada, Alaska, and California. Only four were Americans. Many were new this season, like us, but most were much younger. We were surprised that some didn't even know Jimmy Buffet—the iconic singer most sailors crave on charter—and had never sailed the BVI before. With our own personal charters in the BVI and our Saba Rock history, we didn't feel so green after all.

To dock, we regularly squeezed the fifty-foot-long, fifteen-foot-wide *Orion,* backwards between two tightly placed rows of tall wooden pilings. We had only two inches to spare on each side of the yacht. Our fellow crews enjoyed making it even more difficult. Any day, they could gather at the end of our slip and mockingly "direct" us into our parking spot. "Go this way . . . no, watch that pole," they'd chime, shouting over each other. "Move to the right. Ohhh, you're about to crunch. Slide just a little to the left. Ease it over, baby. Gun it now. Oh, too much." The wildly exaggerated physical antics they'd use to accentuate their directions wouldn't faze Winston though. Like a pro, he'd finesse that baby right into its home every time.

Hurricane Jose provided a fast track for meeting all our coworkers. We'd been crew for only a month when Jose came blowing in. We titled the storm "Back Door Jose," because he came in from the Gulf of Mexico instead of the usual path across the Atlantic. After spending days of prep protecting *Orion* from the coming storm, lowering and removing all the sails, dismantling and stowing the cushions and kayaks, and tying everything down, we were told where *we'd* weather the storm: in a storage locker. Yes, the Windwards stored all their crews in a storage locker on the company's premises, right across from the yacht-filled docks.

It was cramped. It was hot. It was crowded. It was stuffy. But, despite everything, we had a blast. Thirty crew members sat on the floor, backs against the wall, told story after story of days gone by in the business. Winston and I got an ear full. We were told the ropes firsthand and all the rumors as well. Now we belonged. We'd been christened. Thanks, Jose.

Day to day

We were expected to be captain, chef, mate, stewardess, hosts, tour guides, teachers, mechanics, butler and maid for our charterers. At the start of a charter, Winston would greet the guests at the marina office and walk them down to *Orion*. There were lots of ooohs and aaahs when they understood that *Orion* was theirs for the week. They'd climb aboard, pick their stateroom, and stash their luggage. Then they'd come up to the cockpit, for our safety briefing. "One hand on the boat at all times" topped the list. Fire equipment, man overboard, and toilet instruction were included. ("Nothing goes into the toilet unless you've eaten it first.") Then we'd sail off, presenting lunch underway.

We'd ask three important questions: Can you swim? Are any of you allergic to anything? What are the most important things you want to see and do on this trip? We wouldn't guarantee we'd do everything on their list, but we strived to make sure, if at all possible, that they got to do the top three.

Every island stood out for one reason or another. Unless we had an unusually short charter, or terrible weather, we sailed on what we called the milk run.

Norman Island was our first stop, with something for everyone. It was only a two-hour sail from Tortola and offered both shallow and advanced snorkeling, plus choices of Willy T's, a raucous floating pirate ship bar, or a tamer beach bar, Billy Bones. Our people had the option to treasure hunt along the beach, or hike up goat trails for exercise, and they could go out to dinner, or eat on board.

While underway to Norman, I would serve lunch, usually rotis that Veronica had delivered just an hour before, topped with mango chutney and accompanied with a tropical fruit salad. While the guests were eating and watching the scenery sail by, Winston and I would learn more about them.

The first twenty-four hours gave us a good snapshot of who was on board. We'd been given their preference sheet before the trip, but reality usually spoke much more clearly than words on a page. Now we'd see. Did they love to party? Drink at all? Get drunk? Dance up a storm? Sleep in? Get seasick? Were they scared of the water? Irresponsible in it? The first twenty-four hours told us a lot.

We anchored as near the beach as we could (Winston knew a secret spot where most other crews wouldn't go). Then we'd invite everyone to go for their first swim, or take them by dinghy around the tip of the island to the dazzling caves.

My snorkeling directions covered a few key points: 1) Remember you have to save enough energy to swim back to the yacht. 2) Keep your ears above the water so you can hear me call to show you something unusual. 3) Do not stick your hands into any openings; there may be an eel inside who doesn't like surprises. 4) This is a national park, so you can't remove any shells or coral. 5) Be ready to jump in the water, even when you're resting. Surprises swim by fast.

Here's one example of that last point. Having just finished offering coffee in the cockpit, I spotted three dolphins swimming right by the yacht. Without a moment's hesitation, I alerted the guests and grabbed my snorkel gear. They just weren't up to Direction #5 and sat there sipping. I, on the other hand, swam madly after the dolphins. All at once, one amazing creature turned around, looked at me, and swam back to me. It was magical. That dolphin came within reach (though I didn't invade his space) and nodded his head several times at me as if to say, "Hi, thanks for noticing us. Nice to meet you." Then he turned and, in a flash, sped out of sight. It was a once-in-a-lifetime phenomenon. And this was part of my job!

Then I climbed back in the yacht and started breakfast. After that, I didn't have to tell anyone to stay alert and stay close; the novices stuck like glue.

On Norman Island, we'd explore a twenty-foot underwater wall of brilliant, living coral punctuated by caves. I'd guide our timid snorkelers inside to see the cave-dwelling fish, with their saucer-like eyes and short, round bodies. With my "children" following like lemmings, I'd point out eels tucked in holes, shrimp camouflaged in crevices, tiny neon-blue wrasses protecting their lair, and spotlight parrot fish chomping away at the coral. Schools of yellow and black striped sergeant majors swarmed us, looking for food. When we were lucky, a turtle, or two, might be lazily feeding nearby.

In Norman's Bight, the cove where boats could anchor safely for the night, guests could swim a different landscape, one of shallow, calm water and long, low reefs teaming with fish. A sweet spot for beginners, this unnoticed area let them snorkel without the scary depth and darkness of the caves. Not only was it an easy swim from the beach, but I invariably found an absurd array of sea life, including rare and prickly stonefish, odd-shaped box fish, and perfect rooster shells. Sending my newbies on a treasure hunt for these delightful creatures rewarded them and me.

Often we'd cocktail ashore, then Winston would grill vermouth-marinated swordfish and gingered broccoli aboard. Being from California, we saw to it that almost every entré was on the grill. Couples would sit on the bow watching the night sky for shooting stars while eating poached pears oozing fresh raspberry Cointreau sauce. The next morning would bring an early snorkel, breakfast and another sail, usually to Peter Island.

Somewhere between all this activity, Winston and I would de-sand the boat, rinse the snorkel gear, clean the heads, change the towels, make the beds, do the dishes, prepare and set up the meals, and plan the next day's events. There would usually be something to fix too—maybe a door handle, maybe a toilet.

Quite the routine

Winston likes telling my secrets. "Cynthia planned a seven-day menu and then simply recreated it on every trip, with necessary exceptions for food allergies, or special requests. She's never been crazy about cooking, so it made sense to have an easy plan: On day one, we served grilled swordfish; day two, jerk chicken; day three, coconut shrimp; day four, lemon peppered sea bass; day five, pork tenderloin. Filet mignon was reserved for the last night, and we left a night open for a restaurant trip. Breakfast and lunch followed the same system. It was easy until you goofed. On our very first charter, Cynthia jerked the chicken so much it almost stood up and ran away. Our clients, a dad celebrating his retirement with his three grown sons, raved about it, but my mouth felt on fire all night. The guys must have had taste buds of iron. But, hey, live and learn. Those guys presented us with an antique chart of the BVI, signed by each of them. We had successfully accomplished our first charter, in spite of the seasoning, and had a keepsake to prove it."

I'll tell another secret. There's a good rule on charter: be vague about the menu. That way if you ruin something, you just substitute something else. On one early charter, I created delicate, lacy, ten-layer filo dough cups. It was my first experience with filo and I did not understand how quickly it baked. So, I burned them dark brown, in a matter of minutes. Nothing has ever moved from a cookie sheet to a trash can so fast. The guests were snorkeling and never saw a thing. I served the chocolate mousse in champagne stems instead. They loved it.

I suppose my biggest secret as a charter chef is that I don't like to cook. I don't even like to eat really. I could live on cheese and crackers and pizza—though I would die doing it. And I'd never eat three meals a day plus apps and dessert, too. What I love is making great food look fabulous and hearing the ooohs and ahhhs as I present it. Guests were always shocked that beautiful meals could come out of such a tiny kitchen. They would often say, "You must just love to cook," and I'd just smile with a gleam in my eye and say, "What I love, even more, is snorkeling."

Each morning, we'd rise early. I'd go for a swim and then prepare breakfast while Winston checked the systems, prepared the rigging, wiped down the yacht, and planned the day's route. We'd have our coffee while passing dishes and silverware from the galley up the stairs to the outdoor cockpit's dining area. With an array of placemats, I could design a centerpiece to create a different restaurant ambiance for each meal. For me, table setting, and presentation were the joy of cooking on a sailboat.

While everyone was eating, I'd clean up the galley. Winston would chat about the day's run, clear the table, and hand the dishes back down the stairs. I'd quickly wash, dry, and store them so I could get upstairs and help with the rigging.

Then guests would get situated for the sail, maybe up on the bow, hanging along the side of the yacht, or sitting snugly in the cockpit. I'd stow my dishtowel and don my sailing gloves. Now I was mate. If anchored, I'd go to the bow and use the remote switch to hoist the anchor while Winston started the motor and stayed at the helm. After climbing over guests to get back in the cockpit again, I'd help raise the jib and mainsail. Once the sails caught the wind and all lines were safely stored, next on the agenda were drinks, suntan lotion, towels, and snacks.

After a short time entertaining the troops, it was down those stairs again to make beds and clean heads. Next? Prep for lunch, choose the placemats, condiments, and ingredients, and arrange everything as best I could while bracing myself, in a slanted galley while underway. Most items went in the sink for safekeeping. Back upstairs for another gracious "Can I get you a rum punch?" or a professional "Captain, I'm ready to tack when you are."

"When we arrived at our lunch destination," points out Winston, "Cynthia was back on deck gloved and ready at the anchor. Down it would go. As soon as we confirmed the hold was good, we'd encourage swimmers into the water. Taking guests snorkeling was the highlight of Cynthia's day. Whether we were at Cooper Island looking for turtles and octopus, or the Baths looking for underwater sunbeams, she thought of every swim as a treasure hunt.

"Since she was a snorkeling chef, she never went swimming without a watch. Long before she wanted to get out of the water, I'd see her rinsed, dried, clothed, and cooking. By the time the group returned, lunch was on the table. They feasted, and we cleaned up. I sometimes ate with the guests, but Cynthia usually ate on the fly. With lunch finished and dishes handed down, washed, and stowed, if she was lucky, she could breathe for a bit.

"Sometimes we anchored a distance from shore and I'd take the guests by dinghy in to a little boutique, or funky bar for happy hour. Then they'd swim back to the boat. Some of my best fun was surprising guests, by swimming up to them with a full tray of rum-somethings. 'Cocktails, anyone?'"

New place settings complimented my centerpiece of shells on fresh tropical grape leaves. Winston, grill master extraordinaire, would grill the entré while wine and cocktails greeted all. The guests sat down to an evening of great food and tales of the day. Night swim, anyone?

Cocktails, anyone? Winston loved swimming out to guests and surprising them with refreshments.

Dream achieved

Here we were, Winston and I, now actual professional yacht captains. We could hardly believe it. We were living full-time on a fifty-foot yacht, in the British Virgin Islands, taking people on sailing vacation almost every day of the week. We were yacht captains, a rare career almost unknown to us, only a few years before. We'd changed our careers and realized our dream job. And we were good at it. How did we get so lucky?

We often sat under the stars and relived our journey: that lost snorkel that helped me find Winston; that advertisement beckoning us to move to Saba Rock; those freelancing sailing jobs that grew our reputations; the many résumés we spread around and hundreds of calls we made; our connections in St. Thomas to gain more boating experience; even our hiatus back in the States that reassured us we loved our tropical life. Then the phone call that was the surprise opportunity from the Windwards. But maybe it wasn't just luck, after all. We'd worked hard on attaining our goal.

Chapter 10
Sailboat Charters: You Won't Believe What Blew in the Wind

Teaching is reminding others that they know just as well as you.
—Richard Bach

*Sailboats arrive at the new Saba Rock eager
for more crazy vacation memories.*

Tortola to Norman Island to Peter Island to Cooper Island to Virgin Gorda to Saba Rock to Anegada to Jost Van Dyke to Tortola
December 1998—November 2000

Variety is the spice of life

Winston and I ran dozens and dozens and dozens of charters for the Windwards, over almost two years. No two charters were the same, ever. The dynamics of chartering matched against the monotony of yacht maintenance was like a kaleidoscope of colorful energy hovering over a grey, robotic vacuum cleaner. Anticipating that kaleidoscope kept us eager.

Charter guests came in many nationalities, attitudes, abilities, and backgrounds, and with many expectations. All those traits played a part in how their charter went. Here's a sampling of some of our most memorable charters. Each reminded us in some way of our goal of adventure with pay, and the choices we made to attain that goal.

The undertaker

It's great to attain goals, but overdoing it can backfire. Whether the goal is dumping belongings, like we did, or partying your heart out, always consider the consequences before you go full bore.

"Usually our charter guests were quite wiped out, after days of wind, sun, and swimming," Winston says, loving to tattle. "But on occasion, there were non-stop partiers, non-stop adventurers and legendary, old, rabble rousers, especially on the first night of the charter.

"A young undertaker, named Charlie, and his new wife chose the Windwards for their honeymoon. On the first night of the charter, we sailed to Norman Island and the schooner bar, The William Thornton, Willie T's for short. Charlie inhaled tequila body shooters, rumrunners, and belly slammers on top of smoking a cigar. He partied with a group of doctors and won several contests, including jumping off the top of the Willie T's naked. His wife was having a great time, too, but she felt fine in the morning. Charles not so much.

"He'd already puked in his toilet, as well as in his suitcase, before showing his face in the cockpit. I tried floating him in the water with an inner tube and a leash to see if it would help his equilibrium. Charlie just begged to be taken to land. We were anchored quite a way offshore, and the water was rough, but I loaded him into the dinghy and off we went.

"As Murphy would have it, the engine died about halfway to the beach. Now we were rocking and rolling in this little, twelve-foot dinghy. When I tried frantically to restart the beast, the pull cord ripped right off in my hand. Now we were rocking and rolling with no way to start the engine.

"I manned the oars, intent on getting this miserable guy to solid ground as soon as possible. I finally reached another yacht, borrowed a makeshift pull cord, and got the engine started. The dinghy had barely reached the sand when Charlie dragged himself out and crawled on all fours up the beach toward some trees. Poor guy was sick as a dog. His rear end sticking out of some bushes was all that showed for a long, long time.

"In due course, we got him back on the sailboat. The doctors who had been partying with Charlie stopped by, sure that he'd be horribly hung over. They left some medicinal powder to remedy dehydration. With a gleam in her eye, his wife threatened to make the stuff into a suppository, but Charlie got to drink it after all. (She was a real trooper, and by the way had cleaned up Charlie's mess the moment it happened.)"

The banana fish

This couple displayed the ultimate spirit of cooperation and flexibility. Both traits are critical to any couple striving toward a common goal, and the payoff can be rewarding. We're reminded of it every day on our journey.

One of our choice, chartering couples were honeymooners, Rock and Brenda, from the Midwest. Rock's dad owned a small sailboat that motivated Rock's interest in a sailing honeymoon. Brenda, on the other hand, turned green just walking down the dock. Plus, she could swim fine in a pool but was petrified of the ocean.

Why on earth, we wondered, would she take this trip? She answered even before we could ask. "It's a compromise," she said, smiling. "We made a deal. I got the wedding of my dreams. And Rock got the honeymoon of his." Then she went below and came up gushing. "Oh my gosh, there's a real toilet." We discovered her only boating experiences had been with her father-in-law's "little red bucket."

My goal was clear now. I got Brenda to relax in the quiet, shallow waters of the Bight and taught her about the wonders of the sea. At the edge of the beach, I eased her into the water with the security of a long, colorful, floating foam noodle. We sat for thirty minutes, just watching the little fish around us. We ventured waist deep and donned masks and snorkels. After seeing the crystal-clear water, with fifty-foot visibility, and learning to breathe underwater, Brenda started to loosen up. Taking her hand, I swam with her one stroke at a time toward the beckoning reef, with its orange, purple, and yellow corals waving in the current. Soon Brenda was playing hide-and-seek with the fish.

We were swimming back to the boat when she suddenly let out a blood-curdling scream. Something had bitten her, she was sure. Quickly assessing the area, I spied the culprit. There, hovering in the water was an innocent, bright yellow banana peel. Brenda got the laugh of her life and brought the peel back as a trophy. She'd conquered her fear, and I had a new snorkeling buddy. What a great job!

Money talks

Achieving even one small part of our goal always spurred us on to the next. One teenager's entire attitude changed for just that very reason.

We stopped regularly at posh Peter Island, with its five-star resort, inviting beach, and deep, sandy bottom. Too windy at night to keep an anchor secured, Peter Island was a lunch stop. There our guests enjoyed the pleasure of sunbathing in paradise. They'd swim to the pure white sand beach from our anchored yacht, or, if tentative about the considerable distance, Winston would ride them over in the dinghy. We warned them, though, "Keep an eye out for the helicopters landing near the beach. They'll sandblast the tan right off you."

With no coral reefs, there were few fish to see underwater. But spying the fragile edge of a white sand dollar almost totally buried under wafting sand was a treat for almost everyone. This was true for a certain young teenager who, I think, had planned to be rather bored on this holiday. Instead, David not only conquered diving for sand dollars; he begged me to challenge him to sea hunts. He and I were snorkeling one morning when I spotted something green floating near the bottom. I dared him to find it, giving only one clue: it talks. He looked confused and started searching. Then he dove deep. Charging through the water with hands outreached and fins flying, David burst to the surface with a huge smile on his face and somebody's twenty-dollar bill in his grip. Money talks.

Yo, ho, ho and a bottle of rum

Our island godfather had taught us to drop our American attitude if we wanted to live in a foreign country. When we tried doing just that, the feeling was infectuous. We liked infecting our charter guests. When in Rome . . .

"On the way from Peter to Cooper Island, we'd sail past Dead Man's Chest, one of my favorites," grins Winston. "Just a small island between Salt and Peter Islands, Dead Man's Chest never failed to bring out the storytelling in me.

"Ah, legend has it, that's where the famous, old sea shanty got its start. Yo, ho, ho and a bottle of rum. If pirates got riled and tried to mutiny, Blackbeard would deposit them on a deserted island—this one perhaps—along with any gold they were due plus lots of rum. The disgruntled pirates would fight among themselves and eventually kill themselves off. Sometime later, the conniving captain would return to the island and collect the gold.

"Guests would quickly morph into pirates bellowing, 'Fifteen men on a dead man's chest. Yo, ho, ho and a bottle of rum. Drink and the devil be done for the rest. Yo, ho, ho and a bottle of rum.' (from Robert Lewis Stevenson's novel *Treasure Island*) It was always the perfect time to break out the rum!"

Cooper critters

With Hanna, we were reminded that opportunities are everywhere, if you're just brave enough to look for them. Keeping your eyes open is the key.

We often spent the night attached to a mooring ball off nearby Cooper Island. One of our very young charterers was just learning to snorkel, and Cooper proved a great pre-school. Lots of visibility and a shallow bottom made five-year-old Hanna feel safe. Turtle grass covered the sea floor. Only eight inches high, the grass often half-hid a big, beautiful conch shell, perfect for enticing a kid to the bottom. (Remember learning to dive for pennies in a pool? Conch is much more rewarding.)

I pointed out the conch to Hanna and showed her how to jackknife to the bottom, slowly blowing out bubbles all the way down. She tried several times but just couldn't get down. I could see the frustration painted on her little face through her mask, so I dove down and brought up the treasure. Underwater, I handed Hanna the large, white, heavy conch shell and then motioned to her to turn it over quickly. As she did, her wide eyes told me she had seen the sunrise-colored animal, and seen it squeeze back up inside its shell to expose the beautiful coral and yellow sides of the shell. From that minute on, she was a conch hunter, diving with the best of them.

I also introduced Hanna to Barry, the Barracuda, and his four-foot, toothy shadow hovering under our sailboat. Barry was a dependable tenant of Cooper's Bay, foreboding but mostly harmless. He could be counted on to enthrall everyone who laid eyes on him.

Then a sea turtle swam by, and Hanna had a new passion. Turtles would slowly glide along the bottom, nibbling here, nudging a conch shell there, searching for their favorite menu items. Hanna and I hovered with our snorkels, perfectly content to watch. Turtles are fast swimmers and would bail in an instant, if we approached. We never tried to touch the turtles, and never kept any conch shells with animals inside, but finding both were delights for our visitors. Teaching Hanna about them was a joy.

Little Hanna gifted Winston a stuffed parrot to help his pirate disguise. "Hey Captain Winston, I found this at the store on Cooper Island, and it reminded me of you," she giggled. "You act so weird like a pirate you should have a parrot for your shoulder. And look, he has a patch on his eye, too, like the one you let me wear!" Hanna the Parrot still hangs on his mirror.

Whales for company

The subject of making a living in the Caribbean invariably came up when charter guests experienced firsthand the natural wonders of the sea. It certainly had made us want a life here.

"A gray whale, fifty feet long and breathing right alongside your vessel, takes the breath out of even the worldliest sailor," remembers Winston, defending his right to be taken aback by them. "When a whale rolls on its side and looks up at you, or hovers near its young to protect it from you, or raises its tail as it dives deep below, you can't help but gulp.

"The first time I saw one it scared the crap out of me. I saw this huge light-colored area of water right off our bow, and thought we were about to go aground on a sand bar that had never been there before! Then I realized it was a whale and was even more paralyzed.

"Several of our charterers were treated to rare but breathtaking whale sightings, some mamas with babies on the way to Anegada, and one sleeping right in the middle of the Sir Francis Drake Channel. Feeling the power of a whale's tale moving the yacht with just a gentle swoosh reminds me every time how small a boat really is. And standing on the deck as a whale passes right beside the yacht is humbling. Some of our guests' best souvenirs are their photographs of these giant creatures."

Tentacle-licking breakfast

Winston and I are constantly on the look-out for opportunities for adventure. It's what turns our world. We're like children with our eyes peeled for places to play. On this charter, I loved intriguing these youngsters with fun adventures directly under their noses. I hope they'll keep looking.

On a family charter at Cooper Island, we found no turtles, but we met a new friend. One afternoon, swimming to shore around a rock pile, I spotted a pile of empty, broken shells—the telltale sign of an octopus's den. I alerted the three kids, five to ten years old.

Anticipation built as they hovered over the rocks, squinting to make out any living thing. I just smiled. After some sweet time, when I was certain they were invested in the search, I pointed out the puffy blob of spotted flesh stretched out right on top of the rocks, just about four feet below us. The octopus was sunning himself through the crystal-clear water. Staring in disbelief, my little snorkelers witnessed, firsthand, how an octopus eats. He reached down with his tentacles and picked up an eight-inch conch shell. As we watched, he deftly turned it over and wormed his suction-cupped tentacles into the opening. Out came conch—yummy, tasty, delectable conch—though it looked anything but that. The kids' description was "slimy and ugly." After the octopus had sucked the shell clean, he dropped it and casually stretched back to sunning. Back on the yacht, the youngsters couldn't stop chattering about their new discovery.

The next day, we snorkeled back to the den, but first found a nice, big conch to take to the octopus for breakfast. As a bonus, we picked up the leftovers, the now clean and empty conch shell he'd eaten the night before. The kids had a trophy, and a lesson, to take home for show and tell.

Underwater highways to Never Never Land

Exploring new things requires conquering fear and taking chances. Moving to a grass hut was an exploration for us, and look where it led. We reminded guests regularly that taking chances and exploring can uncover all kinds of possibilities. You never know what you'll find.

The Baths at the south end of Virgin Gorda is a wondrous snorkeling garden, always on our guests' wish list. House-size granite boulders piled atop each other seem to have tumbled into the water. Anchoring a yacht at the Baths can be treacherous, though, as can swimming. If the wind changes direction or a northern swell rolls in, the sea can cause boats and bodies to be smashed into those boulders.

On a good day, the Baths offers calm waters, sunlight streaming underwater between the boulders, steep sand beaches, and West Indian vendors selling T-shirts and beach towels. One hiking trail leads up a hill to a restaurant, pool and shops. Another, winds through the boulders, long and twisty, requiring squat-crawling through tunnels, pulley-climbing up boulders, and balancing your way precariously across makeshift wooden bridges.

We'd often arrive at the Baths and swim to the beach before lunch. Expert navigator Winston would lead our pack of snorkelers on foot, up, down, and through the boulder trail, ending at another breathtaking beach and surf. "After they finally were ready—taking some groups snorkeling is like herding cats!—I'd start the adventure. Styling in the latest snorkel gear, we'd all swim through the unmarked waterways, between scenic boulders, through narrow rushing currents, and under ten-foot rock crevices. My favorite treat was the one-way tunnel ten feet below the sea. It looked rather treacherous, but guests loved conquering their fear there. A charter of five young men, from General Motors in Detroit, had a particularly mischievous time at this tunnel screwing up traffic. They'd swim through the tunnel the wrong way, just to scare the crap out of each other."

The day was topped off with a hike up the hill for a drink, a swim and some shopping. Waterproof bags were popular. Guests slept really well that night.

Eagle Eye

Initially we worried that minimizing our belongings might have an adverse effect on our psyche—maybe we'd purchase things we didn't even want, just to build up our "stuff" again. On the contrary, our desire to buy things weakened so much so that, now, we have almost no desire at all. We love window-shopping for tropical furnishings and *islandy* wares but have no desire at all to take any of them with us. You might say we're cured of "gathering." One of our charter guests needed to learn that lesson.

One of Winston's and my secret spots we shared with charter guests was Mountain Point, halfway up the coast of Virgin Gorda. The anchorage offered a cliff of fan corals, a field of massive elk horn coral, and a sea of sand between. It was our favorite place to serve cheeseburgers in paradise for lunch. Usually, we were the only yacht there.

Winston loves telling this story . . . "One day, Jim, our snorkeling-crazed charter guest from North Carolina, started wildly waving his arms and yelling, 'Hey guys! Come see! You've got to see this! We've got to get this!' He was positioned about a fifteen-minute swim, off the bow, of our sailboat. In I dove, to see what the hell he was so excited about. After searching out his booty, I told him he'd just have to mark the spot indelibly in his mind only. It wasn't going anywhere.

"Directly below him was an eighteenth century cannon, camouflaged with coral and crustaceans. It took an eagle eye to see it. Jim was sure he was the first ever to have discovered this pirate treasure and was hell bent on taking it back home to his front yard.

"All day he tried to coerce me into rigging a pulley on the top of our mast and raising the cannon with our sailing winch. (The winch was geared to raise maybe an eighty-pound sail. The cannon probably weighed over a ton.) Move over, Mel Fisher and your $450 million dollar shipwreck, *Atocha*—there was a new treasure hunter in town. Teasingly, he didn't seem to care that we'd sink the boat, much less that he'd be arrested for stealing from the BVI. ('Ah, come on, Captain. Let me have it. Help me out here!') After a tasty dinner of grilled pork tenderloin over lemon jasmine rice, we got him to see the light. His treasure hunting trophy would just have to be displayed in his mind's eye. He signed our guest book "Eagle Eye" and invited us to North Carolina anytime to see exactly where he would have enshrined his prize cannon."

And eagle rays

Serendipity was evident when we first made our scary, career change and again now in our perfect job. In 1990, we doctored a postcard with Winston and I standing next to Bert and Gayla on Saba Rock, and low and behold we lived with them four years later. In 1995, a company asked Winston to be a temporary yacht captain, and now we're full time professional crew. Pay attention to serendipity. It's telling you something . . .

Mountain Point offered one of the best vantages available for watching show-stopping, spotted eagle rays. The six-foot-wide rays are stunning creatures, black with white spots covering their upper surface with a pure white, shiny underbelly. Their tails are as long as their width, and their snouts are shaped like an eagle's, perfect for digging on the sandy bottom for prey.

When spotted eagle rays swim by, they appear to be giant, graceful butterflies under the water, their pointed wings flying as if through the sky. First introduced to them on Saba Rock, I've been lucky enough to see them often when we snorkel, but especially at Mountain Point.

Once, there on charter with five especially enthusiastic people, I told of its beauty and how much I related to this member of the shark family. When I slid into the water with one of my guests, sure enough, three eagle rays cruised across the bottom eating their breakfast. We swam with them, a good distance away but with them just the same. Then one gently turned, looked at me I swear, and followed me to the surface. Though I loved these creatures, it was a little disconcerting to have one follow *me* instead of me following him. We boarded the yacht rather quickly, but as I climbed up the ladder I realized my swimsuit was black with white dots. Lo and behold, maybe he thought I was a cousin.

My guests decided I must have been an eagle ray in another life. I liked that idea and took it to heart. Maybe in another life I had been an eagle ray. On my fiftieth birthday, a fortune teller had told me she saw something like a shark, in my past life. And I was appalled. I didn't want to be a shark, for God's sake. Hmm. Could it have been a spotted eagle ray? They're in the shark family. (This is the same mystic who told me I'd been a sea captain in the seventeenth century and also carved figureheads, the wooden figures on the bow of ancient ships. It all fits, doesn't it?)

The pigs cometh

In our yachting career, a sense of humor has pulled us through many a mishap. Laughter can be a weapon of mass destruction when you want to annihilate some disaster. We keep it handy. And we know two men who do the same.

"Remember we had wanted to pick a special place to spend the Millennium new year," Winston asks, "and that Tonga was rather a bust as far as any celebration was concerned? Well, we ended up for that momentous New Year's Eve at Bitter End Resort, right across from our old Saba Rock. We hosted a charter of Europeans who kept the Bitter End bartenders hustling champagne almost nonstop. A large-bellied guy from Germany was the business partner of a large-bellied guy from Finland, and both were customers of two other Germans, two rather tall, lanky gentlemen. Two men had wives with them, one a very new fresh wife following a recent divorce.

"This group ran hot and cold, for sure. Some nights they were the funniest, happiest crazies at the bar, the life of the party, with pictures to prove it. A big, male German in his wife's bra is hard to forget.

"Other times, these guys argued like cats and dogs. At one point, the newlyweds stomped off the boat to a hotel. The bride called the other men 'pigs' and blamed them for 'corrupting' her dear, pure husband. All this while Cynthia and I were sailing, serving, cleaning, and trying to be as invisible as we could.

"The next day when we got ready to set sail, up came those two big-bellied, hefty 'trouble-making' guys, proud and shirtless. Across each of their guts, written in bright red lipstick in eight-inch letters, was the word 'PIG' with an arrow pointing to the other guy. I loved it. Vacations can bring out the very best in people! Ha!"

Sailing the sheets

Opportunities abound, right under your nose. Sometimes you're fearful of acting on them, but adapting the attitude, "Why not?" (and not answering!) can open you up to some great experiences. One set of charter guests can attest to that.

There's nothing like having a charter during a hurricane, and Category 4 Lenny wanted us to get the full monte. Lenny miscalculated and luckily spared the BVI, but not before making some of our customers nervous. Four out of six women we had aboard our yacht decided to abort the charter and fly home—while flying was still a possibility. But two diehards grinned from ear to ear, incredulous. "We flew all the way from San Francisco for this adventure. Why in the world would we miss the chance to check out a hurricane?"

So, even with the storm looming, we enjoyed one more day on the water with these two risk-takers. Then Lenny forced us to take cover. We brought the yacht back to the dock, where the two women observed, firsthand, the multitude of preparations to protect a yacht from a hurricane. We put them to work, too. After packing down, stringing up, crossing over, tying under, securing on top of, stowing below, and dragging off, we gently patted our yacht good-bye, with a forlorn "see you later." Then the four of us shared one of the last motel rooms available, telling stories and making friends. Lenny blew by in a few days. Then we were back at it, undoing all the security we had so painstakingly created. Now knowing us more intimately than they'd ever planned, our clients wrote in our guestbook, "We sailed the sheets with Winston and Cynthia three out of four days. We'll sail with them anytime. Bring on the hurricanes!"

Bookworms soak up the sea

Work can be play and play work. Isn't it great when you do something you really love, while doing something else you really love? These kids had that knack.

During opposite weather—as in dead calm—a family of four came walking down the dock dragging two extra-heavy duffel bags. The odd thing was, the kids were doing the dragging. Not soon after we set out for Norman Island, the contents spilled out. Books. Books. And more books. Kids' books. With disappointment, we feared these guys wouldn't even notice the sea and never get their noses out of the pages. But, wow, were we wrong. Both children read voraciously, bragging when they finished a book, but they just as voraciously absorbed every bit of nature they could.

One flat, calm day, we motored fifteen miles to Anegada Island. The kids counted one hundred seventy-five starfish on the bottom, sixty feet below in crystal-clear water. They appreciated every drop. We still have the bronze wall sculpture of starfish they gave us. You just can't judge a book by its cover, or a ton of books for that matter.

Bubba-toothed board member

Never be fooled by what you see on the outside, be it a boat, a lifestyle, or a person. Winston and I recalled that lesson when this guy came aboard.

"Watching our new clients walking down the dock usually gave us a good idea of what the week would be like," Winston points out with a snide smile. "Kids running? Couples arguing? Lovers holding hands? One guy really fooled us though. Dressed in a sport coat and tie, we were sure he was a yacht club snob. This guy started complaining the minute he saw the yacht. 'How can this be the boat? What, no air conditioning?' This was *not* looking like a pleasant charter.

"But it turned out to be one of our most fun charters ever. That stodgy, grumpy guy transformed into a crazy nut once the Caribbean washed over him. He donned bubba teeth, got his black, curly, 1.5-inch long hair braided and beaded island-style, and tied on a pirate bandana. He not only conversed with all the natives until he had them in stitches about his bad teeth, he squeezed himself behind a makeshift table under a palm tree next to a local and helped her sell sarongs to the tourists. I couldn't believe it! Cyn would have killed me had I done that!!

"The kicker," Winston concludes, "was a couple of weeks later, when he sent us a photo of him wearing all the same garb to a board meeting in Stamford, Connecticut. What a surprising guy!"

Our old digs

Winston and I had spontaneously grabbed that opportunity to work on iconic Saba Rock. We captured an era in the BVI that disappeared only a few years later. When I think how we might have ignored that opportunity and missed that lifestyle and that grass hut, I pinch myself. Where would we be now if we hadn't moved to that hut? Still in the corporate world?

We couldn't show our patrons our old digs on Saba Rock now that Bert and Gayla had sold the Rock and it had been renovated. The Jimmy Buffet hangout and Pirate Bert were gone. Instead, let's just say the new owners had different values. They wanted a polished feel to the

Underway heading to Norman Island and happy hour at the Willie T floating bar.

place and they wanted it bigger, the island that is. New construction to enlarge the island had buried much of the reef. The renovation had done away with every rusty safety pin on the place (which was a good thing) and replaced it with professional, sturdy, solid-looking beams and bolts (which was a sad thing). Our Rock, the rock we had had the privilege of calling home, morphed from a lively Caribbean shanty to a posh resort. The place was unrecognizable except for Pee Rock, which now had a gift shop built around it instead of sitting at water's edge.

There were six, condo-type hotel rooms above the bar where Gayla and Bert's two-room stone home had stood. Our hut's rickety dock was no more; instead, a big chunk of land stretched over the reef with perfectly kept green grass and rows of picturesque palm trees shading hammocks. There was a separate, glassed-in game room, with pool tables and pinball machines, but not a dartboard or parrot in sight. And there were big slips for yachts to dock for the night—no more dinghy dangling around this rock.

When he sold the Rock, Bert had requested that Pee Rock remain, as well as the natural pond where Feather and Pita had lived. Now it was an aquarium with a few fish, a big moray eel and some weathered, authentic artifacts. The gift store still sold hats and T-shirts, but Bert's face was gone from them. Shipwreck treasures were sold, reminiscent of the gold doubloon Bert had found in the sea so many years before.

We still enjoyed a drink at the bar. And Gonja, the black cat, still wandered around and brought a smile to Winston's face. But, for us, shiny, new Saba Rock had lost its luster. Winston and I were among the lucky few who had known her at her best. We missed the old Saba. Still do.

Foxy's lair

You've heard the old adage, "Work can be play, " even if you don't profess to believe it. We determined not only to believe it but to take steps to find that kind of work! It sure paid off.

One of my must-stop places was, and still is, the island of Jost Van Dyke," interrupts Winston. "We could count on Jost to give us a break and keep everyone off the boat for a while—lunch *and* dinner if we were lucky. Jost had three cool hangouts: White Bay's Soggy Dollar Bar, Sidney's Peace and Love, and Foxy's.

"White Bay had room for only a handful of yachts, but its Soggy Dollar Bar drew swimmers from all around. They'd ferry in from St. John, St. Thomas and BVI resorts. Soggy Dollar's honor bar allowed swimmers to make their own drinks and keep their own tab. That honor bar is a thing of the past now, replaced by rows and rows of cruise ship beach chairs, but it was precious while it lasted. Sidney's Peace and Love boasted some of the best T-shirts in the islands.

"Foxy owned the title for the 'third-best place *in the world to* celebrate 1999's New Year's Eve. The best place was Times Square and, second, Piccadilly Circus. A hole in the wall, dirt-floored bar and restaurant, Foxy's drew tourists from around the globe. The owner, crusty and disheveled Foxy, was rumored to be a millionaire, with a daughter at Princeton, but he looked as country bumpkin as they come—no shoes, bad teeth, swollen eyes, scratchy voice. But when that voice started to croon an ad-libbed fable about someone in the audience, he shined like the North Star. And his ditties weren't limited to people either.

"Foxy could sing a ditty involving any state, or city, in the world, uttering how things about that place were similar to his island, fictitiously, of course," Winston recalls with a smile. "He talked endlessly about his dusty black lab. 'He's a West Indian dog because he's lazy as shit and doesn't know who his father is.' Foxy maintained that Father's Day was the most confusing day in the Caribbean because nobody knew who their father was. To me, he's still one of the icons of the islands. And I've been known to repeat several of his jokes on a regular basis," Winston adds.

Growing pains

Time passes quickly. We were almost fifty when we chucked everything and did what we wanted for a change—adventurous living with pay. As one set of charter guests realized, time moves quickly, so you might as well live it to the fullest . . .

Probably one of the best times at Foxy's was the night with a mom, dad, their sixteen-year-old daughter, and her girlfriend. Celebrating their sweet sixteen birthdays, the girls were eager to dance up a storm, even more so when a group of good-looking young sailors walked in. They rocked and rolled to the music while a very dismayed father looked on. Mom was fine with the scene, keeping a close eye on the girls while letting them feel their oats. Dad was watching his little baby grow up right before his very eyes, becoming antsier with every wiggle of her hips. At last, it was too much for him. His wife slid over to me. "Don's ordered a double." She smiled. "He's never ordered a double in his life."

Another day, after strolling Loblolly Beach, the mile-long, secluded, white sand beach on Anegada Island, this same couple told me with big grins that they'd made "loblolly" a verb! The girls had their own secret fun, too, skinny dipping off the yacht, in the middle of the night. Now that's taking advantage of a holiday!

"Don't forget about the lizard they bought," pipes up Winston. "This family bought a two-foot-long carved lizard from Foxy's to take back to their lake house in Connecticut. And they named it 'Winston.' Ha!"

Thoughts on paper

On the seventh day of most every charter, we'd head back to Tortola for good-byes and plane-catching. Guests, who had just met us a week earlier, would write in our guest book like they'd known us for years.

They documented the crazy adventures we'd led them through . . . As one college-age kid wrote, "I've stumbled home from bars, walked, biked, motor-biked, skateboarded, even snowboarded home from bars, but I had never swum home from the bar until now. What a trip!"

Our guest books proved to be a diary of our yachting career. Including photographs and kids' drawings and letters of thanks and hilarious retelling of stories, these books paint a colorful picture of our life at sea. Sometimes, we scan an excerpt and email it back to the author, just for fun.

Our charterers would walk off our yacht inviting us to their homes, promising to return, asking for emails and postcards, and honoring us with presents to remind us of them. A three-volume, eight-inch-thick photographic collection of underwater creatures, fish, and coral is my most favorite gift by far. (I check off the picture in the books every time I spot a new species.) "Hanna," the eye-patched parrot, still watches Winston brush his teeth every morning. Maps and photos hang in our crew cabin, compliments of and autographed by our many new friends.

A bit of reality—our to-do list

"In between our charters," adds Winston, "when you imagine us stretching out on a lounge chair with our feet up, and taking long dips in the sea, we'd actually be burning the midnight oil preparing for the next group and maintaining the yacht in stellar condition. Not so glorious.

"Besides keeping inventory of materials required to clean a yacht perfectly (like teak cleaner, varnish, sand paper, waxes, deck wash, and stainless polish), we monitored equipment supplies like engine oil, generator oil, air conditioner filters, propane, fuel, spare toilet pumps, and the mechanical parts needed to maintain them (including duct tape!). Then there was the interior with its burned-out ceiling lights and stuck cabinet latches and finger-printed mahogany walls and salt-covered windows and dirty linens and used shampoos.

"I remember one week our repair list included stained upholstery, a ripped canvas window, a broken bar light, a new stereo installation, and the boat name sticker reapplied. In addition, we were polishing the hull, changing the stove fuel, fixing a sail, installing a shelf in a closet, buying a toaster, and changing oil in the generator. And, of course, ordering and purchasing provisions and making the cabins ready for our new, best friends.

Life was often a twelve-hour-a-day grind (which Winston hated) when we didn't have people onboard and 24-7 (not his favorite either!) when we did. But like our young guest had so astutely remarked, we were lucky to be going on everyone's vacation.

And speaking of vacations

In the slow, summer season we took another vacation, in conjunction with my son's wedding overlooking San Francisco Bay. We hosted the rehearsal dinner, topped off with potica, a dessert recipe passed down from my great-grandmother. I took great joy in making the potica, a table-sized, Slovenian cinnamon bread that I'd baked for my family for years. (I could never bake potica onboard the sailboat, because there was no place large enough to roll out the dough! Plus, it takes twelve hours to make.) Just smelling that dough rising was nostalgic. The wedding was lovely, and it was fabulous being with our family and friends again. I missed them. Island living had its drawbacks.

Then we jumped on the Harley and rode to Jackson, Wyoming, to meet up with our friend, Otto. Months before, we'd planned the rendezvous: The Cowboy Bar in Jackson, on the third barstool, at 3:00 p.m., on Tuesday. We arrived two hours early and Otto pulled up fifteen minutes later. How's that for coordination? Heading to Route 66 in Arizona, Otto had asked, "Do you want to go this way to Winslow, or that way to Flagstaff?"

We both immediately picked Winslow. "Oh brother." Otto grinned. "You two just want to go stand on the corner, don't you?"

Devoted fans of The Eagles and their legendary ballad "Take It Easy," we couldn't possibly pass up the chance.

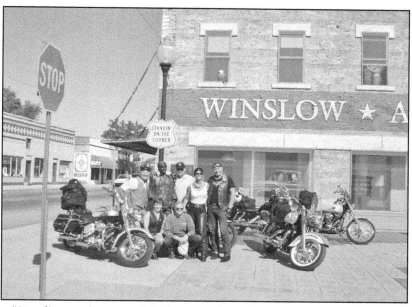

"Standing on the corner" during a Harley ride on Route 66 with friends.
(Winston and Cynthia standing far right.)

Well, I'm a-standing on a corner in Winslow, Arizona,
and such a fine sight to see.
It's a girl, my Lord, in a flatbed Ford
slowin' down to take a look at me.
Take it easy, take it easy,
Don't let the sound of your own wheels
drive you crazy.

Chapter 11
Kicked in the Balls

*Remember where you came from, where you are going, and why
you created the mess you got yourself into in the first place.*

—Richard Bach

*Graduating from a monohull to a catamaran, Winston and
Cynthia get lots more room to entertain guests.*

Tortola, BVI, to St. Thomas, USVI, to St. Lucia
to Grenada to Fort Lauderdale
November 2000—January 2001

Life in the yachting industry had its ups and downs. We'd been
warned by lots of professionals in the business. We weren't prepared,
though, for the hand we were dealt after taking over a new yacht. We'd
heard horror stories of owners firing crew on the spot, and crew being

left high and dry on a dock, but we didn't think them the norm. And we didn't think they applied to us.

Our life aboard Windwards' sailing yachts was a test for us. We'd learned we could:

1) live together in a space that was fifty feet by twenty feet;

2) work together 24-7, with strangers living with us most of the time;

3) and not divorce or kill each other.

That first year and a half, we handled over fifty term charters, most seven days in length but several ten to fourteen days. We were promoted from the sailboat to running a catamaran, a large twin-hulled sailboat with a superstructure between the hulls. This yacht was more stable than a monohull because of its breadth, sailing the seas, without the tilt associated with sailboats. It allowed much more room for guests, too, not only in sleeping quarters but in the entertainment and galley areas.

Our charterers now enjoyed air conditioning, a video screen, and two large trampolines stretched across the bows of the boat for sunning and riding the waves. The catamaran was much more comfortable for us too. Now the interior living space was the same level as the deck outside. It eliminated the narrow staircase we'd juggled at mealtime, and climbing over people to get to the helm.

Every evaluation from our customers came back to the Windwards raving about the yacht, our service, our graciousness, our menu, and our ability to make each guest feel supremely at home. We loved our job, and we were breathing as easily as if we were snorkeling over purple fan coral, watching it sway in the quiet current.

Then we got kicked in the balls. One couple complained, and we were fired.

The sad saga

Two charter guests, after writing gracious remarks in our guest book and presenting us with a nice cash gratuity, complained to our boss. They said we hadn't fed them any good meals and refused to take them to a particular bay (which was off limits for sailboats per the government). What's worse, they said we made remarks like "No f . . . ing way are we going to turn on the air conditioner," and "I'm not your gofer." We were shocked.

Oddly enough, this couple had complained about another charter the year before and had been given a discount, which they used on our trip. Fishy.

Our boss called us on the carpet in her office. We were flabbergasted when she told us we were facing a thirty-day suspension, with no pay, removal from our yacht for thirty days, and possible termination, all because of this couple's review. When we pointed out we had another charter the next day to prepare for, she asked for our rebuttal in writing (between preparing for our new charter). Under this veil of threatened termination, we hosted three guests (Windwards employees from headquarters, no less) on a four-day charter and still somehow showed them a good time. "We should have received an Academy Award," snivels Winston.

Here are some excerpts from our letter of explanation: "We suspected these people might complain because we weathered their comments . . . the water being too cold to snorkel, the wind being too windy, the boat rocking too much at night, the sea being too noisy at night, and not having enough sun. We are appalled to hear the complaint about not feeding them enough. All food and drink items they'd requested were on board and presented with our usual cuisine. And those quotes were lies."

Even after our boss heard and read our explanation and said that this complaint should only require a warning, the next day we were again called into the office. We would be terminated.

Our follow-up

Our emotions ran wild—shock, anger, loss. Fired? How could we possibly be fired? This was our dream job, living aboard a yacht, taking people on sailing vacations, in the most beautiful waters of the Caribbean. We were perma-vacationers with full-time pay. We'd been crewing sailboats successfully for almost two years, hosting over fifty charters with hundreds of happy guests. Our critiques were outstanding. Not one complaint—not from our employer, fellow crewmembers, or charter guests—until now. How could we possibly be fired?

We both felt betrayed, but we each handled it in a different way. Winston was angry and indignant. I couldn't breathe. It was like having my mask and snorkel ripped off my face in a sudden, raging current. I panicked and bawled uncontrollably, telling our boss between sobs that she was ruining our career, that we'd planned to do this forever. Winston was trying to console me and control his anger simultaneously. The boss assured us that "crews always go on to better yachts after leaving the Windwards," her way of consoling us, I guessed.

But we didn't want to go on to anything else. We lived here, in this foreign country, the BVI. We'd lived full-time on this yacht for the past year and a half. It was our home. Now we were being forced to leave? Where were we supposed to go? Didn't they understand we wanted to do this job for the rest of our lives? Didn't they know we loved this job, and our guests loved us? We'd received 'thank you' gifts, long letters of recommendation and lavish gratuities. How in the world did we go from our corporate lives and all our "stuff" to running that dilapidated beach bar to attaining our ultimate dream job as yacht crew—only to have it ripped from under us?

Sunglasses covered my swollen eyes, but nothing hid the hurt and betrayal—and embarrassment—that both of us felt as we walked back down the dock to our yacht. News traveled fast, and our friends came to support us, but we were inconsolable. We felt empty and brimming with anger simultaneously. Devastated and outraged. Our dream career was gone.

Here is an excerpt from our next letter to the company protesting this treatment:

In the past twenty months, we have handled over fifty charters and never once received even a warning letter. We have never had a suspension or been put on probation. Every "Welcome Home" survey response from clients rates us "excellent" in every category. This group has a history of complaining. We have a history of excellence. Who's to be trusted here?

A smattering of endorsements sent to headquarters

"Feeling doomed and pinned against the wall," adds Winston, "we tried one last effort. We emailed all of our past charter guests and asked for their support. They responded in droves. Every time we opened another email, confusion and anger would overwhelm us, while the heartfelt sincerity and generosity of our guests did, too. Cynthia's tears flowed with every read, salt and peppered with pride.

"My wife thought there might have been elves onboard, the boat was so clean."

"Meal preparations were an exquisite mix of Winston's grilling and Cynthia's extraordinary culinary skills, making the experience comparable to that of a gourmet restaurant."

"Cynthia paid special attention to my safety while snorkeling, ensuring that I did not miss a single magnificent underwater sight. Both captains were well known and introduced us to an extraordinary group of island 'characters' with stories we will never forget."

"They are a very special twosome who absolutely adore what they do and make their enthusiasm contagious. They made us feel like we were the one and only group of clients that mattered."

"From the time we first met them, we felt we had known them forever."

And still we got fired

We were dismissed, despite all the evidence. It was officially *because* of the evidence: we were fired "for telling company secrets to past charter guests."

We licked our wounds and made the best of it

None of our fellow crew members at the Windwards could believe our fate. One generous and empathetic New Zealand couple helped us pack our belongings, along with all the gifts our satisfied charterers had given us, onto their boat, and sailed us off to St. Thomas's Hassel Island and the refuge with our dear friends, Glenn and Barb. I was brokenhearted. Winston was furious. Glenn and Barb were a godsend for our morale.

If nothing else, Glenn pointed out, this horrible experience garnered us a file full of incredible reference letters. Bolstered by his optimism, we couldn't let this fiasco ruin our career. We were armed and determined.

Word got around that we were freelance crew available for hire, and we lucked into several temporary situations. The first was filling in for a friend whose partner had fallen sick. He generously offered us the job, knowing we needed the moral and financial boost. We were flown down the Caribbean chain of islands to St. Lucia, where we did a ten-day charter throughout the islands of St. Vincent and the Grenadines, including Palm Island, Mystique (for

Dinner! Winston cleans some lobsters during a sailboat delivery to Grenada.

New Year's Eve), Union, Tobago Cay, and Petite St. Vincent. The trip expanded our horizons immeasurably.

Then buddies, Presley and Pam, needed help delivering a yacht from the BVI to Grenada. Sailing with Olympian Presley was a joy and also a tutorial. His Olympic sailing skills made the trip a university of winds and currents. Passing the smoking chimney of Montserrat's volcano broadened our view of nature. And forgetting our bad luck, we reveled in catching king fish and lobster and sailing into pristine Marigot Harbor. Approaching Grenada in utter darkness, Pam and I spread-eagled across the bow with flashlights, panning for buoys so we wouldn't crash into them. It was a wonderful delivery and good for our souls.

Then reality hit again. We were technically homeless. And out of work.

Our sailing career had changed us. Physically, we were more agile, climbing up and down staircases and bilges and masts, grabbing kids before they jumped in the dinghy and hats before they flew in the drink. Mentally, we were quicker, too, (we had to be!) driving the yacht in dangerous seas and turbulent gusts of wind. Socially we'd changed from being individuals to being a pair, wincyn. Now, instead of having lots of separate friends, we were wincyn . . . if you knew Cynthia, you knew Winston, and vice versa.

Our relationship had changed, too, something we hadn't quite considered. "He does his thing, I do mine," now had become "we do it together or not at all . . . there are no pink and blue jobs . . . where you go, I go." Our moods even changed: Winston had become more tolerable and I more relaxed. Our buying habits changed because, besides less money to spend and nobody to impress, we had little interest in spending it—no magazine ads to entice us, or finely-dressed women to shame us, or brightly colored store windows to haunt us, or hairdressers to beg us to cut that mop. Our goals, however, remained the same: to be perma-vacationers, living and working in a place we love, with adventures non-stop. That's what mattered the most. Our goals stayed the same, despite everything.

It's been said that all things happen for a reason. If we hadn't been fired, maybe we'd never have had the guts to climb to the next level of yachting.

But for the time being, we sat in St. Thomas, weighing our options and feeling dejected. Then we planned a Harley getaway, a sure way to lift our spirits.

Nothing like a motorcycle ride to clear your head after getting fired.

Chapter 12
Sail's for Play, Power's for Pay

*You're always free to change your mind
and choose a different future, or a different past.*

—Richard Bach

*Winston and Cynthia snag their first motor
yacht job on seventy-five-foot Catalina.*

Fort Lauderdale to Abaco Island to Grand Bahama Island to Key West to Houston
February 2001—August 2001

After more soul-searching and evaluating our career choices against our bank accounts, we took a major step. "In the yachting world," Winston loves to point out, "there's a common muttering, 'Sail's for play, and power's for pay.' Sailboats are usually more fun but motor yachts pay much higher salaries. We vowed to transform ourselves

185

from sailors to motor yacht crew, as in mega yacht crew making the big bucks," adds Winston. This was considered blasphemy by many tried and true sailors—crossing over to the dark side, to the stink pots. But cross we did, anxious and unsure.

Nursed lovingly back to sanity by Barb and Glenn on Hassel Island, we massaged our résumé to meet our new goal. We spent a lucrative afternoon absorbing tips from our old friends, Buddy and Susie, who had run the red sailboats in the BVI and also had taken the leap. They were now in St. Thomas running a hundred-foot yacht. We were overwhelmed by the yacht, its massive interiors, its huge engine room, and its tiny crew quarters of sandwiched bunks meant to house five crew members pancake-style. My recurring thought, *I'm blown away that they get to live on this huge yacht.*

"I'm not sure you guys should do this," advised Buddy. "Why would you want to learn an entire new industry? Don't you think you're too old?" God, that damn age thing. We were only fifty-two and fifty-four, still spring chickens in our minds. His comment cut Winston to the quick. "I secretly believed," Winston says, "the Windwards had fired us specifically because of our age. In my mind, Buddy had just confirmed it."

As disheartening as Buddy sounded, we pushed on. With bold attitudes, a brazen plan and perhaps some stupidity, we flew off to Fort Lauderdale, the worldwide mecca of yachting. We were positive that if there was a motor yacht job for us, we'd find it in Lauderdale.

"But first we had to find a cheap place to stay," remembers Winston. "Luckily, in Fort Lauderdale a network of great and not-so-great crew houses offer housing, security and camaraderie to out-of-work yacht crews wandering between employment. The rooms are priced to fit small budgets and offer amenities that crew members need: computer access for job searches, bicycles to get to interviews, group socializing for sharing ideas and building morale.

"We chose our crew house based on two criteria: It had a seasoned mega yacht captain as head of household (Captain Bill owned the place) and it had a pool, a perfect remedy for those can't-find-a-job doldrums. Like Sandra back in San Diego who had pushed us toward Saba Rock, Captain Bill launched us into the world of mega yachts."

Winston and I approached our job hunt much like we had approached our reconnaissance of the BVI, systematically and thoroughly. We introduced ourselves personally to every crew placement agency in Lauderdale. (These agencies are the "headhunters" of the yachting industry, connecting crew with jobs.) But we didn't stop there. On a major tip from Captain Bill, we also introduced ourselves to all the key yacht brokers in the area. When the broker is selling a yacht, often he's asked to recommend crew who could run the boat. The broker sells the yacht and crew become employed—a mutually beneficial combination. "To this day," Winston smiles, "even after twenty years, brokers are our best source of job leads."

And, according to Captain Bill, our age was actually an asset—not a surprise, by the way, to me.

Crewing Motor Yachts 101

Somehow, by the grace of God, we got an audience with the guru of yacht brokers in Lauderdale. Inviting us to his home, he reviewed our résumé and assessed our careers so far. He assured us our sailing expertise would be valued in the motor yacht industry. "Motor yacht skippers can't transition to sailboats, but sailors make excellent motor yacht captains. People who sail understand the effects of winds and currents and waves on a boat; most motor yacht skippers just don't have that built-in asset. You'll do fine. Plus, you offer a maturity not often found in this industry."

Bingo.

Then he mentioned a mantra that has resounded with us ever since: "You guys need to understand one thing. Most motor yacht owners are, to put it gently, different from me and you. They aren't there for play, like your sailing charters. They don't want to be your friend. They want and expect servants. End of story."

Then he punctuated his advice with the real ending, "You two seem like really nice people, so you also need to understand that ninety-five percent of motor yacht owners can be assholes. You're crossing into an entirely new line of work." We took a deep breath.

Duly warned, we went back to the crew house and reviewed our plans. Was he correct about the people we'd be working with? Did we want to risk the change? Could we handle being treated like servants? It didn't sound as good as we had imagined, but we poured two, hefty rum and tonics and plowed forward anyway. "Power's for pay," and we wanted to be part of that.

We made a conscious decision that we wanted yachts that required only two crew full-time, as in a couple in our case. We definitely did not want to go after jobs on superyachts that had six to twelve crewmembers. We wanted some privacy, and we wanted to maintain that sense that we had on the sailboats, that the yacht was our responsibility. That decision limited our choices to yachts around one hundred feet, but that was fine with us. Bigger was not better in our case.

Crew placement agencies connected us with a couple of owners, but we had no serious bites. One relatively green couple from Texas, who had just bought their first yacht, interviewed us via phone for what seemed like hours, picking our brains about how to take care of a yacht and what was involved in chartering. We were very forthcoming and truly gave them their money's worth (though they weren't paying us a dime), even though we were secretly scared shitless about running a motor yacht. They didn't hire us, singing the blues that they couldn't afford us. Later, we heard they hired a crew half our age, with no chartering experience, to take care of their multimillion-dollar yacht. Go figure.

We kept job hunting.

The right place at the right time

We knew that breaking into the motor yacht world, with no previous positions on motor yachts, would be challenging. Not to mention having been fired from our last job. To help even the score, Winston used this downtime in Fort Lauderdale to take some mariner courses and enhance his credentials. We believed in our dream and watched for any opportunities. Being in the right place at the right time is what it took.

Our landlord, Captain Bill, was offered a position he regarded as below his pay grade. "Too small a boat for me," Bill said, "but *Catalina* might be perfect for you guys. It's for private use only, no charters, so you won't be very busy. The owner only wants to hire a captain, but I'll tell him he can get both captain and chef for the same money he would pay me. What a bargain for him, and it's the break you two need." Now we knew what "sail's for play, power's for pay" really meant. Motor yacht salaries were lavish compared to sailboats. Being sold as "two for the price of one" paid us more salary than we'd ever make at the Windwards on a sailboat.

Bill took us to see *Catalina* in the Los Olas Marina. When he walked us through the engine room, Winston broke out in a sweat. The twenty-foot by twenty-foot, walk-in engine room was stocked to the ceiling with equipment. Two shiny white engines, the size of small cars, took up

Winston's new office on the seventy-five-foot Catalina.

most of the room. Along the sides, with aisles in between, were two water makers, two huge generators, air conditioners, even a workbench with every tool known to man. Hefty protective padding around "hot zones" and an intricate, red fire system hinted of emergencies. A built-in vacuum system begged cleanliness. Winston promptly began picking Bill's brain.

Catalina was only a seventy-five-foot boat but had three levels, so she seemed huge compared the fifty-foot sailboat and even the catamaran we'd run. *Catalina's* main level included an outside dining area and wet bar on the aft (rear) deck. The entire interior was bright and airy with light oak paneling and large picture windows throughout. Beautiful silk shades monitored the sunlight. The main salon's sumptuous, beige leather, L-shaped settee (couch), accented with rust and turquoise pillows, sat opposite two matching, upholstered, swivel armchairs reflecting the same colors. Completing the ambiance was a disappearing wide screen television and the classiest mechanical cocktail table I'd ever seen. With the touch of a button, it rose twelve inches and slid toward the L-shaped settee, fitting perfectly into the corner for eating while watching the tube.

Catalina had a formal dining room for eight and a beige leather breakfast nook off a country kitchen galley. That galley, very unlike the three-foot square space in my sailboats, had a normal size oven, refrigerator and freezer, even a dishwasher and trash compactor. It seemed there was miles of counter space. I was in heaven. A curved staircase led to the lower level and three posh staterooms with heads (bathrooms, remember?) for each. The master stateroom (the owner's cabin) was complimented with a double-sink vanity and matching toilets separated by a glassed-in bathtub/shower with mirrors on the ceiling.

Oh, yes, there was one more room, a tiny—and I'm talking tiny— crew cabin. The floor was eighteen inches by thirty-six inches. (Look down, now, and picture that.) Our bedroom consisted of that floor, a standard-size bed squeezed up against three walls, and a closet the size of two bed pillows. One of us would have to stay in bed while the other dressed. Our guru broker's words rang true . . . these were servants' quarters for sure.

There were two drive stations, one just in front of the galley on the main level and one on the fly bridge, the top level of the yacht. Both drive stations had engine throttles, auto-pilot, chart plotter, compass and VHF radios, plus large leather captain chairs which looked really impressive. Besides the drive station, the fly bridge had an enclosed, air-conditioned U-shaped seating area, tables and a BBQ. It also housed a tender (a fourteen-foot inflatable boat with a fifty-horsepower inboard engine and steering wheel, far fancier than the ten-horsepower dinghies we were used to). A crane mounted to the deck lowered the tender to the water.

Luckily for us, Captain Bill was a well-respected captain in the industry. His referral, plus that bargaining chip of a two-for-one salary, got us the interview. *Catalina* had just lost its captain but was scheduled to be in the Bahamas for family in two weeks. Its Texas owner was on the hunt and in a hurry. On Bill's advice, he invited us to fly to Houston, where he lived, for an interview.

Winston was under the gun to upgrade his U.S. Coast Guard captain's license, but I was free. Off I went to interview for a crew position on a motor yacht, having never run one in my life, or even been on one that was moving.

I met owner Dick at his office. A big, tall Texan, he towered over his fine, dark-walnut desk. Carcasses of bear, deer, moose, and some kind of wild cat hung on his walls. I surmised this was not our type of guy.

But we desperately needed to break into the motor yacht industry, and this might be our only ticket. With the blind vision of someone looking through a swim mask covered in seaweed, I talked fast. I concentrated on our impeccable references, just like a politician concentrates on his successes. Yes, we were in for the long term, and, yes, we were available immediately.

Did I say this guy was in a hurry? Without even meeting Winston and knowing we had no large motor yacht history, he hired Winston and me as his full-time crew. We were to take the yacht from

Fort Lauderdale to the Abacos in the Bahamas when Winston finished his classes.

Winston looks back, "By the pure chance of landing in Captain Bill's crew house, we had joined the dark side. Bill toasted us with rum and off we went. We moved our bag of belongings to *Catalina's* crew quarters. Now, officially, we were motor yacht crew.

"We felt the highs of excitement and the blackness of potential death concurrently.

"The first time I started the engines," winces Winston, "the yacht almost jumped out of the water. And so, did I. We were used to sailboats whose motors barely made any noise. When they said, "power's for pay," they really meant power!"

The six-month cram course

Winston continues, "Not being completely stupid, we hired an auxiliary captain, with our own money, to teach us the ropes and make a few trips with us. He had been recommended by Captain Bill and really was a godsend: we were taught the best ways to maneuver this size yacht, the best ways to maintain its equipment, and techniques for interpreting its radar, chart plotter and autopilot. Then he helped lay out the route we should take and the timing for crossing the infamous Gulf Stream, with its strong currents and high winds. It would be our first trip ever to the Abacos, the northernmost group of Bahamian islands. It was scary, for sure, but we basically held our breath, listened to our tutor, and plowed ahead.

Almost two hundred miles east of Florida, Abaco's Marsh Harbour would be our base. It is the fifth largest city in the Bahamas but only seven thousand people live there. The Abacos are green with mangrove trees accented by white sand beaches, just our style. Each morning at 8:00 a.m. we'd listen on our VHF radio for the Daily Chat, a light-hearted round-robin discussion among all the boat owners and captains in the area. They introduced newcomers (like us), reviewed happenings on the island, discussed the weather (that's where we learned the term, "wild white horses" when referring to waves), and always included a joke of the day. The sailing community was warm and inviting.

During the next six months, the owner, his wife and family came aboard for only a week or two, and never traveled with us. We drove that first motor yacht out into the Atlantic and across the Gulf Stream to the Bahamas, back to Fort Lauderdale, south around the Florida Keys, up the west side of Florida, west across the Intracoastal Waterway and across the Gulf of Mexico to Galveston, Texas. By then we were actually confident as motor yacht crew.

Then we were let go.

Let go with no warning. It felt as bad as being fired.

Vagabonds again, this time in Houston

We had just weathered the hundred-year rainstorm of 2001 that flooded downtown Houston. It trashed university medical research archives and floated our seventy-five-foot yacht above its own dock. Having water creep up our legs while *standing on a dock* was alarming enough, but watching the yacht creep up, too, was frightening. All we could do was gingerly feed out the lines that held her to the dock and wait for the ocean swell to subside.

Always happy to get out of the galley, Cynthia uses some elbow grease instead of olive oil.

After only a few hours, the sea's level returned to normal again, but then the mess appeared. The yacht's hull was covered in what I can only describe as gunk, mustardy-yellow, gooey-gunk. Immediately, we started polishing *Catalina's* hull with special sea-safe chemicals to remove said gunk. When we were just about finished with the job hours later, the owner's secretary came trotting down the dock. I thought she was bringing us the new cushions the owner had ordered.

Not.

"You're being let go," she said, void of emotion, oblivious to our scrubbing. "The boss likes you fine, but our former captain has finished school and is taking over this afternoon. Here's your final check. I'll wait while you collect your things."

What the hell was this industry about?

Our questions and protests fell on deaf ears. "I'm just the messenger," she said. This owner had his secretary do his dirty work. Stunned, we gathered our personal belongings and stood on the dock. This was a nightmare. Once again, we were in shock. Numb. We had never heard one word of concern, or disappointment about our work. He'd acted pleased with us—trusted us with his car, his credit card, his yacht. What the hell? If our job on *Catalina* was a temporary gig while the captain was away, couldn't the owner have been honest about it?

Odd though, unlike the trauma at the Windwards only months before, I didn't cry a tear and Winston wasn't livid. It makes me sad to say it, but I guess we'd hardened.

My sister, Deborah, and life-long friend, Judith, both lived in Houston. Maybe that alleviated the boss's guilt, if he had any, that is. One phone call and, at least, we had someone to pick us up and a place to go. We vented to Judith. The unethical owner hired us under pretext of long-term employment, knowing it was only until his captain returned. I recalled his office of dead animals that I'd seen when he interviewed me, and the conclusion I'd made then, but ignored. When you meet somebody and think he's not your type, he probably isn't. Enough said.

But those six months on our first motor yacht taught us so much.

Lessons learned the hard way

"When skippering a Hatteras brand yacht, with Caterpillar engines, directional signs that read "No Wake Zone" mean trouble," starts off Winston. "Even coasting in neutral, Cat engines put out a wake that rocked the shores of the Intracoastal Waterway (the inland waterway which runs just inside the Atlantic coast from Florida to Virginia and along the Gulf of Mexico from Florida to Texas). Homeowners along the Waterway cursed us loudly for going too fast as our wake sent waves up into their yards. Not good.

"Never cross the Gulf Stream if there is an 'N' in the wind direction. Winds that are blowing from the north, northeast, northwest, even east-northeast across almost five knots of current in the Gulf Stream create waves known as "wild white horses." Bucking these waves can be treacherous. It was.

"Never ever follow another boat into a harbor, thinking they know the best approach. We bent the yacht's props on the sea bottom learning that one, even with our hired captain's expensive guidance. The noise created when a four-foot spinning prop scrapes a coral reef haunts you, for a long, long time. I dreamt that sound for months. The repair required two weeks in a boatyard. Surprisingly, our boss took it well. He quoted the old adage, 'There are only two kinds of captains in the Bahamas. Those who have hit the bottom, and those who are about to.'

"Another thing, when you're pulling away from the dock, never put the yacht in gear. Holes can occur—in the dock, or the boat, or both. This was a tough lesson. Looking at the damage, small as it was, caused my stomach to churn. We paid for the repair ourselves, because it was caused by my inexperience. That was one day I considered crawling back to sailboats.

"Double check your rear door and arm it, with a warning alarm. Once, when we were motoring up the Intracoastal, seawater poured into *Catalina's* rudder room and master stateroom before we even noticed. The door, situated almost level with the sea, had been left open. We had our co-captain on this venture, too. He was cool as a cucumber. We were panicked. As a side lesson, a large beige silk carpet dries quickly when spread across a hillside.

"One lesson Cynthia was teased about for a while: Only say 'Mayday,

mayday' over the VHF radio, in cases of life, or death. Calling 'mayday, mayday' during our master stateroom carpet-drenching didn't make the U.S. Coast Guard happy. Those words are reserved for life-threatening emergencies. We were in only eight feet of water in a narrow, well-populated waterway. Drowning was not an issue.

"And," Winston concludes as he shakes his head, "two last important lessons from *Catalina:* If an owner will hire you on the spur of the moment, without even meeting you, something's fishy. And some yacht owners don't have the balls to do their own dirty work."

Graduating, sort of

We took refuge at my sister Deborah's home and again immersed ourselves in the job search via the internet. At least the crew placement agencies knew us by now, and our résumé had grown.

We had survived our own version of "Crewing Motor Yachts 101," had overcome the many obstacles, learned from our many mistakes, and traveled the Atlantic and Gulf of Mexico, the Intracoastal, and the Gulf Stream, with a seventy-five-foot yacht to our credit. We'd accomplished our goal, transitioning to power for pay.

But now we'd been fired from two jobs in a row.

How the hell were we going to overcome that?

Part Two:

Kissing Frogs and Paying Dues

Motoryachting with rich people is sometimes like walking the plank blindfolded.

2001 - 2011

Chapter 13
Adventures Aboard the Ark

What the caterpillar calls the end of the world,
the master calls a butterfly.

—Richard Bach

Aaaarrrrrr. Where's my coffee?

Houston to Palm Beach to St. Thomas to
British Virgin Islands to Fort Lauderdale
August 2001—June 2002

In the right place again

Now out of work, with two sailboats, one motor yacht, and two firings under our belts, Winston grabbed the chance to fly to San Diego and squeeze in a Harley-Davidson ride. I stayed with Deborah and her husband, Ernie, capturing treasured times with my young niece and two nephews, and having lots of girl-talks with Deborah and Judith. Even bad times bring blessings.

After about three weeks, I got a call out of the blue from the newbie yacht owner couple who had picked our brains on the telephone so many months before. They'd drilled us on the ins and outs of chartering and then hired inexpensive youngsters instead of us. Well, seems their first crew hadn't lasted—what a surprise. They wondered if we would be interested in running charters in the British Virgin Islands on their sixty-five-foot Horizon motor yacht, *The Ark*. *The Ark* would be rented for a week at a time through charter brokers. A captain and chef were included in the price.

Trying to hide my ecstasy, I asked where they were located and when we might meet. Unbelievably, they lived five miles from Deborah, right there in Houston! Meant to be? We all thought so. It was serendipity for sure.

Winston put his Harley to bed and flew back for the interview. There was one small glitch we had to consider: it was these people's first yacht, so we knew we'd be potty-training them for a while. One example, they presented us with a thirty-page manual of crew duties which elaborated more about vacuuming and polishing than it did about engine maintenance and safety. Despite their odd priorities, we had a good interview, focused on the positive and, even with their manual, accepted the job.

Winston loves this next part. "The owners flew us to Fort Lauderdale, where the yacht was docked. Rather than have us drive *The Ark* in rough seas, they opted to ship her to the Virgin Islands on Yacht Mover Limited. The yacht transport company carries many hundred-foot yachts with ease on seven hundred-foot ships. Engineers fill tanks in the ship to lower the ship's deck below the water, so yachts can float right on. Then underwater divers secure the yachts to the sunken deck. The tanks are then pumped dry and the deck rises again. The ship sets sail with its cargo all secure on its deck. Yachts move all over the world this way, floating on and floating off a large ship. Yachts arrive at their destination in perfect condition. As pricey as it is, it eliminates the wear and tear on the yacht, its engines, and its crew, plus saves the expense of fuel required for four thousand-mile, open ocean journeys. I loved the idea.

"This was our first time ever maneuvering a yacht over a big sunken deck. And knowing there were divers in the water made it that much more treacherous. Listening for cues on the VHF radio was critical. Yachts had to line up in designated order, so the correct size yacht went into the correct designated spot. Think of it as yachts treading water, waiting their turn. That, in itself, can be a challenge, if there are high seas or high winds. And driving a yacht over a sunken deck, while scubas divers are securing others underwater, tightens the sphincter muscle for sure.

"But the process went off without a hitch, loading and securing yachts of all sizes in just a few hours. Later we watched the deck rise and the water drain. Sure enough, there sat *The Ark,* tightly packed in among the other yachts, strapped down like a Harley to a flatbed. She was ready for her journey south. So were we. We hopped a plane to the Virgins to meet her. *The Ark* arrived, perfectly intact, six days later."

Impressing the charter brokers

Chartering a motor yacht in the British Virgin Islands would be a piece of cake. We knew the BVI like the back of our hands. We'd handled over fifty sailboat charters like champs, with the Windwards, and had the references to prove it. And *The Ark* had a "personality"

Reflections of a Caribbean sunset.

that both charter brokers and charter guests would love. She had been named in honor of her owner's devotion to the Humane Society, and the yacht's decor was all animal.

Winston explains, "Charter brokers recommend specific yachts for their clients' vacations. They annually travel to 'Charter Boat Shows' around the world to see the charter boats firsthand. It's not just finding the right yacht; brokers want to find the right crew to match their clients' personalities. Besides touring the yacht and learning its amenities, brokers interview crews (typically a captain and chef) about their style and history together."

Crew proudly present their yacht in full regalia, from gleaming stainless railings to spotless heads. They display their water toys like kayaks, snorkel gear, and inflatable rafts, fill the boat with tropical flower arrangements, and dress the tables with creative place settings, as if she were ready for charter. Talking with up to a hundred brokers over three days is both exhilarating and exhausting.

"These boat shows were new to us," Winston notes. "At the Windwards, we'd never met a yacht broker. The company always arranged our charters, with no effort by us at all. In this new world of private yacht chartering, we needed to market ourselves and our yacht in order to get charters. We had to impress the charter brokers. This was going to be fun."

For our first British Virgin Islands Charter Boat Show, Winston and I held court on *The Ark* for three days straight, introducing ourselves and becoming friends with almost seventy-five charter brokers. *The Ark* was the only new motor yacht available for charter; most were sailboats. And in all her grandeur, *The Ark* was the queen of the boat show.

Sixty-five feet long, *The Ark* slept six guests in three staterooms and had four heads. Her outstanding feature: she offered three decks of creatively themed décor. Her aft deck piqued visitors' curiosity, with a gleaming oval table and a pair of comical, two-foot-tall giraffes lounging ridiculously. Wide double glass doors invited guests into an interior of high gloss rosewood, white, silk settees and white carpet. Throw pillows of leopard and giraffe prints complemented the rhino sculptures atop the disappearing television and the zebra placemats on the dining table. The lavish staterooms each housed a resident animal, or two, from beautiful but hilarious monkeys entwined in the bookcases to three plush and over-stuffed elephants lollygagging on a queen-size bed. The fly bridge (that top level) housed the drive station and the BBQ, a frig and a curved dining area, and some wildlife. A large, padded, sun pad spread across the bow for sunbathing. Alongside it sat a basket full of beach towels, *"The Ark"* T-shirts and matching hats. And at sunset, her expansive windows glowed with a full-length mirrored reflection of the sparkling sea and blazing sky.

Back to those zebra placemats, a multitude of exquisite dinner china reflected many intricate animal patterns, a creative mix-and-match option that gave every meal a new look. Casual breakfast china was bright blue and yellow, with lots of napkins and placemats to change its look too. Fine crystal for evening and blue goblets for daytime accented the place settings.

One of the many "animal" place settings on The Ark.

A funny note, though, with all the elaborate choices of china and place settings, the galley—where all the food came from to fill those plates—was tiny. And I'm not exaggerating. The galley's floor was two feet wide and four feet long, quite the opposite of *Catalina's* huge, country kitchen to which I'd grown accustomed. But the black marble counter tops and gleaming appliances promised great things.

So, as I was saying, showing off *The Ark* to charter brokers at the BVI Boat Show was a pleasure. They loved the theme, they loved the history, they loved us.

Winston grins as he remembers, "All our old sailing buddies came by to say hello and get a tour. Less than a year before, we'd been fired from the Windwards. Now, everyone asked, 'How in the world did you get this job?'"

Shock treatment

Our newbie owners took our advice fairly well, but once in a while we had to provide a little shock treatment.

The wife was having a fit about provisioning expenses and let me know via some rather irate emails. (Provisioning expenses include everything necessary for a successful charter, i.e., food, booze, linens, flowers, etc.) Her email read, in part, "Why on earth did you buy Evian water when cases of cheap water could be had for twenty-five cents a bottle at any grocery store? And there is absolutely no reason to spend seven dollars on edible flowers!" In the same email, she also demanded I stop sending the sheets and towels to the professional laundry.

Micromanaging a seven-dollar expense seemed obsessive but no matter. It took several hours to compose a professional explanation— sans emotion—because I was pissed. This was her money, and she deserved an explanation. I pointed out the few dollars' worth of colorful edible orchids earned rave reviews from almost every female charter guest I served, and they always were mentioned on comment sheets that went back to the brokers. As for the Evian, the grocery stores here didn't offer cases of cheap water. All bottled water was the same price, and Evian was the most impressive to guests. Plus, the bottles fit perfectly when stacked in the tiny refrigerator. Space was always a key concern.

Her response to my explanation: she would go with me to provision for her next trip on *The Ark* and see for herself. This was my chance to educate a millionaire. Couldn't wait.

Soon after she arrived, I walked her over to the laundromat I would use, if I did the linens myself. The place was full of locals and their kids.

Most dryers had no front panel and displayed rusted guts. Half of the washers were out of order and the other half all busy swishing noisily or knocking out of balance. The only folding area was sticky with soda spills and used chewing gum. Did she really want *The Ark's* Egyptian cotton, custom-fitted, seven hundred fifty-count bed sheets going into these machines?

For the next exercise, I hailed a gypsy cab driver and explained we'd use him all day for our ongoing shopping trip. My boss indignantly asked him who he worked for and where his taxi license was. I explained that gypsies were the cheapest and best choice, they had no license but were the normal mode of transportation on the island, and if you waited for a government taxi, it could take hours plus cost three times as much.

For *Island Shopping 101,* I took the owner to every store on my route, demonstrating how cost conscious I was and how much trouble it was to be that way. We traveled to this store for local fresh fish and this other store for meats, that store for canned goods but never grains because they're soggy, this market for breads, that place for almost everything else, K-mart for some liquors because they are cheapest there, and the specialty shop for wines because they give great discounts to charters boats. The trip took five hours. All the while, our cabbie waited patiently for every load.

And we weren't finished yet. Once we arrived back at the marina, we had to carry all the groceries down the dock, then carry them up the stairs and into the yacht. Dock carts were rarely available at our marina, so it often took four, or five, trips.

At the end of that day, an exhausted but more understanding owner smiled at me and said, "You can buy anything you want, Cynthia. I trust you. And, yes, do send out that laundry." For her graduation from *Island Shopping 101,* I brought her a glass of Chardonnay, with a delicate, edible, purple orchid on the side.

The Ark's herd

Charter guests on *The Ark* included an angelic little girl with a great sense of humor who loved pointing her little finger at Winston and bossing him, "Listen, Mister, you'd better do what Cynthia says!" to charter guests who tied themselves to the table on the last day, chanting "We ain't going. We ain't going." We coerced them off the yacht with promises of rum. (Over the years, we've rendezvoused with them several times, staying in their homes in Texas and, later, California. Good friends. Great charter guests.)

Who's your worst charter guest? (Move over, Italians)

Guests always asked continual questions and soaked up every fable we recited. "Who were your worst charter guests?" they'd invariably ask, hungry for titillating tattle tales. With a grin, Winston's pat answer was, "Well, this charter isn't over yet, so you're still in the running!"

It seems a funny question, but it's no laughing matter. You'd be surprised how much unsafe or rude behavior can hurt a charter, especially on yachts like *The Ark*, with only two crew to police everyone while keeping them safe, making them happy and providing over-the-top service. The captain's nerves can wear thin if he's constantly barraged with ridiculous requests or abusive retorts. He always maintains his cool. My job is to deflect that pressure by steering guests toward realistic and equally enjoyable offers. On some charters, that can be a full-time job.

The Coast Guard and/or national park rangers have strict rules where motorized boats are concerned, no matter what size the vessel. An extensive and specific book, *U.S. Coast Guard Rules of the Road,* outlines every rule a boat driver must adhere to. Yacht captains are expected to know all the rules, and to follow those rules to a T. Any breach by a charter guest is considered a breach by the captain. U.S. Coast Guard licenses have been revoked over some of those breaches.

Letting guests know that, while remaining their fun-loving charter host, is an art and a requirement.

Our outrageous, Italian charter from way back in Blunder Bay days had held the record as our worst charter, since 1995. Then came Mike, on *The Ark* . . .

"OK," says Winston, "picture a clan of five run by a 'know-it-all, I'm right/you're wrong' man, his soft-spoken blame-it-on-my-husband wife, and three unsuspecting children, twelve, ten, and six years old. In seven days, this family proceeded to ruin their reputation with us, with a scuba diving company, with the Bitter End Yacht Club, with Anegada Reef Hotel, and with another crew.

"The mother asked Cynthia to come to the staterooms, showed her three, black trash bags full of dirty clothes, and said, 'Mike wants you to do this laundry.' Cynthia apologized in that there was no way she'd be able to handle that much laundry. We only had a small washer/dryer combo, and Cynthia was quite busy with their sheets and towels, plus lunch was due, and the kids expected her to take them snorkeling. The mom replied, 'Well, then, could the captain do it?'"

I won't describe the look on Winston's face when he overheard that, or the words he muttered, but if he'd been wearing a swim mask, it would have been shrouded in steam. I asked Bitter End Resort if they might accommodate her laundry, but it was a holiday, and they were swamped with their own guests. I offered to do a few T-shirts and underwear to help out, but she didn't take me up on it.

From that day on, each morning I would find a pile of wet towels on the floor in each of the three staterooms. They were determined to make me pay.

Each day, this group continued to astound us with their ingratitude and rudeness. Realize that on much larger yachts with more crew and more equipment, crews are often expected to handle much more, to go above and beyond. It's just that on a sixty-five-foot yacht, with only two crew and limited resources, there are certain constraints we can't ignore, as much as we'd like to.

"Oh, and the parents thought nothing of inviting people they'd just met to come aboard for lunch, with no notice and no offer to purchase extra food," Winston complains. "It's great trying to make lunch for two adults and three children, which all of a sudden becomes lunch for eight, or nine. (On a sixty-five-foot yacht, the fridge and freezers accommodate exactly what's needed for the guests on board for the week, with little room for extras.) After the second time Mike pulled this stunt, Cynthia had to make it clear not to do it again—her 'please' was accompanied by her index finger pointed for emphasis. In one ear and out the other . . .

"They also thought nothing of allowing their six-year-old to take the tender out by himself, without telling the captain, no less. The tender was the yacht's 'taxi,' a fifteen-foot, inflatable boat that transported guests to bars and beaches when they didn't want to swim. When I first noticed the tender was gone and saw the parents and two older kids still onboard, I was sure it had been stolen. Then the kid appeared in the dinghy, spinning around like a maniac out in the anchorage—unsafe and unlawful. What a jerk. Thank God no one died in that fiasco.

"And speaking of dying, Mike insisted that I schedule five scuba dives for everyone but the youngest. The professional scuba company that we hired for the dives radioed us on the morning of the second dive and cancelled. They explained Mike didn't listen to directions, or cautions, brought extra people on board when told not to, showed massive disregard for the safety of pairing when swimming, and, in a nutshell, were the most dangerous scuba diving parents they'd ever seen. All I could say was I understood. Unfortunately, the cancellations meant Cynthia and I had to be with them that much more.

"And another thing . . . just thinking about this gets me pissed. These people were traveling in tandem with six people on another private yacht. We rendezvoused one afternoon, supposedly just for a swim. True to form, big-mouth Mike invited them all over for dinner. When the chef of the other boat declined, because neither yacht was equipped for more than six people, and she already had her rack of lamb roasting, Mike stole her people and said 'Just put the lamb in a bag and bring it on over.' That chef telephoned her boss that instant and quit on the spot. She didn't even discuss it with her husband. In all likelihood, her guests had been every bit as horrible as ours," Winston concluded.

But as my mother used to say, there's a blessing in every misery. And she was right. Even with all the rancor we still have for Mike, he saved the day when Winston ripped his hand open while manhandling a runaway anchor. Mike was a surgeon and repaired Winston, with professional finesse. He was complimentary of Winston's fortitude, too. He'd handled the pain with no anesthetic except for—you guessed it—some Cruzan rum.

As if things weren't eventful enough, on the morning of the last day when we were driving *The Ark* through Sir Francis Drake's Channel back to St. Thomas to get this group out of our lives forever, we struck a submerged object. We were in the middle of the channel in sixty feet of water with no designated warnings marked on the chart. Both Winston and Mike were at the helm, and neither saw anything in the water. We never knew what we hit, but after limping to the dock and diving under the boat, we could see both four-foot props were badly bent. It must have been something big.

We were very happy to see this group walk off the dock and out of our lives. Calling the owners about the prop damage was almost pleasant compared to dealing with those people for another day. They still hold the record as our worst charter guests.

Our first delivery north

Our bosses traveled to the BVI, checked out the prop repair and then played on their yacht in the islands for another week. That's when they notified us they had some grave financial difficulties. They'd be selling the boat when we could drive it back to Florida.

Thus ended our first season of chartering motor yachts. We were bummed, but learning fast about the instability of this industry we were so eager to join. We hired a third eye to help us deliver the boat north and set out for Fort Lauderdale. The two-week trip took us to Puerto Rico, the Dominican Republic, Turks and Caicos, and the Bahamas. It was necessary to stop often to buy more fuel and wait for weather windows.

When we were underway, rules were especially critical. With a three-man crew, we stood watches in pairs of two, alternating while the third crew member slept. "Standing watch" means driving the yacht and watching for other boats, debris in the water, even whales. One person, the skipper, drives the yacht with the helpful eye and backup of the other crewmember. Crew monitor radar, the route, weather conditions, latitude and longitude and distance travelled, and record all that information in the yacht's log book every hour. Also necessary are hourly engine room checks to assure that nothing has gone haywire with the engines, generators, stabilizers, water makers, air conditioners, etc. You only relax when you arrive.

We were delayed in the Dominican Republic because, after taking on fifteen hundred gallons of fuel, our boss's credit card wouldn't work. Oops. And, no, we didn't know his mother's maiden name. Crap. And we couldn't reach him. Murphy's law. So now what? We had to hire locals to "watch" the yacht, bribe them with extra cash and *"The Ark"* hats and T-shirts. We were escorted to a bank by armed guards, then waited, until we finally could reach the boss hours later. He arranged for a bank transfer to pay the bill, and that evening we were back on the yacht drinking heavily. (By the way, there is absolutely no drinking allowed when the yacht is underway.)

Near Bimini, our yacht was boarded by the U.S. Coast Guard. After hailing us by VHF radio, five Coast Guard guys with guns climbed aboard, while we were underway no less, and went through the entire yacht, from the lowest bilge to the highest storage locker and everything between, provisions included. They checked that we had the proper life jackets, the correctly dated emergency flairs and life rafts, the proper official documents showing ownership and proof of insurance. We had to show all fire extinguishers and where they were located, life rings and evacuation directions . . . everything needed to insure a safe, responsible trip. It impressed them we had created a document for each stateroom telling guests where various safety equipment was located and how to use it. The end result: they gave us a "Good as Gold" rating and bid us farewell. We're still very proud of that acknowledgement.

After almost being hauled off to jail in the Dominican Republic and being boarded by the Coast Guard, the rest of the trip was delightful and uneventful. Understand that on a delivery, we drive, sleep, eat and fuel, and not much else. There is rarely enough time to explore the islands, so we saw little of them, only their ports and their customs agents. But our résumé was growing and our understanding of motor yacht owners broadening. Would we ever find a normal one? What could we expect next?

When we landed in Fort Lauderdale, the boss sold the yacht, and we took a break. We flew back to San Diego to begin a four thousand-mile Harley ride, this time to hook up with two sets of friends in big-sky Montana: Dave and Roxy from Windansea days and Barb and Glenn, our Hassel Island *compadres* who were touring there. White water rafting and Glacier National Park were both on the agenda.

We could look for our next job later.

Chapter 14
The Sweet Life

Your friends will know you better in the first minute you meet
than your acquaintances will know you in a thousand years.

—Richard Bach

Grand Bahamas to Fort Lauderdale to St. Thomas and BVI to Fort Lauderdale to New York City to Newport, Rhode Island, to Martha's Vineyard to Nantucket to New Orleans
June 2002—June 2004

It's who you work for

Via telephone, we interviewed with seven, different, potential bosses, during our motorcycle recess. A husband-wife team was a rare commodity at the time, and our reputation was blooming just when we needed it most.

I was stressed about getting another job, knowing our bank accounts were dwindling, but we still turned down quite a few opportunities, because we recognized red flags early in the conversations. One criterion we held fast to was being allowed to have family on board occasionally, when owners were not. This may be unheard of on most megayacht, but we specifically tried to choose yachts with casual atmospheres and trusting owners who would allow it. We were determined to find a job that fit our casual, adventurous, perma-vacationer lifestyle, and we would work hard to earn it. This might not be industry standard, but it was our goal and we would stick to our guns until we found it.

Recalling our mentor's warning about the ninety-five percent assholes rule, we treasured the day we got the call from the Catholic doctor running a Jewish hospital. He'd have to have a sense of humor to survive that scenario, right?

We were Harley riding in Montana, rendezvousing with our Virgin Islands friends, when Dr. Jerry reached us. His yacht broker had recommended us as matching his needs perfectly, and he'd gone to great lengths to track us down. "I'm about to purchase a motor yacht in the Bahamas," he'd said, "and I want to charter it in the Caribbean. I know I want you two to run it and *only* you two." (ta dah!) "Will you fly with me to the Bahamas to take a look at her?" (duh!) After a lengthy and delightful phone interview sitting on the bed in our Motel 6 room, we knew we had struck gold.

Ideally, the doctor wanted to fly us first to New York the next day, for a weekend trip with his wife, Donna, on his current boat. But we were in the middle of Nowhere, Montana, with no place to store the motorcycle and no airport, so that idea was dumped. A week later, with our bike conveniently receiving a check-up and oil change plus storage at a Harley dealership in Salt Lake City, we flew to Fort Lauderdale and then on to Freeport, Grand Bahamas.

There, looking down from the top of a long airport escalator, we got the first glimpse of our new boss. His huge smile, welcoming outreached arms, and casual shorts and T-shirt sealed the deal. We liked him immediately. The feeling was mutual. Jerry told us later he knew he liked us when he saw Winston wearing a Leatherman (that indispensable fix-anything gadget sailors wear).

The *Sweet Life* was indeed sweet. We were surprised by her ivory color, contrary to the usual gleaming white of most yachts. But we soon understood that ivory softens the sun's glare considerably, a definite asset in the tropics. Inviting furnishings throughout the main salon, galley/dinette, pilot house and staterooms made the yacht light and comfy. The separate crew quarters off the engine room offered only twin beds but a double set, plus an extra crew lounge for washer, dryer, microwave, and fridge. It was quite an

One of the many yacht interiors Winston and Cynthia enjoyed.

improvement over *The Ark*. And the boss insisted we use one queen-size stateroom when no one was on board.

The crowning glory of *Sweet Life* was her hot tub atop the fly bridge. Tucked in around two curved settees, a shiny barbecue, a drive station, and a fifteen-foot tender, the hot tub could be covered with an upholstered sun pad or exposed for some watery pleasure—perfect choices for charterers.

Jerry completed the yacht purchase while we had dinner with Donna and their friends. When he took official possession and wanted to celebrate, there was a welcoming bottle of wine but no wine opener on board. Not to be deterred, Jerry grabbed a screw and a screw driver from the engine room and *voila,* bottle opened, and toasts flowing. Grinning at each other, Winston and I knew this guy would be a keeper.

From that moment, literally, we were in charge. Jerry and Donna flew home, and we prepared *Sweet Life* for the trip across the Gulf Stream from Freeport, Bahamas, back to Fort Lauderdale, in the U.S. Simultaneously, we alerted a hundred charter brokers that we'd be bringing some really, sweet life to the BVI that fall: "Prepare your clients for the time of their lives, hot tub included. Keep your eyes peeled for rubber duckies."

Haunts in the night

"Only a day after taking possession of the yacht, still in Freeport and before we had even uncovered all the nooks and crannies aboard, we were rudely awakened to the seedier side of the docks," grimaces Winston. "After noticing that our blue, bank pouch wasn't where Cynthia had put it the night before, we began retracing our steps. Some cash and our passports were inside that pouch. I was sure we had it on the yacht the night before and had stashed it in our traditional hiding place.

"We searched throughout the yacht, with panic silently creeping in. Then, 'Would you have taken it up to the fly bridge, Cynthia?' Sure she hadn't, we climbed the stairs anyway, opened the glass hatch, and, in awe, stood among piles of receipts, my driver's license, credit cards, and, thank God, our passports, strewn all over the deck and blowing in the wind.

"Stunned, we figured that somebody had entered our yacht while we were sleeping and found not only the blue, bank pouch but Cynthia's purse as well. She hadn't even noticed that missing. Quickly gathering up our papers and assessing what was missing (three hundred dollars and my cell phone), we started canvassing the dock to see who else had been robbed. The yacht next door was hit, as well.

"Police reports were filed, but no one was ever caught. The best that police could figure was that the cleaning crew hired by the broker had searched for booty instead of dust, and then left an out of sight hatch open. The fact that they were aboard, going through our things while we slept, was eerie. But, eternal optimist, Cynthia, reminded me bad things can happen anywhere. We refused to let it bum us out."

First things first

Sweet Life needed a bit of maintenance and, remember, we still had our motorcycle in Utah, so we headed with the yacht to Fort Lauderdale. We made the eighty-eight-mile ocean trip in record time. Our boss's broker and his financial advisor were our deck hands. The Gulf Stream seemed asleep for a change (no "N" in the wind direction). How nice.

In Lauderdale, we maneuvered *Sweet Life* up the New River to Lauderdale Marine Center, where she was hauled out and readied for new bottom paint. Perfectly timed, we beat feet it back to Salt Lake, retrieved our Harley, and finished our trip back in San Diego. We parked the bike in our friend Tim's garage and tucked it in for the winter.

Flying back to Fort Lauderdale (on the boss's dime), we approved the work done by the yard and arranged for *Sweet Life* to go south aboard Yacht Mover Limited, the same company that had transported *The Ark*. British Virgin Islands, we're back!

What makes you two so good?

Once again, the Caribbean boat shows found us marketing a showcase motor yacht among a bevy of sailboats. Using 3-D marketing techniques from my corporate heels-and-briefcase days, we made sure brokers would remember the crew with the hot tub. (Hot tubs were rare on our size yacht at the time.)

Each was given a yellow, rubber ducky—well, more precisely, brokers had to fish them out of our hot tub. Until you've seen two hundred bright yellow, red-beaked, rubber duckies decked out in black sunglasses, advertising our website floating in a hot tub, you can't quite get the impact, but it was significant. Our little guys, sitting on the desk of a charter broker right next to the computer, would be the perfect reminder to recommend *Sweet Life* first.

Those ducks became our trademark and from then on, we were labeled the "Rubber Ducky Crew." Each year we'd hand out different rubber ducky characters—the next year: mask and snorkels.

Boat shows were a major deal, and we enjoyed preparing for them. *Sweet Life* was immaculate, inside and out. And we rehearsed.

Winston and Cynthia weren't called the "Rubber Ducky Crew" by charter brokers for nothing.

Winston and I reviewed every question we might be asked and knew all our answers. But, this time, there was one question we weren't ready for.

The matriarch of charter brokers, a woman with probably the most clout in the industry, was sitting on our settee, casually enjoying a stuffed mushroom, when she popped the question. "I tell you, I've been walking these docks all day, and constantly I've been hearing, 'You've got to see Cynthia and Winston' and 'Winston and Cynthia are amazing. Make sure you meet them.' What I want to know is, what makes you two so great?"

Floored, we couldn't think of anything to say. We'd rehearsed a lot of questions but not this one. Then I meekly answered, in the presence of this charter guru, "Because we're old, I guess." She laughed and agreed. We had the breadth of experience to talk with almost anyone about almost anything. And, we could make people our friends almost immediately. Most other crews were at least fifteen to twenty years younger, if not more. Old was good. Age was an asset.

To us, the formula to becoming celebrated charter crew combines enthusiasm, flexibility and professional preparedness, plus a penchant for marketing. Lowering your expectations and being a jack of all trades helps a lot, too. With Winston and I there are no pink and blue jobs; we take responsibility for everything that contributes to the ultimate charter experience for our guests. We invest in their interests and see that reflected back at us time and time again. Being a long-term couple doesn't hurt either.

You have to keep your goals in mind, if you're choosing a new career, and not be sidetracked. Some crew want to show off their French cooking; others are expert scuba instructors; still others prefer the silver service, white-shirted epaulet style. Sticking to our own goals, we present ourselves as Jimmy Buffet casual crew. Making that clear to charter brokers has sealed our success, because we get the type of guests who prefer the same. We don't expect every charter to be wonderful, but we're determined to make the most of every charter. (One more thought . . . as a little kid, I always wanted to be an airline stewardess—travel adventures, showing people a great time, keeping them safe, and making money. Funny how that's sort of come true.)

Sweet life aboard Sweet Life

We hosted many, many charters aboard *Sweet Life*. Not one did we regret. Our best was with owners Jerry and Donna themselves, but memories include many characters.

Jerry and Donna brought two of Jerry's right-hand men—except they were women—on one charter with us. Shirley and Susan were overweight, to put it gently, and very unsure of themselves in the water. They loved to laugh and eat and drink, and they toured every bar and shop in the BVI. But I wanted them to love the water. And my triumph was making both feel secure, floating with Styrofoam noodles tied to a safety line behind the boat. Soon they were so comfortable that one lady kept unhitching herself to explore, floating off toward the horizon. After retrieving her for the third time, we anchored her as well. Those two were a real joy to have aboard.

"Another time, Jerry and Donna brought their son and grandson aboard," laughs Winston. "Four-year-old Trenton knew boats like a sailor. He knew how to enter via the gangway and how to keep his knees loose when walking around the boat underway. He also knew that things don't usually fly off the boat. Sitting in the salon one day, looking out the window, as we were underway, Trenton suddenly saw our large, white-vinyl sun pad go flying by. 'Oh, shit!' the little guy blurted out. 'Get the life jackets!' The sun pad had worked itself loose from the bow and gotten away. After three days, an ultra-light pilot spotted our pad caught against, I swear, the only piece of ragged, vinyl-ripping, chain-link fence on the BVI coastline. Helped by the local garbage barge driver, we could barely lug the massive, sopping wet sun pad up onto his deck. It was like pulling a thoroughly-soaked queen-size mattress up a staircase. She was repairable, though, and we were happy to have her back."

Sweet Life had a few quirks. One of them was caused by a faulty breaker that, at will, would switch the hall light on and off. We jokingly said these idiosyncrasies were caused by *Sweet Life's* resident jumbie, Luigi. A precious little charter guest named Lila, who was as sweet as she was pretty, was enthralled with Luigi stories. Needless to say, Winston and she connected. They palled around constantly. But this little cherub shocked us all one day when her mother was standing on the stairs telling us a story and overlooking Lila's plea for attention. Suddenly, Lila's frustration got the best of her, and she literally bit her mother's thigh. Stunned beyond belief, Mom promptly hoisted Lila down to her stateroom and shut the door. We heard lots of crying and sobbing, then quiet, and then more crying and sobbing. Ultimately, Mom reappeared. "When I asked her what possessed her to bite me in the leg, she answered through sobs, 'Luigi made me do it!' When she could see I wasn't buying that story, she added, 'The electricity got really strong and made my teeth bite down.'" That's the last time we explained boat quirks with kids in the room.

"We still converse with a family of three stair-step boys plus a large mom and dad," Winston says, thinking back. "They were with us for a week, but it was evident the first day that drawing those boys comfortably into the water was going to be difficult. Soper's Hole on Tortola was our first stop, and it offered a perfect non-threatening snorkeling hole to tease the boys into relaxing underwater. None had snorkeled before, so Cynthia was in heaven with fresh 'fish.' After sitting waist deep on the edge of the beach, testing their masks and snorkels, Cynthia and her troop were ready for fins. Seeing tiny fish underwater had broken the ice.

"Soon they graduated to three-foot-deep water, where they knew they could stand, if uneasy. Cynthia pointed out shell after shell, and they, being competitive brothers ready to outdo each other, dove for them wildly. I could just tell Cynthia felt more rewarded than the boys. Later that day, we moved the yacht to a deeper anchorage, twenty feet of water. The now-broken-in and brazen boys vowed they'd all jump off the swim step together (not climb down the ladder into the water the sissy way). But after no action on the third count of one-two-three, their one hundred fifty-pound mama in a bright, royal blue swimsuit yelled, 'Bomb's away!' and flew off the fly bridge—fifteen feet high over the boys' heads, soaring through the air, before landing with a splash and a 'whoopee!'

"OK, boys, if you won't do it, I will!" A charter guests shows up her sons.

Instantly, three boys jumped in together, no count needed. The entire anchorage could hear their screams of success. In gratitude for opening up their new world of snorkeling, the boys presented Cynthia with an iridescent, stuffed mermaid. I bet those guys still talk about their mom's motivating splash."

Probably one of our most impactful charters was with Rob and Bobbie and their son and daughter. Those kids, maybe ten and twelve, were open to everything we suggested, from mango chutney to blowing conch shells. And, every time I climbed to the fly bridge, our rubber duckies were arranged in yet another creative scenario.

So why was it so impactful? Ten years later, we were docking a yacht on Block Island, off Newport, Rhode Island, when a dockhand yelled out, "Hey, did you used to run a yacht named *Sweet Life*?" "Yeah, we did," I nodded with smiles. Then the young man introduced himself. "I'm Andy of Rob and Bobbie. You took me on the best vacation of my life and changed my dreams. I now have my own captain's license and am going to work on a mega yacht next season. You two are the reason for my career." Andy had recognized me by my voice and the sailing gloves I always wore when docking. Winston and I are proud to have influenced him so significantly. We stay in touch, too. He's been crew on a one hundred sixty-foot Feadship for several years now. One of our own charter guests went after his dream, and got it!

In this vagabond lifestyle of ours, connecting with family always rejuvenated us. My son, Jason, and his wife were lucky enough to take advantage of *Sweet Life* in the Caribbean, staying on the yacht with us for several days and then beaching themselves at the Cooper Island Resort for a few more. Thanks to our boss's enthusiasm and a nice discount at the resort, they enjoyed the best of both worlds—a luxury yacht honeymoon (albeit with Mom) and a secluded, romantic cabin on the beach. How terrific it was to offer them that fiesta, and to spend time with my son again.

How dare we help

"Not every experience was cheery," inserts Winston. "Cane Garden Bay was a lovely bay that we'd been enjoying since 1990. A quaint hotel and several good restaurants complemented Quito's live reggae at night. Like Saba Rock, though, Cane Garden had changed since our sailing days. We found this out rudely at 6:00 a.m. one Tuesday. Our sweet life turned sour.

"Anchored in the bay, with a father, mother, sixteen-year-old son, and his friend as charterers, we went to bed in calm waters with full stomachs. At about midnight, all hell broke loose. A shift in the wind and current sent a large, north ocean swell rolling into Cane Garden Bay. Cynthia and I awoke to banging on the hull.

"Up as quick as lightning, we were at the bow with flashlights. (Cynthia and I slept fully clothed on charter for just this type of emergency.) A twenty-five-foot runabout motor boat had dragged its anchor and tangled it in ours. Banging repeatedly against our hull, it had already gouged deep ugly scrapes into *Sweet Life*. We ran for fenders and tried to drop them between the two boats, hoping desperately to stop the contact. But we just didn't have enough hands.

"We rallied our two, hardy, teenage guests to help, and they sprang into action. I shimmied into the motor boat and tried to start it, to no avail. I futilely tried to raise its anchor, too. Impossible. So, I climbed back off the dipping and diving boat and ran to the engine room for a tow line. Meanwhile, Cynthia and the boys were using all the strength they had to run in tandem along the sides of *Sweet Life* with the heavy fenders. The adrenalin kicked in and the boys became determined gladiators, trying to repel the attacking rogue boat, as it bounced and swung violently in the waves.

"I climbed into our dinghy, motored over to the rampaging offender and secured my tow line to her. With no other course possible except letting our boat be destroyed, I released the runabout's anchor chain. It immediately descended to the bottom and the abusing runabout was loose. With the boys' help, we towed her back to her fleet, tying her behind a sister boat.

"Moving someone else's boat in the middle of the night is a risky thing to do. But if I had just let her go, she would have travelled hell-bent into the rocks. I could never let that happen. So, we towed her to safety," Winston said with a shrug of his shoulders. "We all felt good about saving her."

At first light, I slipped into the water with snorkel gear in order to find the anchor. At the same time, a large, ranting West Indian rowed his kayak out to our boat. Bellowing almost incoherently all the way out to our yacht, the man insisted we were trying to steal his boat and were responsible for its four hundred-dollar anchor. With his continual threats, we couldn't get in even one word of explanation. He screamed that he was calling the police and rowed away.

We were floored. Instead of rowing over to thank us for saving his boat, he came over raging about losing his anchor. We went on the defensive instantly. Winston wanted to follow the man back to land, but I nixed that. Who knew what he might do? We decided to get the guests started on breakfast and then go ashore—with four hundred dollars in our pocket just in case.

As we were explaining to the parents why they'd be on their own for breakfast and encouraged them to be entertained by their boys' storytelling, we eyed a BVI policeman on the beach. Good or bad news, we didn't know.

"We rode our dinghy to the dock and approached the man with 'POLICE' blazoned on the back of his navy windbreaker. Our enemy started yelling as soon as he saw us, and even the policeman couldn't get a word in edgewise. We asked to go to the police station to make our statement, so we could be away from the maniac. In the quiet of the station, he took our story, line by line.

"The outcome," adds Winston, "was bullshit. The maniac was a bigshot in Cane Garden Bay, and the policeman's hands were tied. He advised us to pay the four hundred dollars (twice what the anchor was worth) just to get the bully off our backs. If he wanted to, this guy had the pull to get us and our boss's yacht thrown out of the country for good. We greased the crook's palm, and, what a surprise, he settled right down. Asshole."

We rarely went to Cane Garden after that. As far as we know, that irrational being is still there, harassing the tourists and annihilating the bay's beautiful aura.

Covering a lot of water

After each winter season in the Virgins, we'd drive the yacht north through the Caribbean and Atlantic, then up the Atlantic Intracoastal Waterway from south Florida to Norfolk, Virginia, and New England.

More about the Intracoastal: Extending both north and south from Virginia to Florida and east and west from Florida to Texas, it's three thousand miles of natural and manmade canals dug out of rock inside the eastern coastline of the United States and the Gulf of Mexico, built originally so ships could maneuver, if war occurs. It provides safe passage to move a boat to the northeast without having to take it outside in the big bad ocean. The downside is that it's very slow. Yachts can travel only six knots (about 6.9 miles per hour) through much of the passage. And there are a hundred-plus bridges over the Intracoastal, some so low they must open to allow boats to pass under them. Some bridges open on demand; many adhere to strict schedules. Timing on the Intracoastal is everything. It's not pleasant trying to lie dormant at a bridge for hours, waiting for it to open.

The first leg of the trip through the Caribbean from the Virgins to Florida is twelve hundred miles. We hired extra crew and had shifts of three hours on, six hours off most of the trip. We always had two crew at the helm for safety and drove day and night. One trip found us directly under a fierce, lightning storm for almost twenty-four hours. It was traveling at exactly our speed and headed in the same direction, and, of course, the worst of it was in the middle of the night, in the pitch black. If lightning had struck the yacht, all systems could be dead, including our two electronic diesel engines. How we avoided being struck by this electronic light show was a miracle. Our nerves were shattered by the time we reached the dock in the Bahamas. Another time, because customs officials couldn't find the time to come to our dock for two days, we sat tied to the pilings, unable to legally go anywhere on land, watching perfect, weather windows pass by. My dear, happy Captain Winston got grumpier by the hour. But everything worked out, as it usually does. It just takes time. Sometimes, lots of time. Patience is critical for yacht crew.

This was when we'd remind each other, "This is the dream we wanted. Now deal."

Intracoastal blues

Our boss dreamed of cruising the Intracoastal with us on *Sweet Life*. The Intracoastal extends one thousand five hundred fifty miles along the Atlantic coast from Norfolk, Virginia to Florida Bay. Larry looked forward to stopping at delightful historic towns along the way: Daytona, St. Augustine, Savannah, Charleston, Georgetown, Cape Fear, Cape Lookout, and Norfolk, Virginia, and then through the Chesapeake to New York and Newport, Rhode Island. Regrettably, his dream got cut short—twice.

Owner Jerry was skippering *Sweet Life* up the Intracoastal, on the second day of our voyage, his chest expanded and face grinning ear to ear. Winston had schooled him in navigation rules. "'No Wake Zone' signs mean no wake at all—in other words, coast at idle speed," he warned. "Continually glance behind *Sweet Life* to make sure you aren't making a wake, and that you're in the middle of the channel."

Jerry and Donna were up on the fly bridge steering the yacht. I was in the galley preparing lunch, and Jerry had sent Winston down to grab a sandwich. Seeing a tall bridge up ahead, Jerry and Donna started studying the chart. They forgot the rule about the wake.

Winston relates the episode frowning, "I glanced out a porthole just in time to see a twenty-five-foot runabout almost flip over, two fishermen yelling profanities and steadying themselves while beers and coolers floated everywhere. Jerry's speed had thrown a wake that rocked those fishermen like a tidal wave. I ran to the bridge and yelled 'Jerry, slow down!' but of course it was too late. Being a good man and a physician to boot, Jerry was mortified. He turned *Sweet Life* around straight away. Our offers to help the still-ranting fishermen fell on deaf ears, and poor Donna could take only so much cursing. After assuring, from afar, that there were no injuries or damage, we calmed our nerves and continued up the Intracoastal. But not far.

'I spotted a county sheriff vessel headed toward us, noting the names on the sterns of every vessel it passed. I knew right then they were looking for us. (Apparently the angry fishermen had done more than just curse.) Sure enough, three officers asked to come aboard. We explained that we had unwittingly rocked that boat but had gone back to check on the fishermen and were sure they were OK. Then things got weird.

"The officer in charge said not to be alarmed, but that he had to read Jerry his rights. That got everyone's hearts pumping, especially Jerry's. This was serious. The officers separated us and proceeded to interview each of us about the incident. 'Tell us what happened in your own words,' and we all told the same story because it was true. Then there were a few more questions like 'What color was the boat?' and 'What side of your yacht was it on?' But then we heard the question that sent us into tailspins:

"'What about the other boat?'

"It was obvious to the officers that we were each completely taken aback by that question. None of us had any knowledge of another boat being waked. But, in fact, before I had looked out that porthole and seen the fishermen, Jerry had driven by a dock where a woman was launching a small boat. *Sweet Life*'s wake had rocked her right out of the boat onto the dock, her story went. And she was very injured, her story continued. Her husband was the one who called the authorities in the first place—not the fishermen. The authorities didn't even know about them.

"The officers believed our stories, luckily. But they warned, in that neck of the woods, some homeowners along the Intracoastal lie in wait for nice, big, extravagant yachts to make a mistake. Then they're on the way to the bank.

"We had to backtrack all the way back to the scene of the crime, where we waited, and waited, and waited, and waited for a new set of authorities—criminal investigators this time. There was no dock to use, so for about three hours, I had to keep maneuvering the yacht to the side of traffic while not allowing it to go aground. Talk about tense.

"After more interrogation and lots of form-signing, we were released. We never did get to meet the accuser, but Jerry had long months of dealing with her lawyer to settle the matter. We'll never know if she was injured, or not, but when cops warn you that you'll never win a court battle with Intracoastal landowners in that county, you believe them.

"And this was only the second day of Jerry's thirty-day dream.

"Then, just when the yacht's cheerful atmosphere was almost revived, shit struck again.

"Jerry still wanted to drive, and I reminded him again about the rules: 'Stay inside the channel markers, not outside. Go slow and watch that wake. Make sure you stay in the center between the red and green markers, or you'll get off course and maybe hit a shallow spot. When that happens . . . well, you don't want to know.' Jerry swore he'd be vigilant but impishly grinned, 'I think you should know that Sea Tow knows me on a first name basis.' How could you not love this guy?

"The Intracoastal is unforgiving at its narrowest sections. Jerry, in his enthusiasm, had inadvertently forgotten to look back (again) and wandered off center. Hearing the loud screeching, scraping sound of two forty-eight-inch props dragging across rock got everyone's attention, especially Jerry's. We limped to port in St. Augustine, the mood completely deflated.

"The bad news was we had a badly bent prop and the swim step's hydraulic stairway was damaged as well. We'd be beached in the boatyard for probably two weeks. (Thank God I wasn't driving.) Jerry, God bless him, in all his good humor, smiled with chagrin and bought us all a drink. More than a little shaken from these first days of his adventure, he said he'd return when the props were repaired. Off he flew to his home in New York."

Well, long story short, Jerry didn't make it back, until we were in the Chesapeake Bay. Duty called, and he got busy. Winston and I drove the Intracoastal alone. We had the yacht to ourselves.

History lessons up the coast

Charleston

Approaching Charleston, at Mile Marker 469, from the south, we ventured into a narrow passage called Elliot Cut. As luck would have it, we met two huge commercial tugboats coming our way, face to face so to speak, blowing their warning horns. We had no choice but to spin the yacht around (a very tight squeeze I might add) against the current and drive back out the cut, until the tug boats passed. A bit of a pucker factor . . .

If we had the time, we'd absorb some history in every town, usually from a tour guide in period clothing running a horse and carriage. Sometimes it varied with a ghost tour or haunted house lecture. Charleston probably had the best stories—or at least the most adept story-tellers. We had a ball there.

Myrtle Beach

The scenery on the way to Myrtle Beach was picturesque, reminding us of the Old South, with Spanish moss draping off the live oaks and lots of snakes and other swamp creatures swimming their day away.

Then we approached a seven-mile section of the Intracoastal known as the "Rock Pile," the last part of the Intracoastal to be dredged. A ledge of sharp, jagged shale threatened from either side. The "Rock Pile" was hairy, especially for a yacht our size, and we had to stay exactly in the center to avoid scraping those ledges. On approach, we radioed ahead to see if there was any southbound traffic in that seven-mile stretch. We certainly didn't want to have to pass anyone . . . or back all the way out either!

About midday we pulled into a quaint, little dock for fuel, Wacca Wache, in south Myrtle Beach. We were advised to stay the night, because we wouldn't make it to the next bridge opening in time. We wondered how to fill the day. Remarkably, it was Bike Week—a motorcycle rally taking place right down the road. We enjoyed a surprise rendezvous with thousands of bikers. Since Winston had lived in the area a lifetime ago, in the Air Force, he was right at home.

The Beauforts

Then there are Beaufort and Beaufort, two cities with the same name but different pronunciations—and personalities. Beaufort, South Carolina (say "Bew-fert"), and Beaufort, North Carolina (now say "Bo-fert"). In both cities, you can feel the reality of traditional southern hospitality: Krispy Kreme donuts on the dock first thing in the morning, daily newspapers delivered with coffee and a smile. No matter what we asked, or what we needed, everyone was at our beck and call. We'd check in with Jerry daily, and knew he missed this part most of all.

Coinjock

One of the must-stops on the Intracoastal is the little-known village of Coinjock, North Carolina, about twenty miles south of the Virginia state line, with a population of under five hundred. Coinjock is known throughout the mariner community for its dockside restaurant: Eat an entire thirty-two-ounce prime rib and you get it free. Many have tried, and most have failed miserably, but crews and owners treasure the stop as a highlight of the long trip. Arriving there for the night in time for the feast is a real challenge. The relatively short fifty-mile trip from Beaufort, NC, to Coinjock takes a full day and maneuvering between the high and low tides, and bridge closings and openings, requires perseverance but yummy rewards.

Norfolk

The mouth of the Chesapeake between Portsmouth and Norfolk, Virginia, marks the official Mile Marker 0 of the Intracoastal, though it continues unofficially through the Chesapeake and the Delaware Canal to New York City and beyond. Norfolk's huge, Navy base intrigues every mariner who dares to enter the busy shipping channels. We were dwarfed, and on guard constantly. The huge harbor was full of escorted ships and virtual trains of cargo barges, moving in all directions. We certainly were sharpening our driving skills, readying ourselves for New York City.

The Chesapeake

Our boss couldn't wait to have us travel the full-length of Chesapeake Bay, with its quaint coastline towns and scenic vistas, and he joined us for the trip. Unfortunately, our Chesapeake baptism was comprised of cold, blowing winds and pouring rain. Winston buried beneath winter jackets and foul-weather gear, in June, kept nudging Jerry, "So this is the wonderful northeast you've been so eager to show us, huh?" The wide open space going up the Chesapeake was like being in the middle of the ocean compared to what we'd just driven through. The contrast between cities like bustling Baltimore and tiny St. Michael's drove home the uniqueness of the beautiful Chesapeake, rainy or not.

New Jersey to Nantucket

When we made it to New York City, Jerry based us for a month in Weehawken, New Jersey, just down the street from Frank Sinatra's Hoboken and directly across from New York City's 34th Street Ferry and Broadway. He chose that marina specifically, so we'd have a spectacular view of New York's skyline across the Hudson River. Plus, he lived in Manhattan and it was an easy hop, skip, and jump to the yacht for him and Donna.

We couldn't wait to savor our first cup of coffee sitting on the aft deck, monitoring the Hudson River traffic and gazing at the Big Apple. Then we physically tried to do it. Due to horrific metal joints that connected a snake of metal docks like a monstrous undulating train moaning and groaning in constant protest of the waves crashing against them, we could barely hear ourselves think, much less speak. Day in, day out, morning, noon, night, it didn't matter. Due to 9/11 (two years earlier), the PATH tunnel under the river was closed, so ferries ran nonstop. Our awesome New York City skyline views were, forevermore, enjoyed from inside *Sweet Life's* glass doors.

Navigating the waterways around Manhattan and Long Island is no easy task, and Winston mastered it like a champ. Hell's Gate (aptly named) comprises two opposing currents rushing between narrow, curved embankments. We motored around the Statue of Liberty and Ellis Island like experts, though Winston's sphincter muscles really got a workout. Still chartering, we entertained charterers for river runs up the Hudson, enhanced with limo-laced tours of mansions, West Point, and across the Sound to the inner sanctum of posh Sag Harbor.

Working on a yacht, as luxurious as it seems, can take a toll on your private life. You live in your "office" and are on call 24/7. You may not be working with guests on board, but your responsibilities never end. Getting off the yacht for some play time is wonderful medicine for the mind.

We relished living near New York and took full advantage every chance we had: Broadway plays, city tours, Central Park art exhibits, a Yankee game by ferry, Ellis Island where my grandparents from Slovenia are commemorated, the glorious Statue of Liberty and the sobering raw sight of the Twin Towers' Ground Zero. We watched our cash carefully and ate at almost every locals-recommended hole in the wall joint we could find. We scoped our way around the city like natives. The main limitation, with our New Jersey location, there was no ferry to the marine store. It was a hundred-dollar cab ride.

Our boss was busy with work that first season, which afforded us lots of time to take quick road trips through Vermont, New Hampshire, and northern New York State. Again, time away from the yacht multiplied our enthusiasm for time on the yacht a hundred-fold. We rented a car and took in the Amish settlements in Pennsylvania, and toured the Harley-Davidson assembly plant in York, Pennsylvania. (I wanted to tour the York Peppermint Patty factory, too, but it had moved out of York. How could they?)

We also got in some family time. You know, we're living a dream lifestyle, one we strived for and cherish, but we do get lonely and miss family and friends. Family visits inject me with new life. My future son-in-law asked permission to marry my daughter, Andrea, on *Sweet Life*. How cool is that? My older brother, Jim, and his wife stopped by while seeing his children in New York and I met Andrea's future in-laws there, too.

Good-hearted Jerry and Donna offered me lenient time off to spend time with my ninety-year-old parents in Tyler, Texas. That's the beauty of working for a wonderful owner and having a wonderful husband who would take care of the yacht without me. My mother had suffered with Alzheimer's for almost ten years and visiting her was healing for both of us. I read aloud her diaries from age sixteen to twenty-five and watched her relive those memories as if they had just happened yesterday. I learned a lot about my Mother during that time and will forever be grateful for those intimate moments. Mother died that season, and every grandchild from around the country travelled to Texas to celebrate her life. Winston and I attended. Being on *Sweet Life* during this time was phenomenal. We couldn't have been working for better people.

That brings to mind the warning we'd received when we first considered moving from sailboats to motor yachts, that about 95 percent of owners were assholes. Jerry and Donna were definitely in that rare 5 percent.

New England, new rules

Travel-hog Winston loved that New York wasn't our only base on the east coast. Like many yachts escaping the hurricane season in the Caribbean, each summer we chartered between Newport and Block Island in Rhode Island, and Martha's Vineyard and Nantucket in Massachusetts.

"As we sat in the marina in yachty Newport, RI, the 'cog' in the nautical wheel of New England marinas, we watched yachts come and go from the Carib. More than once, we shared a hearty beer and pizza with crews we'd not seen for months, or even years.

"Each New England area was pretty impressive, with its own set of docks, fancy provisioning, and fog-ridden schedules. And, man, were there new rules! Dock reservations had to be made months in advance, at a very hefty price. Fog didn't count as an excuse for cancelation either. Pay up, buddy, full price, even if you can't make it. One dock master even required bribes. I started thinking there were no more pirates left in the Caribbean because they were all here in New England! This definitely wasn't the friendly "we'll find you a place" atmosphere we'd enjoyed down south."

Hooked but not caught

Reminiscing about New England, Winston recalls one of his most heartwarming stories about Nantucket. It centers on a poor, little seagull. "This seagull sat perched near water's edge with a four-inch, three-pronged, very colorful fishing lure hooked on his beak," he sets the stage. "My heart went out to this poor guy and I was determined to help. The seagull hadn't quite got the message though. Every time I got close, the gull would fly back up to a rooftop, fishing lure swinging in the breeze. While he was up there, we watched him trying to bat the lure away with his foot. This went on forever. Eventually, he had his foot caught in the lure, along with his beak. Now he was really in trouble. He was able to fly back to the water, but just barely. And there, on a pile of ragged rocks just barely above the surface, he sat.

"So, just as a sightseeing ferry loaded with tourists pulled into the harbor, I squatted down, stretched out and started belly-crawling across the barnacled rocks and low tide water. Now intrigued, my ferry audience went silent. Leatherman tool in hand, I was determined to catch the bird, clip the hook of the albatross and free this poor little guy. Talking softly in what Cynthia calls my 'birdy language,' I shimmied toward the gull, alternating between elbows, beer belly, and knees, trying to convince him I meant no harm. Finally, on my third attempt, he stopped hopping away. The seagull, balancing on one foot, with the other attached irreversibly to the lure in his beak, eyed me suspiciously. But, at the same time, he seemed to have a bit of hope in his eyes. I noticed a short fishing line dangling from the lure and grabbed for it. Then I knew I had him. Slowly pulling in the line while balancing on my belly, I reached out with both hands, cupped him and gently tucked him under my arm. Sigh of relief. Then I sat up. (God was my body sore!) I untangled the fishing line, clipped the barb off the hook and pulled it through his beak and foot. Off the seagull flew, free at last, to the boisterous applause of the ferry riders."

(I'd like to add that Winston's entire chest of beautiful curly hair was puffed up like a penguin, the entire rest of the day. And he still has that lure. It's a trophy.)

Fog firsthand

One of the bigger challenges of yachting in New England poses the most earnest threat—fog. It never shows up in brochures, but it often showed up in our dream job unannounced. You must be prepared to take the good with the bad, even in dream jobs.

We've been caught in fog more than we care to think about, but two events are forever seared into our memories. One involved inching blindly along in a total whiteout, blowing our fog horn while checking the radar screen every few seconds. Next thing we knew, a huge, black cable appeared fifty feet from our bow. After two heart attacks and an almost involuntary, 90 degree turn, I found the words to scream, "Barge and tow ahead!" Why we hadn't noticed the barge on radar, we'll never know. But, had we not seen that ominous cable crossing in front of us, it could have sliced *Sweet Life* in two and barely noticed a bump. Our guardian angels deserved double pay that day.

Another time, a whiteout during a sudden powerful storm had us holding on for dear life and our bosses braced on the floor, trying to be brave. They even donned life jackets in fear. Cabinet doors were swinging open, and only outstretched feet kept liquor bottles from spilling onto the floor. Winston felt his way through the fog without incident, but laptops were no longer in laps, and dishes no longer in dish trays. Our hearts, on the other hand, were finally back in our chests.

A sweet routine with benefits between

In May, we'd driven *Sweet Life* all the way from the Caribbean to New England, and in the fall, when it was time to return to the tropics, the owner shipped her rather than risk rough seas and all they threaten. As a bonus, we got time off while the ship was underway.

That's the way our seasons unraveled on *Sweet Life:* Virgins in the winters, New York and New England in the summers, working our schedules around time off when we needed it. When my son's daughter was born back in San Francisco, my first grandchild, Isabella, we were on charter in the British Virgin Islands. But I got to listen to her birth live, via a cell phone speaker in the delivery room, and meet her a month later. Our life was good.

A nostalgic final voyage

Then Jerry gave us advanced notice that, after the next winter season in the Caribbean, he was moving the yacht to New Orleans. No more chartering. No more Caribbean. He'd made a career change and was going back to his old stomping grounds. He would keep *Sweet Life* on Lake Pontchartrain.

By then, we weren't surprised by any owner decisions. But this time, we were heartbroken. We loved these owners and always looked forward to Jerry coming aboard dressed in a big smile, shorts and T-shirt, crooning, "I'm home, I'm home, I'm home at last!" To his credit, he was kind enough to give us six, full months' notice.

Many of our charter guests rebooked trips with us, and things were going great. We were making money and saving some too. We used some of our gratuities to buy a polo green Corvette (just what we needed, right?) and stored it at Jerry's new home in New Orleans. It was Winston's dream car and I spoiled him rotten (which he deserved more on some days than others, if you get my drift)—besides, he needed that carrot to keep him laughing.

From fun-loving guest to possible boss

We directed six more charters that last season on *Sweet Life*. And one was quite important. A family of five from Scandinavia chartered the yacht for a week, three young kids and the nicest parents you'd ever want to meet. We had such a neat time with this group we even rendezvoused with them after their charter when they were hanging out at Bitter End Resort. That's when they posed the question, "If we bought a yacht, would you two be willing to be our crew?"

Winston and I were stoked by their offer because 1) we knew our time on *Sweet Life* was ending, 2) we truly liked this family, and 3) they offered to pay us a *retainer,* until they found the right yacht. That was the kicker. We could finish our work for Jerry on *Sweet Life* and be collecting a partial salary from our new bosses, until they bought a yacht. Ah, our sweet life, now with extra sugar, sprinkled on top.

We finished our Caribbean charters on *Sweet Life* and delivered her back to Jerry, at his new home in New Orleans, on Lake Pontchartrain. The trip took us from St. Thomas, through the chain of islands— the Dominican Republic, Turks and Caicos, the Bahamas—then up Florida's west coast, and across the Gulf of Mexico, hugging the coastline where we could. The trip was similar to the one we had taken on our first motor yacht, *Catalina*, returning her to her home in Houston. Ironically, both trips ended jobs.

This yachting industry kept taking the wind out of our sails.

When Winston would begin to shut down, I'd always reminded him we had to lower our expectations. Rolling with the punches was the name of the game. Each setback—firing from the *Windwards*, sudden unemployment from *Catalina*, boat sale from *The Ark*, and now our favorite bosses cutting us loose—somehow kept bringing us closer together, and more resolved to make this damn career last.

I do, I do

Still on retainer, we really made the best of our paid time off while our new, almost-boss searched for a yacht. We splurged and bought

Winston and Cynthia wed on Windansea Beach in La Jolla, CA.

another Harley, this time a long distance cruising model with saddle bags (since my butt was becoming sore on our aqua "Softail"). So now we had two Harleys and a Corvette—completely crazy since our career was waterlogged. But they were fun, and we played hard on them, hooking up with family around every curve. Then we did even more.

After being together for fourteen years, we decided to tie the knot, and not once but twice. Our first wedding was on May 1 ("Mayday, mayday" seemed appropriate) in Tyler, Texas, at my dad's bedside the day before he died. My brothers and sisters were there. Poignant and momentous.

For our second wedding, the one I'd always envisioned, we gathered our children, their families, and a few important friends on the sand of Windansea Beach, in La Jolla, CA. It was the very spot where we'd met and lived, and from where we launched our phenomenal second career. Our make-shift invitation (bought at a local marine bookstore) pictured a long, wooden dock stretched out over the Caribbean Sea. We were barefoot and casual. A deep green, Hawaiian *maile lei* draping Winston's shoulders and a fragrant crown-like garland called a haku lei replaced a veil for me, both freshly-flown-in gifts from Winston's long time friend, Janet. She brought them from Hawaii for the ceremony. (Janet had gone on our first date, to make sure she approved of me. Luckily, she did, and now we'd come full circle.) The "La Jolla Air Force"—fifteen pelicans flying in perfect formation—punctuated the wind-blown ceremony just as the rising surf lapped at our feet.

Still having time off and still on retainer (maybe we'd be lucky, and they'd take a year to find their yacht), we chose not one but two honeymoons to match our double weddings.

Winston loves reliving this time in our lives. "For our first honeymoon, we drove our new (wedding present!) 2003 black and silver Harley-Davidson Heritage twenty-four hundred and fifty-one miles on the historic Mother Road, Route 66, from beginning to end, Chicago to LA. We paid $66 for the pleasure of joining one hundred other bikers on this journey. Two saddle bags and one backpack stored everything we needed. I road our bike from storage in San Diego back to Chicago with our friend, Tim, while Cynthia squeezed in sister time in St. Louis. We rendezvoused in Chicago at her brother's home. Then on a sunny, Saturday morning we sat at the official beginning of Route 66, engines roaring and Cynthia's black leather fringe ready to fly. Seven days later, we arrived at Santa Monica Pier in Los Angeles. There is much nostalgia in the small towns dotting the old highway and so much history too. We'd covered Chicago, St Louis and Joplin, Missouri, Oklahoma City, Amarillo, Gallup, New Mexico, Winona, Kingman, Barstow and San Bernardino, right on in to Santa Monica. Just like the Eagles' song says, we got our kicks on Route 66.

"Then, as if that were not enough honeymoon, we rafted down the Colorado River, through the Grand Canyon. We travelled on a motorized, inflatable raft with two guides and fourteen other people, including Cynthia's sister, Suzanne, her husband, Paul, and, yes, again, our friend, Tim. (He went on both of our honeymoons!) We camped every night, slept under the stars, hiked the canyon at least once a day, roared over ten major rapids including notorious Lava Falls, and floated quietly, sans motor, the rest of the two hundred sixty-mile trip. No one in our boat fell out, a testament to our death grips on the hand-holds. And no one got hurt either, though that release they make you sign says you could die at every turn. Hearing the history of adventurers, who first challenged the river, made our rubber rafts seem like limousines. Seeing the canyon from the bottom up was life-changing. We constantly shook our heads at our insignificance. Oh, and I impressed our river guides so much that they asked me to be a 'guest guide' for the week. I declined. The last thing I wanted was to be responsible for people on a charter!"

And so went our summer, sweet good-byes to *Sweet Life*, sweet hellos to marriage, and sweet anticipation of our new boss.

Chapter 15
A Yachta Misadventures

Your only obligation in any lifetime is to be true to yourself.
—Richard Bach

Whether chipping away at an icy deck or high in the sky repairing a satellite dish,
Winston and Cynthia shared crew responsibilities.

**Dania Beach, Florida, to Newport, Rhode Island, to
Key West to Clearwater, Florida, to Daytona Beach to
Nassau to Atlantic City to Palm Beach to BVI to St. Maarten
to St. Bart's to Staniel Cay to Palm Beach to San Diego
to Newport Beach and Santa Catalina Island. Whew!**

June 2004—November 2007

Dreams turn to nightmares . . .

The years with the fantastic owners of *Sweet Life* were sugar sweet. We knew that fact constantly when, over the next several years, we weathered a series of exceptional adventures, with mostly miserable bosses.

Living in close quarters is often tricky. When you're stressed out because of a lousy boss, you teeter on the brink of leaving the industry almost daily. Leaving your spouse creeps into your mind occasionally, too, in the heat of those "We should stay/We should quit" arguments. Our goal, an adventurous life with a job we loved, hit a brick wall with some of our next bosses. The adventurous life was there, for sure, but loving a job with a less-than-great boss was a compromise that left us dissatisfied.

We were still free of "stuff," and never tired of that. It remained exhilarating. We regularly found even more stuff to shed as we packed and unpacked from various boats . . . t-shirts we tired of, favorite but worn-out flip flops, an old hair brush, usually several ball caps. (How they accumulate I'll never understand!) But packing and unpacking got old as we landed one short-term job after another. We had crew friends who stayed forever with one owner. Why hadn't we found a job like that? Were we spoiled to expect even more out of life?

One thing for sure, the next few years gave us experience on many kinds of yachts with many kinds of engines, generator, AC systems, etc. And we were based in lots of new locations. So, our résumé was fattening up at least. We had only to keep an eye out for those elusive opportunities.

We knew the standard rule about first time yacht owners ("Stay away from them if at all possible."), but we hadn't been exposed to another rule: "Wonderful charter guests don't necessarily make wonderful owners."

Those Scandinavians, who had paid us a retainer, purchased an eighty-foot, Italian-built baby named *Dreamweaver*. Into it, they crammed a fifteen-foot circular floating trampoline, two jet skis, seven sets of scuba gear including tanks and regulators, a two-person kayak, a snuba machine for scuba diving *without* tanks that sounded like a jackhammer gone wild, plus a fifteen-foot sailboat complete with mast and sails.

We took our boss and his family to the Bahamas for a ten-day maiden voyage. Picture us anchored in a serene aqua bay, owner's laundry flapping on the railings tackily, trampoline, sailboat, jet skis and the noisy snuba monster floating off our stern. At one point we had fifteen different toys in the water—not being used. It was a tedious and tiresome cruise. But, alas, the trip was cut short by Category 4 Hurricane Francis, spinning right at us. This marvelous-guest-turned-difficult-owner refused to acknowledge any danger. "We're used to storms where we live and ride bikes in forty-knot winds. This is nothing."

Hurricane Francis was not nothing. His thinking was completely irrational, like thinking you can breathe in a wind tunnel because you are wearing a mask and snorkel.

Winston's eyes glaze over when he talks of this incident. "After a few days of worsening weather, I became a volcano about to erupt. My blood was smoldering. Cynthia braced for impact; she was my only outlet, and I needed venting. She managed to slow the lava, but she got burned in the process, too. We would mutter teeth-clenching curses, every time we passed each other, on the way to smiling at the guests. (Talk about taking a toll on a relationship!)

"This stalemate lasted several days, the kids unaware, the toys floating, me seething. The longer we delayed, the sharper the words between Cynthia and me. Finally, as the storm was about to bear down on the Bahamas, I erupted. Marching out to the owner, I gave my ultimatum, 'It's noon. I hate to have to tell you this, but the last plane leaves this island today at 4:00 p.m. The airport is closing due to the hurricane. Unless we start packing up every last toy this instant and head for Florida, Cynthia and I will be on that plane.

"Silence.

"Four hours later, we'd packed the yacht and were headed to Lauderdale.

"We located an empty dock and even before we were secure, the owner and his family high-tailed it out of Florida on the last plane to Europe. We harnessed *Dreamweaver* using every trick we knew, double-boarding fenders so they could ride up and down the pilings, securing chains around the dock cleats and attaching our dock lines to them so the lines wouldn't chafe on the pilings, securing bow and stern anchors, and lashing and storing everything inside and out. After thirty-six hours of violent wind and rain, Francis passed right over us. Remarkably, the yacht endured. Beaten to a pulp by the sheer anxiety of the past week, Cynthia and I slept for twenty-four hours straight."

After that experience, the owner got cold feet. "I make a better charter guest, than I do an owner." We agreed.

Work can be play. We'd proven it. Life without stuff is terrific. We'd proven it. Making a living in exotic places we love is possible. We'd proven it. Perma-vacationing with full-time salaries can be a reality. We'd done it. Yachting is a challenging career that requires hard work and perseverance. And opportunities appear every day. They certainly do. All we have to do is recognize them, and act.

Madame BJ meets Katrina

With the luck of the Irish and the help of our almighty yacht brokers, we moved from our not-so-perfect *Dreamweaver* to a stunning, eighty-foot, private yacht named *Madame BJ*. Its University of Tennessee alumni owners wanted the yacht for private use only—no charters. They dreamed of driving her up the middle of the country via the Alabama River and the Tombigbee Waterway to Tennessee, to one of the largest on-the-water tailgate parties in the United States.

Unfortunately, *Madame BJ* was a lemon—a really sour lemon. It had broken steering, wrong props, inadequate stabilizers and shore power complications. Plus, there was a hole in the hull from electrolysis.

Even after myriad repairs, the owners were dogged to take their dream voyage. We drove *Madame BJ* down the Intracoastal and up Florida's west coast to Clearwater, where, alas, a critical steering mechanism failed. Six days and five technicians later, we were headed for the mouth of the Alabama, when we faced the colossal and final bump in the road—Hurricane Katrina.

Katrina's wrath annihilated any cruising plans in the area. Our poor, disenchanted owners, deflated beyond belief, finally surrendered. They had us deliver the yacht back to Fort Lauderdale and, you guessed it, sell her. We were notified yet again of losing our job, this time due to broken parts and broken dreams.

Our boss asked us to remain as crew on *Madame BJ*, so we could look after his asset while we researched other job opportunities. Good thing, too, because guess what blew in? (It was a bad year.) Wilma. This hurricane blew a bathtub through a hotel wall and sent furniture flying from the fifteenth floor right over our marina. Cleats on our dock were ripped from the concrete, and several mega yachts went floating down the Intracoastal, unmanned but still secured to six pilings dragging along beside them.

When the weather finally settled down, we renewed our relationships with yacht brokers, crew placement agencies, and our network of crew friends. The first interview we landed was with a seventy-five-year-old nudist couple. We kept looking.

Personal biz squeezed in

Being unemployed had its benefits: personal time. My relatives rendezvoused again at the Buffalo River in Arkansas, where we'd spent seventeen, consecutive, family reunions. There we spread my parents' ashes, letting Mother and Dad float down the river like they'd done on canoes for seventeen summers. It was heartwarming to see my kids, brothers and sisters, and all our nieces and nephews in the place that meant so much to my parents.

Nine to five, for a change

Homeless mariners, we hung out in Prescott, AZ, and took a few road trips on the Harley, but paychecks were beckoning, and we had to succumb. With no luck finding a yacht via long distance, we cut short our "sabbatical" and traveled back to Fort Lauderdale to hustle in person.

That's what it took. We got a job offer.

Just an aside . . . Call it karma, serendipity, or just God winking at you. We got a wink, in Daytona, FL. Early one morning on the way to an interview, we had a very flat tire. When we asked for help from perfect strangers parked next to us, they turned out to be lifelong friends of Winston's mother and dad, Queenie and Holly, some sixteen hundred miles away in New Brunswick, Canada. Unbelievable. They remembered Winston as a little boy and also as young punk. He remembered them, too. Also, unbelievably, they had a tire pump, so after some warm stories and a heartfelt good-bye, we were on our way to the interview. Once again, we enjoyed the power of fate. And we got the job, too.

Our life aboard the private yacht, *You,* differed from any job we'd had so far. The boss furnished us a condo, and a nine-to-five workday—a new concept for us, living away from work, and going *home* every night. He only required a bottle of wine every night and two meals a week (chicken parmesan and lobster were his routine choices). We actually went to work nine to five. We were headquartered in Daytona, but spent time at the elegant Atlantis Resort in Nassau, too.

Our extracurricular activities educated us. We attended the Daytona 500 Race and learned about it personally from several drivers whose yachts were docked near ours. We explored NASA, touring the museums and speaking with astronauts. The major highlight, after two aborted attempts by NASA because of weather, we witnessed the launch of the NASA Space Shuttle. The sight of that rocket spiraling into space was one of the most awe-inspiring moments in all our travels.

Another of our goals checked off, Winston finalized his U.S. citizenship application and took his oath while we were working on *You*. A Canadian citizen and a Green Card holder for more than thirty years, he needed U.S. citizenship in order to expand his coast guard license to run larger vessels. (Always preparing for our next opportunity.)

Then one day, a broker called, asking us to interview with his client. We drove a few hours down the coast and met a couple who seemed high maintenance, with lots of red flags. But before we could call the broker and turn down the offer, the choice was made for us. Our boss got wind of our "disloyalty," as he called it, and promptly sent his minions to fire us. That day. Then and there. Get your stuff and leave! Needless to say, we accepted the other offer.

Winston concludes without a smile, "The red flags fluttered like the ominous dark clouds before a storm."

Another horizon blurs

Elaine Lorinda was our third Horizon yacht, this time with an eighty-two-foot LOA (length overall), sleeping six guests. She was a beauty, full of tawny-colored, glossy wood accented with a shiny, black marble wet bar and galley. The main salon featured a raised circular ceiling, inset and glowing with the night sky's stars and planets. The dining area was an oval space with curved bench seating for four, plus two padded stools for extra guests—nicely compact, but tough on formal dinner parties. A bright yellow and white striped settee (couch) on the aft deck was continually highlighted with three square vases of fresh, yellow flowers. The yacht even had a built-in, drop-down treadmill, used daily. The mechanical systems and electronics were very familiar, and we adapted to them easily. But that was about all that was adaptable.

Two couples owned the yacht, one as high-strung, loud and ostentatious as the other was tranquil. One was over-the-top demanding (I had to change the crystal bread bowl for a more expensive one in the middle of a dinner party), the other gently asking, "Don't we have some old, cheap dishes we can use?"

Unhappily for us, the demanding couple used the yacht most of the time. For our first, formal dinner party on the yacht, the screamers (as I nicknamed them) demanded the thickest veal and the highest-rated wine. I'd never even bought veal before, much less cooked it. We hightailed it to Fort Lauderdale, the mecca of yacht provisioning, and found the perfect resource. We purchased enough sixty-dollar veal slabs for dinner and an extra for practice. The man behind the counter described precisely how to grill them, and we left well-prepared. The meal was a tremendous success with praise all around. The screamers would have died if they knew we bought that veal at a Crown Liquor Store in Fort Lauderdale. They considered Fort Lauderdale "Hicksville!"

The low-key, nonchalant partners who owned the other half of the yacht thought our traditional turkey and dressing dinner was "the best dinner we've ever had on any yacht anywhere in the world." Go figure. Too bad we rarely, if ever, saw the gentle owners and had to do double time with the difficult ones.

Luckily for us, the owners liked moving the yacht. We skippered *Elaine Lorinda* to the Bahamas and throughout the Caribbean. Because the demanding couple wanted over-the-top service, we had the luxury of hiring our friend, Harley riding sailor Ron from St. Louis, as a mate, to help both on deck and inside the yacht. We enjoyed glorious backdrops in St. Thomas, the British Virgin Islands, St. Maarten, Anguilla and St. Bart's. That's where the glorious part stopped.

No matter what the beauty—rude, condescending, ostentatious people dissolve it as quickly as the sun sets.

Mrs. Boss took delight in bragging to her guests at the dinner table about "stealing" a twenty thousand-dollar pair of earrings at the expense of a poor, St. Thomas salesperson who gave away her commission. I cringed. That salesperson was our friend who sells jewelry for a living.

Like I said, this couple was hard to take. Mrs. Boss summoned our mate, Ron, down to her stateroom to photograph the fifteen, decorative pillows arranged on her bed. "This way, you can check how I like them, and put them exactly this way every day." Ron was a licensed marine engineer, a full-fledged licensed captain, a retired firefighter and paramedic, a huge asset to the yacht and our team. Now pillows were his problem. We almost lost him that day.

Mrs. Boss lived for shopping. I made what I thought was a very clear and easy request. "The yacht could use a cheese board. It needs to be unbreakable, easy to use, easy to clean, and easy to stash in a cabinet." What did she bring me? My jaw literally dropped when she triumphantly unpacked a cheeseboard made of sterling silver (yes, the kind you must continually polish) and glass (yes, the kind that shatters). It had five parts to be disassembled for cleaning, and could not go in the dishwasher. Thanks for nothing.

Here's another example of her not listening—or not giving a crap anyway. She wanted candles, but like many crew, we'd shunned real candles because of the fire risk. She said she understood totally, and promptly went shopping for an alternative. Did she bring back battery-operated candles? No. Way too easy. She couldn't contain her excitement as she unpacked two delicate crystal (breakable into slivers) oil lamps (yes, requiring flammable oil that could spill). And that's not all. To assemble this idiotic, candle substitute, I had to balance a small crystal lampshade on four toothpick-like projections that came out of the oil lamp's neck. She didn't understand my "no, no, no, no, no, no, no, these won't work" protest. "Oh, come on, Cynthia. They're so gorgeous. We'll only use them when we're docked, when the boat's not moving." Oh, yes, that's it. Let's put them on the cocktail table, where all your wine-drinking friends can try to manipulate their finely manicured hands between the hors' d oeuvres, the wine glasses and the tall, lighted, crystal oil contraptions.

Mr. and Mrs. Boss's friends were as stubborn and rude as they were. We warned them soberly about the hazards of going swimming in the "James Bond" Thunderball Grotto on Staniel Cay in the Bahamas. Snorkeling there without fins was treacherous, unless timed perfectly with the strong current. One large gentleman knew better though. He could swim, and it was slack tide, and frankly, he said, we didn't know what we were talking about. Ten minutes later, I was swimming madly halfway around the bay to rescue him. Using the lifeguard hold, I pulled him to the nearest boat, and they kindly brought him back to our yacht by dinghy. Mirroring our boss's attitude, not a "thank you," not a "you were right," nothing.

"Listening to our professional advice was impossible for these owners," says Winston in an exasperated tone, "even after incidents that damaged the yacht and broke a guest's foot.

"We were anchored outside St. Bart's awaiting our turn to dock when the owner insisted we lower the tender. 'Winston, the women *must* get to the island to go shopping,' he informed me, frantically. The seas were very rough and lowering the tender on a crane from the top deck to the waterline would be like lowering a pendulum from a moving rolling coaster. 'It's too dangerous,' I said, but the owner screamed at me so loud and for so long that I finally gave in. 'It's your yacht,' I said, and lowered away. Our deckhand almost went overboard trying to control the swing. As I'd predicted, the tender crashed into the side of the yacht and removed a nice chunk of her fiberglass. Luckily Cynthia was standing guard, so it didn't hit any guests. But, by God, now the women could go on their cherished shopping spree.

"On this same trip, after the yacht was docked," Winston continues, "a male guest was too proud to take our helping hand and suffered the consequences. With rough seawater surging against the concrete wall we were tied to, he insisted on walking across the *passerelle* from the yacht to the dock by himself. (A *passerelle* is a long narrow ramp used for boarding a yacht. It moves and sways with the movement of the yacht, and we always help guests maneuver across it, holding their hands and carrying whatever shoes, hats, beach towels, books and satchels they're taking along.) Not this guy. A sudden rush of the sea jerked the *passerelle* sideways and catapulted him, headfirst, into the bushes on the other side of the dock. Even a broken foot didn't make this guy admit he was wrong," Winston concluded.

How about lying about my food? Perhaps some yacht owners have an unwritten contest about how "my chef is better than your chef." I'm no Julia Childs, but I have served some gorgeous meals. However, when docked in St. Bart's, a minute's walk from some of the best French bakeries in the world, why not offer their decadent French delicacies—you know, the kind you can't even figure out how to eat much less how they were built? My boss agreed, and off I went to the bakery. Later, I heard her bragging that her chef (me) had made these impossible-to-create desserts. I didn't even have enough room in the fridge to keep them, much less the tools to make them! I pulled her aside and with an emphatic index finger stated, "If I ever hear you lying about my food again, I will expose you in front of your guests." She got the point. It never happened again.

Lacking even a smidgeon of that Jimmy Buffet atmosphere on board, we were forbidden to call these owners by their first names. It was strictly Mr. and Mrs . . . (We understand this is standard on many yachts, but it doesn't come natural to us at all.) Hard to handle was that their friends actually tattled on us, if they heard us mention anyone's first name. Then the boss would come to us, shaking his head, "My guest told my wife that she heard you use Mrs. Boss's first name."

That's one-upmanship for you: "Your servant behaves worse than mine."

An incident in the water drove home this point again. A guest was having a terrible time snorkeling, and our mate impulsively snorkeled out to his rescue, "Hey, Bob, maybe you should try my mask. It might make snorkeling a lot easier for you." The guest accepted it eagerly and swam away happy. However, later, the mate was reprimanded for using the guest's first name. It's odd how a guy could put his own mouth on the mate's personal snorkel without even thinking, but tattle on him for speaking his first name. There's no figuring.

The time I consider our lowest on the yacht was when the owner gave us a tongue lashing, after his invitees had left. "Never, ever speak to our guests. Period. They are not interested at all in anything you have to say. Their worlds revolve around very influential people. You are unimportant. They couldn't care less about you." That censure still ranks as the worst insult in our entire career. Two hours later (after I had calmed down), we told the boss and his wife expressly that. Did it matter to them? Not one iota. The wife said her husband didn't mean it. Yeah, sure.

Remember, we took this job because we got fired from *You* for interviewing with this couple. At least, we kept saying to ourselves, we were receiving a paycheck. We bought a Toyota FJ Cruiser there in southern Florida, just to keep ourselves in the driver's seat, so to speak. It was bright yellow, a nice contrast to our Caribbean colored Harley. (Our Corvette was back in California.) Now if we needed to get out of town, we could. The FJ gave us a sense of security, sort of. (Funny, the only major things we owned all had wheels. What does that tell you?)

Then there was the yelling. My daughter, Andrea, was having her first baby on the West Coast, and we had full permission to spend a few weeks there while the yacht was undergoing some maintenance. Mr. Boss told us to leave early, which we did eagerly, arranging for another very capable captain to babysit the yacht in our absence. But while in San Francisco at my daughter's home, the boss called, shouting at the top of his lungs that we were overdue and had better get back right then. My granddaughter hadn't even been born yet. We told him no and sent him the written schedule he'd OK'd before we left. That was the second-last screaming fit we put up with.

Time with Andrea, coupled with Jason and his family, was cherished. We were right down the hall at the birth of our second grandchild, Lassen. Winston held her in his arms, the smallest human he'd ever set eyes on, much less touched. Soon after, he returned to the yacht and I helped Andrea through the first harrowing weeks of motherhood, a significant time I will always treasure. Then I flew back to Florida, and helped prep the yacht for a ten-day trip to the Bahamas and then north to Annapolis for the summer.

The next and final screaming fit detonated while we were docked near Atlantis, in the Bahamas, awaiting an additional crew member to help deliver the yacht north. (Our mate, Ron, was long gone, taking his pillow photograph with him.) Mr. Boss phoned with a nonstop rant, about our lousy choice of dockage in Annapolis—the sole dock space available by the way. I'd been on the phone almost daily for weeks trying to coerce dockmasters into giving us a space. We'd only been able to secure it because of our local connections. Mr. Boss accused me of never even trying to get a good dock. Worse, he also accused me of hoping we'd be in a bad location, just to spite him. That was the last straw.

Drained by constant disrespectful and unfounded accusations, Mr. Boss's final insult fueled my clarity. I hung up the phone, looked at Winston, and said quietly, "We're quitting this job."

"When?" he asked.

"Right now."

This was, and still is, the only time I've ever abruptly quit a yachting position without notice, even as bad as some were. Winston has been ready to quit many times; I'd always convince him to stick it out, afraid of not having a job, having too little money, being homeless, being blackballed, etc. I'd always change his mind. Winston was shocked at my decision.

But he was all for it. Winston had been champing at the bit to quit for a month at least, but I'd kept smoothing things over in my usual style. But now we were finished, emphatically. We crossed back over the Gulf Stream to Florida and parked the yacht back in its little home dock right under the tyrants' penthouse, removed our belongings, and left. We called the other owners (the nice ones) to forewarn them and apologized for having to quit so suddenly. Not surprisingly, they understood. We drafted a clear and concise resignation letter and delivered it via email to both owners. It outlined the unsafe conditions, extreme demands, untrue accusations and rude treatment we'd encountered. With that, we left with a clear conscious and our ethics intact.

Again, finding ourselves between jobs, we took a break to travel, our usual antidote and best benefit of being out of work. Boy, was it an attitude lifter. On the schedule was my grandparents' homeland in Slovenia with my brothers and sisters, sweet times with Andrea, Jason and their young families, plus another Harley road trip through the West.

Westward, ho!

And west we went, not only for a motorcycle trip but for our next yacht position. Expect more out of life and you'll get it!

*Winston and Cynthia always found time to
do what they enjoyed most, here on a beach
in Dry Tortugas National Park.*

Chapter 16
Five Thousand Miles of the Rugged Pacific

Perspective. Use It or Lose It.

—Richard Bach

*Alaska cruising offered new horizons
for Winston and Cynthia.*

San Diego to Puerto Vallarta, Mexico, to Juneau, Alaska, to San Diego
November 2007 – August 2008

No Clorox bottle this time

Production yachts are often nicknamed "Clorox bottles" because they bob on the surface rather than slice through big seas. We found just the opposite, *Oyster Pacific,* a one hundred fifteen-foot, well-built yacht based in Southern California that needed a couple to run her. Our positive thinking was paying off.

255

Winston liked this yacht a lot. "*Oyster Pacific* was a staunch and sound classic. She was built for the sea, not for posing on yacht club docks like some of the boats we ran. With a high-sided bow and wide, safe walk-around aisles, she was sturdy inside and out. A hot tub crowned the fly bridge, and that wasn't the best part. The captain's quarters (our bedroom) had a dozen large drawers, a full-length closet, a desk (and even a chair), and a walk-around queen-size bed. Now this was a real captain's stateroom.

"She was a perfect charter boat, too, because she offered four identical staterooms, not the usual king and a couple midsized beds and then the rejected twin room for guests.

"The owner was sturdy, a seasoned fisherman and yachtsman who usually appeared in Hawaiian shirts and wrinkled shorts. He'd owned many boats and weathered many storms. Yet, he was as laid-back as we expected a West Coast owner would be. He interviewed us on the yacht, invited us to his hilltop home for Christmas dinner, and offered us an enticing program. First stop was Puerto Vallarta, Mexico, for the winter. Next stop, Alaska in the summertime.

"There was another benefit: this yacht was too large for us to run by ourselves. The owner had hired two extra, full-time crewmembers. So we were going to be managing crew for the first time. It might be nice, for a change, to have someone else to talk to besides each other, and someone to help with the work. (We originally decided to work on motor yachts needing only two full-time crew, for privacy, as much as anything else, and that kept our options under one hundred feet in length. It was nice to get a chance to try having roommates, for a change.)

"We inherited an experienced engineer hailing from Vancouver, Canada, Greek by nationality and bizarre by personality. Ari knew *Oyster Pacific* like the back of his hand. He had babied her for six years and was full of expertise as well as funny bullshit. We also inherited a pretty young stewardess who helped Cynthia with the interior and washed the boat in her bikini, driving all the other deckhands crazy."

Certifiable

Number one on the agenda was a license upgrade for Winston, from his U.S. Coast Guard 100 Ton license to a 500 Ton. Back to school in Fort Lauderdale, Winston traveled, on our own dime, to take the two-week, nail-biting study class and then sit for the exam. The all day test is overwhelming in many respects, even with years of sea time under the belt, but Winston returned victorious, a 500 Ton captain.

The first thirty days of this gig began in a boatyard. It allowed us the time to get to know *Oyster Pacific* and learn more about the owner, too. He had a penchant for showing up at the yacht at around 4:30 p.m. and staying until 8:30, with lots of "While you're relaxing, could you guys . . ." (He meant right then, while he was there.) We'd put in a full day's effort and were ready for dinner, but he'd regularly find us a project. He was very

One hundred fifteen feet of sturdy design made Oyster Pacific *a truly ocean-going vessel. Cruising north to Alaska and south to Mexico, Winston and Cynthia shared crew quarters on* Oyster Pacific.

predictable and witty, truth be told, and his demeanor so easygoing, we could hardly find fault. When we'd retort, "But it's dinnertime, and we can do it tomorrow," he'd consistently answer with a big smile, "Aw, come on, guys; it's easy. It'll only take a minute."

Winston pipes in, "Let me just say, there are almost *no* jobs on a yacht that only take a minute."

We mocked the owner so much about this frustrating little saying of his that one day we took the best revenge. We bought a bright-red, four-inch, round "EASY" button from Staples Office Supplies and pressed it every time he appeared. He laughed, and we used it even when he wasn't around, just for kicks. "That Was Easy!!"

Mexico bound

Our delivery to Puerto Vallarta was fantastic. We had the owner, his wife, and our crew aboard. Seas were relatively cooperative. We stopped in Cabo San Lucas, at the end of the Baja peninsula for a night, three days into the trip. Cabo was colorful, vibrating and full of spicy Mexican fare. After margaritas, enchiladas, mariachis, and a night's sleep, we pulled away from the dock and ventured south on the thirty-six-hour journey to Puerto Vallarta on Mexico's mainland.

Two thousand-pound mamas and one-ounce babies

No one ever tired of trying to capture those spectacular moments when whales rose to greet the yacht.

The whales were by far the premier attraction in Puerto Vallarta. Humpback, gray, and killer whales annually swim south from Alaska, to bear their young in warm Mexican waters, and they put on quite a show. One day on a twenty-four-foot "ponga," a modest-sized fishing boat owned by a friend, we were surrounded by seven whales breaching and spouting right in front of us, dazzling and scary at the same time. We could have been overturned with a swish of a tail. They had approached us, so we just floated there obediently, until the show ended. Encore, we wished.

Another stellar memory was the day I hiked to a beach where baby turtles were being released. Not any larger than my big toe, hundreds of these squirming little babies wiggled their way down the beach, and rolled back up in the surf, and down the beach again, and back up in the surf, many times over. So intriguing to watch and satisfying to help. The poor guys would roll up the beach and land on their backs, and I'd get the pleasure of righting them. Then off they'd scramble toward the sea again. I've snorkeled for years with grown sea turtles. Now I've observed their endearing beginnings, and even helped some reach the sea.

After a weeklong Mexican vacation, the owners returned north and stayed there much of the time that winter. We had the yacht to ourselves, and between upkeep and maintenance on the yacht, we and the crew had one adventure after the next. We rode horseback on a rocky trail through the jungle, across streams, and up mountains. Unfortunately, Winston's horse lost its saddle—with him in it—on the edge of a cliff. "I will never mount one of those GD creatures again." The crew ziplined over the jungle for the first time—each of us harnessed to a steel cable suspended over a forest of canyons. One push from a guide and gravity propelled us whizzing and screaming over and through the jungle. On a calmer note, we kayaked in sombreros too.

We kept our stewardess/deckhand busy, mostly on the deck. She plugged away responsibly but was eternally ready to play too and had a great sense of humor. Male deckhands from other yachts hovered around our dock like a swarm of bees, so much so Winston jokingly put up a sign, "Please wait until your number is called. Now serving number 23," just to tease her.

Mexico was full of interesting sights—from seven people packed on a scooter maneuvering through the main drag's traffic, to famous waterfalls hidden in the jungle above the city. We road tripped south to a lush resort, and then across the mainland to Guadalajara to help Ari renew his passport.

Cramming for Alaska

"After a Mexican winter, with only a couple of charters and one trip with the boss, it was time to trek north," Winston recalls. "Back to San Diego for provisions and maintenance and then off to Alaska. We had a schedule to keep. A ten-day charter was to begin two weeks after arriving in Juneau. We didn't know anything about southeast Alaska and needed time to learn the waters and the sights. Our planned schedule allowed three to four weeks to get to Alaska and two more weeks to learn everything we could about the area. However, as we had seen in the past, scheduling is the most dangerous thing on a yacht.

"First off, we got a late start. We'd missed a perfect weather window because the boss had a funeral to attend, and he was delivering the yacht with us. After the funeral, the weather predictions sucked: fifty-knot winds, fifteen-foot seas. He insisted we go anyway due to that damn charter schedule. This was a warning flag we hadn't expected from this seasoned seaman, but there we were racing against dangerous seas, on a two thousand-mile journey. Halfway up California's coast, conditions were horrible. There was no place to pull in along the rocky steep coastline, and no way to turn around either. We had to keep plowing north. That's when I began to really dislike the west coastline.

"We were able to catch our breath when we stopped for fuel in Vancouver, British Columbia. We still had one thousand miles to travel, but at least we were on dry land for a night. Desperate for some alone time, Cynthia and I took full advantage. We found one of the most lavish hotels in the city and blew a wad on luxury that didn't rock and roll.

"We made it to Juneau, albeit unnerved and exhausted from ten days of twenty-four-hour rough seas. We had the treat of hiring a talented sushi chef, who began provisioning without delay. A Russian family was coming aboard in just three days, for their charter. In those seventy-two hours (without the advantage of Google because it didn't exist for us then), we picked everyone's brains we could about the perfect charter route. We hired a fishing/camping guide for the Russians, who had expressed interest in roughing it for a night, or two. And, remarkably, we even found a Russian translator to help us give introductions, welcome information, and safety instructions since the man, his wife, and their twelve-year-old son spoke only Russian.

"With all our preparations accomplished," smiles Winston, "we were bent on exploring at least a tiny bit of this vast new territory, before the charter began. We donned our 'Alaskan tennis shoes' (tall, brown, rubber boots worn by virtually everyone there) and set out.

"Our first personal venture away from the yacht didn't take us very far, just to the nearest glacier outside Juneau. But we received the royal treatment when this cute, little black bear, who seemed oblivious to our presence, ambled by. He walked across the parking lot and sauntered down a raised wooden path winding deep into the woods. We just couldn't let it disappear. So, we followed it. The bear was just ahead of us, then around a corner, then ahead of us again. It took us all of maybe ten minutes to come to our senses: There we were, two idiotic tourists, tracking a wild bear down a raised, railed wooden path. If that bear had decided to turn around, we had no place to go but maybe into his jaws. With that thought, we high-tailed it back to the parking lot and into our rental car.

"Our next bit of excitement—keep in mind that we had to jam in as many exciting moments as we could in this morsel of free time before our charter—was the ice. Yes, a large chunk of coveted blue glacier ice lying right on the beach offered itself up to us. How it got there, who knew? Who cared? Regardless, we wanted that chunk. We'd heard stories of mixing picturesque cocktails over this aqua ice, and here it was.

"We lugged the thing back to our car, plopped it in the trunk, and drove back to the marina. Then we got a little nervous. Was this allowed? We discreetly moved the ice to a dock cart and covered our prize with some stray cardboard Cynthia found, then rolled it on down to the yacht. Not sure if this was absolutely proper, or not, we tried to avoid everyone. Turns out it's perfectly OK to take the ice, if it's on the ground melting anyway. And, by the way, the cocktails Cynthia made were show-stopping."

The milk run—Juneau to Glacier Bay to Sitka and Petersburg

Considering we had no actual sea time in Alaskan waters, our charter with the Russians went well. We took them to Glacier Bay, an

THERE'S A YACHT MORE TO LIFE

eight-hour ride up the bay among whales, sea life, and puffin birds, to a humongous wall of billion-year-old ice. What a sight—and sound too! We watched pieces of the glacier break off the top edge and crash into the water below—global warming right in front of our eyes.

We traveled to the Norwegian village of Petersburg, toured a fish cannery, and watched bald eagles devour the remains, jockeying for political rights, as they perched and dove in line with their hierarchy. (We didn't know it then, but years later we would have the CEO of that fish company as a guest on our yacht.)

Our Russian guests wanted to become one with nature and camp on shore, so our fishing guide dragged lots of camping gear onboard, and we planned a route to the ideal spot. However, watching the bears skulk along the shoreline as we cruised by, they decided those woods looked just too ominous to snuggle up to in the dark. Camping canceled.

Taking our charterers on a Southeast Alaska tour included towns full of history and culture. A forest of hand-carved totem poles struck a grand pose positioned among tall trees and lush greenery. There was a walkabout to satisfy every whim. We even found an official midnight marathon for a moonlit jaunt. And the village of Sitka, a bastion of Russian heritage, was an eye-opening delight.

At anchor, way outside the cities and villages we enjoyed, the silence of the water in remote bays was mesmerizing. Often at dawn, right near the yacht but invisible through the low-lying fog, whales sang every tune they knew, breathing quiet but eerie breaths that permeated the atmosphere and our imaginations. For me, the serenity of those mornings will never be matched.

The rock

"Everything had gone along as smooth as silk so far," says Winston with a far-off look in his eye. "The Russians were nice. They liked the food and had a busy time photographing everything in sight. They saw wildlife and caught fish. They sipped drinks laced with glacier ice and bought keepsakes.

262

"And then we hit the rock.

"It wasn't a very large rock, but it was invisible in the water. It was marked on the chart, but we'd unknowingly drifted off our course in some intense current. The sound was horrifying. The yacht shivered and shook and stopped dead in the water. Its bottom teetered on the rock's pinnacle. My heart stopped.

"We immediately donned life jackets on everyone and raced feverishly through the yacht, inspecting the structure above and below deck. The bilges were dry, thank God, and we could find no visible holes. But we were definitely pinned on the rock, and that could mean only one thing: keel damage.

"After calling the Coast Guard and alerting passing seamen to our plight, we radioed a diver, who came in a flash and checked out the damage. Believe it or not, the diver also spoke Russian, so he translated to the guests what was happening. Our three guests, adorned in fashionable orange lifejackets, with whistles and lights, were loving the excitement. (I'm not sure they understood the gravity of the circumstances.)

"The diver's diagnosis was dire. I can hardly think about this without feeling chills. We were indeed stuck on a rock, which had protruded through the bottom of the boat and into one of our water tanks. The diver advised us that once the tide raised, we would float free and could be on our way—with the hole, of course, but with no risk of flooding. Only the keel and the water tank were damaged. The good news was that no seawater was entering the rest of the yacht.

"We were escorted to a nearby port, where the diver took a more detailed look, camera in tow. The hole was about twelve inches long, right along the very bottom of the yacht. He assured us there was no danger of sinking or of the hole worsening. We made the dreaded phone call to the boss, who took it amazingly well. He agreed that the yacht was a sturdy one and that it would be safe to continue, if the guests requested it. 'Give them the choice,' he said.

"With our makeshift in-house translator, we explained our plight and laid out the options. We could 1) end the charter two days early, thereby earning them some credit, or 2) continue on with some water restrictions. There was no deliberation. These crazy Russians enthusiastically voted to continue.

"As we embarked again, I was nervous as hell. All the crew were apprehensive to be sure, but once the hull earned our trust, we performed like pirates who had just weathered a head-on cannon shot. Rounding out our ten days with the Russians included some rewarding fishing, mouth-watering sushi, and another trip to a glacier. I opted to cut the glacier journey short, however, when icebergs started floating by. (The *Titanic* came to mind.) The Russians disembarked at Juneau, just as originally planned, with a fantastic vacation story to tell. Our story—not so much fun.

Closing the gap

"Ari and I quickly went to work investigating boatyards to repair the yacht. The only one capable in the vicinity was one hundred miles away. To research the yard before driving the yacht there, we boarded a seaplane and inadvertently saw Alaska from another viewpoint—the air. It was fascinating even though our problem lay heavy on our minds. The trip did prove purposeful. No way would our one hundred fifteen-foot yacht fit in that yard and be repaired promptly.

Driving one thousand miles with a hole in the boat

"The only option," Winston frowned, "and the owner agreed, was to drive his yacht back to Vancouver, where we were confident she would be repaired correctly. We not only had to carefully maneuver through tree-size floating logs and debris along the way, but we had to do it at very slow speeds . . . seven to eight knots (8–9.25 mph). For safety we anchored every night rather than risk running over a log we couldn't see. That was undoubtedly the longest thousand miles I've ever driven.

"The yacht was hauled from the water directly after arriving at the yard, and, oh my God, how the damage had grown on the trip. Our photos of the original hole now compared with an opening four to five feet long, right along the bottom of the hull. The force of the water, even at those very slow speeds, had literally peeled back the keel. Realizing we'd driven one thousand miles in frigid water with that major damage made me almost vomit.

"The boss arrived from San Diego, took one look at the hole, and gave us comforting words about how shit can happen. I was never so relieved. Then he took us to dinner. He figured the boatyard would apply a quick Band-Aid and we could get right back to chartering. However, I knew that plan wasn't safe for us or the yacht. I refused to go back into dangerous water with only a Band-Aid repair. The boatyard agreed. Their insurance company wouldn't allow it.

"Since there was no question the yacht had to be repaired correctly, the boss decided to get a lot of other issues fixed as well. He added a bunch of projects that would take more than a month to complete and flew us back to San Diego to wait. That's what his story was anyway.

"In reality, he was letting us go. Just like other yacht owners we'd encountered, he didn't do it directly. The final sad blow came after many friendly emails saying he wanted to get us paid as quickly as possible, then began arguing over expenses he had already approved. Our hearts just weren't up to a fight. We felt cheated, but at the same time felt horrible about damaging his yacht. We decided to write the whole thing off as bad luck. At least we didn't drown or sink the boat. It was a small price to pay in the long run."

The best part

Winston and I agree the best part of working on this yacht was meeting Ari, the sharp-dressing, motorcycle-riding, multitalented engineer from Vancouver who we still see whenever we're in the same city.

Plus, we were back in San Diego again, our city, in our room at Tim's.

And another grandbaby

While all this commotion was going on in our yachting lives, something wonderful happened in our private life. Isabella got a brother. My first grandson was born just outside San Francisco. Baby Jameson had eyes as mischievous as they were blue. He was named after his dad, Jason, and his grandfather, James. We met him at age three weeks.

Chapter 17
The Dry Spell

*But the sky knows the reasons and the patterns behind
all clouds, and you will know, too, when you lift
yourself high enough to see beyond horizons.*

—Richard Bach

*In 2008 when yacht jobs dried up and Winston and
Cynthia couldn't find a boat to live on, they found the
next best thing, a houseboat in Sausalito, CA.*

San Diego to Sausalito, California, to Nassau to New York City to South Miami Beach
September 2008—February 2011

Then the national banking fiasco slammed into our future. In 2008, the country's economy dropped to record lows, and so did the yachting industry. Unemployment saw record highs, among them yacht crews and us. Crews were walking the docks, looking for work, in every port city in the United States.

Never ones to let unemployment get us down, we took off on our motorcycle, visiting the kids and tripping across California and Arizona. Adept at marketing, we were in constant conversation with yacht brokers, crew placement agencies, and charter companies. (Sticking to your dreams really takes work!) After contacting more than one hundred connections, our diligence and optimism paid off once more. Overcoming Winston's negative outlook, my intrepid philosophy of "expect what you want" came through again.

"Wait a minute," interrupts Winston, "I admit I'm often the negative one, but this time I was dead right to be pessimistic."

We'd never make you move in bad weather

We were offered a position on a one hundred eighteen-foot yacht stuck in the Northern California fishing town, Crescent City, awaiting a safe weather window to slide down the Pacific to San Diego. Currents and winds were raging. We reluctantly joined the yacht on her southerly delivery, mainly to see how well she handled. The current captain was about to retire and would be a helpful source of information about the yacht's systems and idiosyncrasies, as we made the journey south.

"As soon as we set foot aboard, however, the captain's plans changed. Now he was leaving pronto on vacation, knowing we were there to babysit his charge. We soon figured out that he hadn't left at all. He'd bailed!

"The weather off Crescent City, bad at almost any time of year, had even hardened fishermen tied to the dock. To make matters worse, the former engineer of the yacht, a friend of ours, had advised us that this boat twisted badly in bad weather. He called it a 'paper mâché hull.' Plus, our two inherited crewmembers were novices, not experienced at all with bad weather. After babysitting the yacht for three weeks, with no sign of the returning captain, or of better weather, we knew the owner might ask us to drive her to San Diego ourselves. Hmmm, what would we be willing to do to secure this gig? Then something made the determination easier.

"Five veteran world sailors—all women on a forty-foot sailboat equipped to round Cape Horn—blew into the marina, in the middle of the night. One woman was so shaken by the seas that she fell in the water, as she was trying to get off the boat. All were frozen and totally wiped out. We invited the five, plus the skipper's elderly dad who was a guest on the trip, to join us for some food and a steamy soak in our hot tub. The stories they told as they munched and boiled were indeed bone-chilling: sliding sideways down a twenty-foot wave going twenty knots, for instance. Even they, with all their world-sailing prowess, were expecting their boat to pitch pole (flip head over heels, in layman terms) at any minute."

I have to interject here. The amazing thing was, these women, while in the grips of possible death driving down that wave, told me they looked at their speed and actually cheered about racing that fast! I'm telling you, the sea grabs your soul in ways you never know. Ok, Winston, continue.

"Just shortly after we heard that wild story, our yacht owner's agent called, needing the yacht in San Diego in four days for a boat show. I flatly refused the request. Cynthia backed me 100 percent. We weren't familiar with this yacht, hadn't even taken her off the dock, and had only young, unproven, nervous crew to rely on for help in an emergency. And the weather still raged.

"The agent argued, cajoled, threatened—all to no avail. (Nothing galls me more than an agent sitting in a nice, plush office looking out his window, telling me how the weather is just fine.) I'd been in fifteen-foot seas and fifty-knot winds before; I wasn't about to do it again intentionally on a boat I didn't know, with crew I didn't trust. Flat no.

"So we waited out the storm. When it finally cleared a week later, and the official captain returned to his skipper's seat, we sailed peacefully and safely into San Diego Bay. Just as soon as we set foot on the dock, we were promptly let go. Our pleasure.

"We wanted nothing to do with this agent, this owner, or this boat, regardless of the economy. Back in San Diego with our friends, we celebrated escaping yet another dangerous owner."

That agent wore blinders. He never considered our view of things, much like a snorkeler who concentrates so much on the pretty little blue fish in front of him that he misses seeing the shark swimming alongside. In life, like in a mask and snorkel, you have to look in every direction to see all the potential.

From quaint houseboat to bustling town square

It was clear we would be out of work for a long time. Yachts were being hauled out of the water, crews let go, and yachts sold at auction. Times were tough. So, what did we do? No, not travel this time. We fell back on our old careers, me in marketing, Winston in construction. But we had our Harley close by; good tonic for our minds. I went to San Francisco near my son, Jason, and helped him market his solar company. Winston traveled with his old partner to New Mexico to build a cancer treatment center.

Working for Jason had unique benefits. Besides a little income, I now lived in the same area as two of my grandchildren, for the first time ever. (Andrea and Lassen had moved to Stamford, Connecticut, by then, for her husband's work.) After searching the neighborhood for a house to rent, I could not picture Winston and me living in suburbia. Then I walked onto the docks in Sausalito, and was saved. Discovering a community of four hundred fifty houseboats, I felt at home in an instant. I notified Winston and rented the only one we could afford. I perused Craig's List for the basics: couch, bed, TV. I brought my kitchenware and a few household goods from storage at Tim's in San Diego and quickly got used to using them again. Our two-story, wide-windowed houseboat came with a dock to sunbathe (though there was little sun) and a potbelly stove for heat. Grandchild Isabella spent the night often, and we spent every weekend exploring together.

After three months, Winston finished the cancer unit in New Mexico and settled into our houseboat. We fit right in, being surrounded by boat people, casual and kooky, friendly and fun-loving. Birds of a feather . . . Oddly, we were driving through Sausalito one day and noticed a license plate reading "Saba Rock." What a shock! Turned out the owners were the same couple who had purchased Saba Rock, from Gayla, and rebuilt it so many years before. Here we were living a few blocks from each other, almost four thousand miles from the island.

Things were going well for us, but there was one predicament. We were freezing. We weren't used to the wind chill of San Francisco. Our houseboat sat in 58 degree water, and, yes, the bedrooms were on the bottom floor. We slept fully clothed most of the time just to stay warm. Our visitors, though, who included my daughter from Connecticut and Winston's sister from New Brunswick, Canada, didn't mind at all. Neither did granddaughter Isabella or Baby Jamo.

One winter season of this, and we decided to try another new-to-us venue. We moved to the small warmer community of Petaluma, thirty minutes north of Sausalito near Napa Valley, and could still be near my work with Jason's company. This time we rented a place in a modern, multiuse apartment building, smack dab on the newly renovated

Shedding her water wings, Cynthia takes a break on Route 66 in legendary Seligman, Arizona.

town square. Again, we had a blast. The town square right below us was alive with music, festivals, farmers' markets, and art shows. The parade of humanity was never ending—as were the wine and the Harley riding.

Winston broadens his horizons

Try as he might, Winston could find no maritime work worth doing. The salary for skippering San Francisco ferries was unthinkably low for a professional captain's skills and the accompanying duties: minimum pay and maximum responsibility for others' lives. Tour boats were the same: miserable weather, the bay's notorious wind conditions, and lousy money.

The mood broke when Winston met a houseboat neighbor who ran the International Tour Management Institute (ITMI) based in San Francisco. Since we took people on tours regularly in the yachting industry, it seemed a natural way to expand Winston's credentials. The classes filled his time, too. Winston graduated from ITMI that spring and provided tours in San Francisco and, later, San Diego.

Deciding to tighten our belts money-wise, plus get warm again, we moved late that summer back to San Diego, to our friend Tim's. He was already storing one motorcycle and a few other personals. We rented a bedroom from him, which helped both us and him financially. He needed the mortgage subsidy, and we secured a place to have available, long-term. That began a rental relationship that continued for almost ten years. We could depend on having a place to stay when we needed one, and Tim got the benefit of our rent.

Windwards crew link up

Former crew from the BVI played a role in our lives even in California.

In San Francisco, we often caught up with two ex-Windwards sailing friends, from our sailboat days. They had a home on a lake near Sausalito. Sharing memories, several nightmares and lots of laughs reminded us that we'd come a long way. Even scrambling to find whatever work we could, we were still enjoying the journey.

For work in San Diego, Winston hooked up with another old crew-friend from our Windwards sailing days, who now owned a small fleet of sailboats in San Diego Harbor. Winston provided three-hour harbor tours, handled San Diego city tours and occasionally held a burial at sea.

I helped our ongoing roommate, Tim, with sales calls and still worked via the Internet with Jason's solar company. Continuing to email our yachting network regularly, we just kept adding to our résumés. No long-term positions turned up for what seemed like forever. But short-term gigs—yacht deliveries—kept our heads above water.

Sailing again but with waterspouts

"Speaking of old friends from our sailing days," Winston adds, "another one turned up with a trip for us. The captain and his wife needed extra crew to deliver his boss's Lagoon fifty-foot catamaran from the Bahamas to New York City. Ready for a change of scenery and eager to get back to our old life, we grabbed the chance.

"You'd think we would have faced our share of bad weather by now, right? Well, think again. The trip was a blast; Cynthia even got to snorkel with the splendid-looking but dreaded lionfish. We'd never seen one before in the wild. But, then, there was another thing, we'd never seen before.

"One hundred miles offshore, the sky turned black in all four directions, though blue sky shined right above us. Then we spotted a perfectly formed waterspout off in the distance, identical to the shape of huge tornados featured on CNN. Just as we were snapping pictures of this phenomenon and oohing over its breadth, we witnessed the birth of a second waterspout. Then a third and a fourth sprouted, ominously. In all, five waterspouts joined sea to sky and encircled our sailboat, closing almost every escape route we tried. This was no laughing matter.

"Putting on life jackets and preparing the life raft for launch, we stood together in apprehension. This was probably the most fearful I've ever been on a sailboat. We didn't have enough power to outrun the spouts and didn't know which way to turn anyway. We were surrounded. We hunkered down, the sobbing captain's wife huddled in a corner almost frozen with fear, the rest of us bracing ourselves for the worst. We alerted the Coast Guard and the boat's owner, then just sat there, holding our collective breath, staring at the sky, ready to launch the lifeboat at a moment's notice. Then, unexplainably, the danger passed. After what seemed like hours, we watched all five waterspouts dissipate into the atmosphere, as if they never existed at all, just a figment of our imagination. Shaking our heads in disbelief, we assured each other that, indeed, we had just witnessed horror and, indeed, we must be living right."

We made it to New York without other incidents but not before the captain's wife swore she'd never set foot on a sailboat delivery again. And she never did.

Moving on in our saga of freelance jobs, when you need a job, you need a job. We'd gone from the raging Pacific on California's coast to a frightening gang of Atlantic waterspouts. We didn't know it, but next on the agenda involved chipping ice.

How in the world was our dream career disintegrating so quickly?

Having established that to find professional yacht positions, we needed to be on the East Coast, we high-tailed it back to south Florida. There, we joyfully retrieved our Toyota FJ from storage. Homeless again though—we needed to save every penny we could.

The Van

Believe it or not, we literally lived in a friend's van. Yes, we lived in a van. From a mega yacht to a van. When I said our dream was disintegrating, I wasn't kidding.

A captain friend of ours living in South Miami Beach had a camper van void of campers. It was parked at a marina in South Beach, Miami. He generously offered it to us, and we jumped at the chance. Free rent, plus we had never experienced *life in a van*. Another first . . . oh boy!

The van was fundamentally a really comfortable bed and a place to store our few clothes. Our bathroom/shower was the very convenient and spotless marina bathhouse; being in Miami Beach makes for some swank bathrooms. Let's just say we were homeless in style.

We parked our latest "home" in the marina garage, right next to our FJ. Though we felt out of place and somewhat degraded at times, mostly we just lay in that van and laughed at our plight. Weren't we yacht captains, one of the most sought-after and rare professions on the planet? Hadn't we just been living on a luxury yacht? What the hell happened?

My children were sure we were nuts. They couldn't figure out why we kept sticking to this ridiculously unpredictable industry. "If we have to explain, you won't understand," was our only retort. We hustled brokers, now in person rather than with emails, since we were on the right side of the United States again. Fortunately, the part-time freelance opportunities kept coming.

One thing is for certain: when you live in a van, moving out is easy.

Now the part about chipping ice

Our next paid escapade involved snow shovels, ice picks, and borrowed winter clothing. A just-auctioned Hatteras motor yacht needed crew to bring her from Newport, Rhode Island, to south Florida, and the owner wanted to play on her ASAP. Could we be crew? It was December 23.

"Of course we could," pans Winston.

"Of course we accepted, and were flown to the frigid Northeast. It was a good choice because it 1) brought us money, 2) got us back in the motor yacht world, 3) allowed us to see Cynthia's daughter and her family on Christmas, in close-by Connecticut and also catch up with a long-lost friend from our Virgin Island sailing days, 4) came with a co-captain who was familiar with the yacht, and 5) meant we'd travel down the Intracoastal again. But what was this white stuff on the docks?

"After seeing the yacht across a parking lot buried in snow, the first thing we did was head for the hardware store to purchase plastic snow shovels. I joked about how we hadn't even seen one in years, much less remembered how to use them. We arrived at the boatyard, during a blizzard, of course. The yacht's heads were still winterized and unusable. Tromping to and from the boatyard bathroom required snowshoes, which we, of course, didn't have. I watched Cynthia make five snow angels in the deep snow on the way to the bathroom. When she came out, all five were already obliterated with fluffy new powder.

"Even the docks were buried in snow that covered a slippery icy base. Cynthia almost fell on her butt more than once trying to get on and off the boat. It snowed two more feet, before we could get the ice chipped off the decks of the yacht. But we persevered, laughing and snarling simultaneously, until we were underway. (Cynthia says it was mostly snarling.)

"We pulled into Beaufort, North Carolina, at 10:00 p.m., on New Year's Eve. Our co-captain had to disembark due to a personal issue. He hooked us up with another captain, Faith, whose friendship continues today. She and her daughter ran a yacht delivery service up and down the Intracoastal. After hosting us in her town and introducing us to fabulous pulled pork and mouth-watering barbecue, she toasted the New Year with us, and we snuggled into our crew beds. We were underway early on New Year's Day, headed down the Intracoastal."

To Winston's chagrin, the yacht owner met us earlier than expected in Southport on the Carolina border. He just couldn't stand to wait until we got to Florida. A nice guy but a newbie yacht owner, he was intent on running the yacht himself once he reached Florida. So, our daydream of landing a full-time position on this boat melted with the snow. So, Miami Beach, hello again, this time to a gracious friend's apartment.

Chapter 18
Zodiac: A Boat Born under a Bad Sign

You seek problems because you need their gifts.

—Richard Bach

*Spending summers on New York City waterways
filled with tankers and ferries and fog honed
Winston's navigation skills and offered some
of the most famous sights in the country.*

**St. Maarten, St. Bart's, Anguilla to BVI to St. Thomas
to Palm Beach to New York City, Sag Harbor, and
Montauk to Newport, Martha's Vineyard, and
Nantucket to Fort Lauderdale to San Diego**

February 2011—October 2011

It's amazing that even with our history of being let go several times, quitting a couple times, bending a prop in the Bahamas, and hitting a rock in Alaska, our reputation was still stellar. Brokers' consensus: "Hey, when you've been in yachting as long as you two have, things happen. Your experience is what we want." So, age *and* calamity can be overcome. See?

Important to our brokers were our integrity, our accountability, our honesty and our general likability. We never once let them down. They appreciated that we could identify with anyone in any walk of life and could speak about myriad subjects on a moment's notice. That's one trait I love most about us, too.

St. Maarten to New York City

Another job came our way via a broker who, for years, had been watching us and the yachts we'd been running. A South Florida couple needed crew desperately, for their eighty-two-foot yacht, in St. Maarten, in the Caribbean. The urgency? Their daughter was marrying in a month, and her honeymoon was to be on the yacht, and they'd just fired their captain for having wild parties aboard. The yacht's itinerary was St. Bart's and the Virgin Islands, then Palm Beach, New York City and Montauk in the summer. Besides family trips we'd have a few charters, too, which opened the door for interesting people and much-appreciated gratuities.

Doing our research about this boat, we noticed a field of large red flags flapping up a storm: This owner already had been through seven sets of crew. The most persevering had lasted only seven months. Translation? The boss was probably tyrannical. The word was that he was a micromanager, accusatory, obnoxious, cheap, paranoid and constantly threatening to sue. But the apartment we were borrowing was getting smaller by the day. So, despite these reservations, we took the job. Maybe we could settle him down.

For the most part, it was the boss's loud, grating, degrading tone of voice that put us off almost every time he spoke. His "don't you know anything?" attitude instantly set us boiling inside. (Sometimes, when he'd be particularly obnoxious, I'd envision myself underwater with mask and snorkel, unable to hear anything but the silent sea.) It wasn't that he just talked to us like lowly servants, he talked to us like we were *really stupid* lowly servants.

But, as usual, despite challenges we had some great times on *Zodiac*.

The honeymoon in St. Maarten went smoothly, other than Winston saving the bride from a phantom shark she was convinced was tracking her. Off the couple flew to their new life together. Then we waited for our next company.

For anyone who's been to St. Maarten, the landmarks are recognizable on both the Dutch and French sides of the island. The airport next to the beach is famous for landing jumbo jets over the heads of bikini-clad bathers, often sandblasting them backward into the water. Vacationers line up against the fence awaiting the rush that could kill them. And the beach bar sitting adjacent to that scene is a virtual circus of kooks and drunks and partying social butterflies. At the weekly, Wednesday night food fair, in the town of Grande Case, the main promenade showcases local art and luscious cuisine surrounded by live music and people spending money. Then there's the French side with its fabulous restaurants (which were way too expensive for our budget) and infamous Orient Beach for skinny dippers and gawkers. We spent several months in this haven, and no number of red flags could negate the silver linings we enjoyed in our spare time.

We hosted *Zodiac's* owners on St. Maarten, St. Bart's, and Anguilla for several weeks, and really never saw their bad side. Like many owners, they chose not to make the trip north and sent us off on our own. We delivered the yacht to Florida in early May, stopping for fuel and rest, in the Dominican Republic, Turks and Caicos and the Bahamas along the way. The voyage took two weeks. Back in Palm Beach, we had back-to-back owner trips, mostly south to Miami Beach, with a few friends. Soon it was time to head to New York, where our boss had an apartment in Manhattan. He had booked several charters for business acquaintances there.

Our skipper friend, Faith, from North Carolina, joined us for the delivery north. Up the Intracoastal, we went once again, arriving in New York in heavy fog. We loved the city though. Driving a yacht among the skyscrapers, under those famed bridges and around national monuments never got old.

We based *Zodiac* at a marina, on the tip of Long Island at Montauk, a place I'd been once during my marketing suits-and-heels career. From there we took several charter groups on tour that summer.

Compared to all the charters we'd ever managed, one charter on this yacht was unparalleled. It held the record in several ways: the good, the bad, and the ugly.

The family that stays together

"I get to tell this part," insists Winston. "This charter included a very unusual combo—a female executive/mother, her forty-year-old daughter and twelve-year-old granddaughter, the grown daughter's ex-husband and also her current fiancé and his young son, plus her ex-in-laws. Now *that's* a family. And they were as cool and fun-loving as they were weird.

Sewers suck

"Unfortunately, during the first of their two charters (yup, two), *Zodiac's* gray water tank backed up and overflowed into a guest's shower. The tank was supposed to automatically empty itself but apparently was full to the brim. After sending all the guests off to a casino for the day, the cursing started, and I radioed a pump-out boat for help. Pump-out boats regularly remove black water tank sewage from yacht tanks, by attaching a hose from it to a fitting on a yacht's deck. But we had no fitting on our deck; this was a grey water tank which was supposed to empty itself. I talked the maintenance guy into slithering his four-inch, hundred-foot-long hose into our yacht, down the mahogany staircase, around the silk wallpaper, and into the stateroom where the gray water tank was buried—under the king-size bed. Due to the ridiculously shitty planning of the yacht builder, the tank had no gauge to monitor its level. And a pump that was supposed to regularly pump the gray water into a treatment tank wasn't working. And worst of all, there was no way to reach the pump to remove or repair it. It was four feet down in the bottom of the tank, which was almost overflowing with dirty water. And if that wasn't enough, the built-in, non-removable bed base all but blocked the eighteen-inch opening to the tank.

"With lots of pulling and shoving and cursing for at least a half-hour, our hundred-foot-long sucking solution just narrowly squeezed into a four-and-a-half-inch slot, the only space accessible at the top of the tank. We joyfully but carefully monitored the long, save-the-day hose through the yacht and watched it throb and heave four hundred gallons of gray water off our boat and into the working boat's reservoir. Just when we were starting to breathe a sigh of relief, we discovered the hose nozzle was stuck in the bottom of our tank. Now visualize that the tank's only access was four and a half inches wide, and it was more than four feet deep too. No possible way to crawl in and free our angel of mercy's valuable hose. Just as I was contemplating the cost of a new hose with a hacksaw in hand, Cynthia miraculously wrenched, bent, twisted and twirled the huge snake loose, and out it came.

"The good part in all this was that the guests never had a clue as to how the mess had been solved. They returned from the casino loaded (in both ways), and off we went across the water to our next stop, Sag Harbor. It was just another day of miracle-working in yachting—or so we thought."

And if that's not enough

"Now the ugly part." Winston continues. "Halfway across the sound to Sag Harbor, Cynthia went down to the engine room, for the hourly check. Because there was a particularly odd, high-pitched sound coming from the starboard engine, she immediately alerted me about the noise. That's when it happened. Just as I was using the emergency shutdown buttons for the engines, we heard a resonant, low pop. Now, with both engines stopped and the yacht dead in the water, I went down to the engine room. It was engulfed in smoke. Thank God, Cynthia had gotten out when she did. The starboard engine had blown a hole in itself the size of a basketball. Hot blackened metal parts laid like shrapnel on my gleaming white floor. But there was no fire. And the other engine seemed undamaged. (Now I sound like Cynthia looking on the bright side, right?) Calm and with only some low-level cursing, I explained to the guests why we'd stopped so suddenly. We limped on one engine into Sag Harbor.

"The poor guests couldn't believe their bad luck. They still had two days left of their charter, and we were short one engine. The trouble didn't faze the matriarch, because once, she told us, she'd sunk her own yacht while it was tied to the dock right in her own back yard! 'If it's a boat, it's going to break,' she smiled. The family departed with big hugs and a promise to take advantage of our boss's offer of a discounted charter later in the season.

"Turns out our boss had anticipated this issue. This engine had experienced major trouble, after running only three hundred hours (they're usually good for five thousand). He had wanted it replaced then, but the builder only repaired the lemon and extended the warranty. Now the boss faced a lost charter and a loss of thirty days of his own yachting time while the engine was replaced. He was suing and that was that. The company ended up paying, but he seemed to spiral downhill from there."

Once back in Sag Harbor, Winston and I were forced to anchor outside the marina, because management wouldn't allow a broken boat in a slip—afraid we'd never leave, probably. Once we were anchored and secured with our snub line (a safety line that hangs under the bow and secures the anchor chain, taking pressure off the bow), Winston and our boss drove off to research a fix-it yard on Long Island.

On the yacht, all seemed quiet, until an unexpected fifty-knot wind drove its way across the bay, yanking and grabbing at Zodiac so hard that I was alarmed. Then the snub line was jarred loose, and the full weight of the one hundred twenty-eight-ton yacht was lurching drastically, held only by the metal anchor chain snapping furiously against the stainless anchor windlass with every gust of the wind. The windlass is an expensive steel device bolted to the bow (pointy end) of the boat that raises and lowers the anchor. The anchor chain runs through cogs in the windlass and, unless secured to a snub line, feels the full brunt of the anchor's pressure. The yacht was swinging back and forth 180 degrees continually, an extremely precarious situation. Try as I might, I could not refasten the snub line. The force of the wind threatened danger. I feared the anchor chain could snap at any moment, the windlass could be pulled from its mounting, or the anchor itself would break loose from its hold on the sea bed.

I started our one remaining engine to prepare for a dreaded breakaway and then radioed a new acquaintance, Captain Kevin, who had befriended us the last time we were in Sag Harbor. Kevin's yacht was safely tucked into a slip in the marina, and when he heard my call for help, he jumped in his tender and was at our yacht in a flash. Together, he and I created a makeshift anchor chain brace that acted as a snub and relieved the yanking pressure on the windlass. We were still swinging 180 degrees, but the yacht wasn't being hurled forward and back every five minutes.

Kevin had come to my aid so fast, and he barely knew me. That's our yacht crew fraternity: whatever you need, someone helps; there's a real sense of security. We've run into Kevin over the years, in Florida, Seattle, British Columbia, and even Mexico. We value his knowledge, his friendship and his kindness.

Replacing an engine, one part at a time

Winston had never even dreamed about the procedure he was about to witness—repairing that blown engine. "Tucked into the northern fork of Long Island lies a capable, little marina with access to a huge crane and lots of skilled engineers," he says. "Both were required to remove our blown engine and replace it with a new one. Plus, the yard agreed to our boss's demand, that the repair be completed in thirty days.

"Keep in mind that *Zodiac's* engine was as large as a small car and weighed thousands of pounds. To be removed, it had to go out of the engine room through a narrow bulkhead doorway thirty inches wide, then down a narrow hallway, and up some seven stairs to another door maybe thirty-six inches wide. The only possible way to remove this monster from the boat was to disassemble it.

"The well-coordinated team of dirty, sweaty, super-strong yard workers earned every penny of their salary that month, I'll tell you. For thirty days, Cynthia and I watched as they painstakingly dismantled the damaged engine and craned it out, one component at a time. Then the brand-new engine, which had been shipped to us from Spain, arrived. The engineers took this brand new one hundred thousand-dollar engine completely apart, craned all those parts into the same small space in the engine room, and painstakingly reassembled the entire thing. These human and metal puzzle pieces moved continually, until we had a shiny new engine mounted inside and a huge pile of disfigured ruble on the outside. It was a masterpiece of a repair. And the owner didn't have to pay a cent of it."

Birthday wish comes true

Right after our yacht's surgery, Winston and I rolled out the red carpet again, for the divorce-friendly family. When the ex-father-in-law had been asked what he wanted for his seventy-fifth birthday, he smiled, "Just to go on *Zodiac* again, sit up top with Captain Winston and hear stories."

He got his wish and as a surprise, too. He thought he was going on a different boat, on a day ride through NYC harbor, but when he walked down the dock, Winston and I greeted him with champagne and a brand-new captain's hat. Needless to say, we were glad to see the whole family again. They came aboard with a two-foot-tall birthday cake in the spitting image of *Zodiac,* complete with tiny deck chairs and satellite TV antennae made of icing. Every detail was spot on. And this time, the charter went off without a hitch.

Goodnight, Irene

Even in New York, we couldn't seem to escape hurricanes. Rare Hurricane Irene threatened the New York area with one hundred eighty mph winds, a Category 5 storm arriving in the dead of night. Warnings projected a twelve-foot surge, which would make most yachts float right off their pilings.

We outlined the best place to secure *Zodiac,* based on our experience with eleven other hurricanes. But our stubborn, know-it-all boss insisted we take the yacht up the Hudson River, where he thought it would be safe in a tiny little marina adjacent to a condo project. We disagreed wholeheartedly,

The small dark boat is Zodiac *and the fine diagonal line running top to bottom shows the path of Hurricane Irene.*

but he remained adamant that he wanted her upriver. And it's his yacht. Just as we entered the East River off New York Harbor, passing much more secure dockage, we got a call from the tiny marina's dock master. "Sorry, but you can't bring your yacht here. The condo owners are all up in arms, afraid your big yacht will smash the marina to smithereens." (And they were right.)

So now, we faced no place to go, no reservations, and Irene barreling directly toward our yacht. On a weather map, her projected path literally cut us in two. Muttering secretly to ourselves about cursing the boss, we jumped on the radio, trying to secure another berth. Eventually we found one, just where we had originally recommended we should be. We high-tailed it there. Mr. Know-it-all made haste for his New York apartment, leaving us to prepare for the worst.

After stowing everything that wasn't fastened down, prepping the yacht with every line, fender, and chain available, and securing her with the expertise earned from the myriad hurricanes we'd been through, I called the boss. His baby was secure, I told him, and we'd be going to a safe hotel when the storm got too dangerous.

Oh my God, his screams reverberated through the phone lines. Winston could hear them across the room. "How dare you leave my yacht? I forbid it. She is your responsibility! You have to stay with her." According to him, we could not leave *Zodiac* under any circumstance. It was our job. "I'll sue you two! I'm calling my lawyer right now. You have to stay on my yacht!" he railed.

We weren't surprised at his outrageous overreaction to a very necessary and potentially life-saving situation, because that's how the man reacted to every situation, from refueling to provisioning to guest entertainment—with screams and threats and self-installed power.

Quietly, I repeated: "We told you when you hired us, that we never stay on a yacht during a hurricane. We have done everything feasibly possible to secure your yacht, and have photos to document our expert work. According to the Jones Act, the ultimate mariner law that protects the rights of seamen and outlines their responsibilities, the captain has the final word regarding the safety and handling of the yacht. We're in the right here. No boat is worth our lives. That's what your insurance is for."

Remember the red flags we mentioned, and the seven other crew? The shortcomings of our boss were adding up. Invariably, he argued with us about every expense we incurred. He called us while we were on charter to warn us about burning too much fuel, and when we didn't answer because we were busy serving dinner, he called the charterer and told her to get us. His degrading tone of voice was one thing. Screaming was another. Suing us for exercising safety was over-the-top. Then we observed him cheating charterers out of fuel money. Plus an unknown gentleman, who encountered him lambasting a young dockhand, took extra time to come over and warn us, "You guys need to get away from that man. He's dangerous."

Bye, bye, bossy

"Shortly thereafter, we presented a resignation letter, providing a two-week notice that allowed us to get the yacht back to Florida," Winston relates, still smiling thinking about it. "We had lasted nine months, the new record. Shocked that we were leaving, the boss asked if we'd please do him a favor and stay an extra week in Florida to show the yacht in the Fort Lauderdale Boat Show. He was putting *Zodiac* up for sale, blaming the fact that he could never get good crew. We agreed, knowing we had no place to go anyway, and might make some good job connections at the show.

"We had a smooth trip down the East Coast minus the boss, crossing paths with yacht crew friends along the way. It was the time of year when yachts aimed their bows south, for the mother of all boat shows, the Fort Lauderdale International Boat Show. The show gave us the opportunity to contact our brokers for another gig and also meet potential owners considering buying *Zodiac*. While juggling interviews and boat showings, Cynthia and I went the extra mile to assure that the yacht was in immaculate shape—not only for our boss, but for our own integrity."

Boat show connections

"We made three good connections at that boat show," Winston thinks back. "The first was an introduction to a joyful couple looking for a yacht; they met us and decided, then and there, that we were the crew for them. We had instant rapport. As soon as they found the right yacht, they'd hire us. They were the light at the end of our tunnel, we thought, until we heard they'd been looking for a yacht for two years. No, they couldn't put us on retainer, but we'd stay in touch. Eventually they decided to buy a condo on the beach instead. Hopes dashed.

"The second connection was with a neat two-man crew; Cynthia and I met them when we both interviewed for the same job, and were turned down. We liked them immediately and exchanged leads throughout the show. Our boss hired these guys, even though we tried to warn them as gently as we could.

"The third and most significant connection was meeting a broker from Seattle when he brought a client to look at *Zodiac*. He'd seen *Zodiac* the year before, and thought then she was in terrible shape. Now, revived after nine months of our tender, loving care, he couldn't believe the difference. His client didn't buy the yacht. But another client in Seattle was crew hunting, and the broker called him to announce 'Your hunt is over. Without a doubt, I've found the couple for you.'"

Some side notes

While we were slaving away prepping for the boat show, the stork was slaving away in San Francisco delivering our fourth little grandchild. Now we had Isabella, Lassen, Jamo (short for Jameson) and tiny new Ava Rose seducing us, whether we were within eyesight or not.

The guys who took over our position on *Zodiac* lasted a whopping three weeks. They telephoned Winston in the middle of the night to say they were quitting that minute. Something about screaming over the salad. Guess they'd already been exposed to one too many tirades.

On the other hand, that tyrant of a boss truly appreciated our extra efforts on his behalf at the boat show. He paid us our full vacation pay, which, frankly, no other yacht owner of ours had ever done. And we found our next position by being on his yacht.

Silver linings are often unexpected. Always remember to keep an eye out.

Chapter 19
Life in the Van

*Don't turn away from possible futures before you're
certain you don't have anything to learn from them.*

—Richard Bach

*Any ship in a storm . . . Cynthia offers a
tour of their home in the hardtimes.*

South Miami Beach to Norfolk, Virginia, to
Bermuda to Tortola to South Beach to Trinidad
to St. Thomas to Fort Lauderdale
October 2011 – May 2012

After the boat show, homeless again, we returned to the camper van
in the Miami Beach marina. (Our friend's apartment was occupied.)
With lots of spare time, we busied ourselves riding the twenty-five-
cent bus everywhere in South Beach, or lounging on the warm, white
sand beach around the corner from our marina. We still laughed that
we were professional yacht captains living in this van for a second

time. The mirth didn't wear off luckily, but only because we had several yacht deliveries as temporary escapes.

Bermuda for the first time

Our South African friend (the waterspout captain) needed extra crew to deliver his boss's sailboat from Norfolk, Virginia, to the British Virgin Islands via Bermuda. We'd never been to Bermuda before and we were grateful for the income, equally for the escape.

We flew to Norfolk and had a long, six hundred forty-mile sail to Bermuda. Averaging seven knots, this first half of the voyage took almost four days. Bermuda, a British territory in the North Atlantic Ocean, is a pristine number of little volcanic mountain points sticking out of the ocean about six hundred miles southeast of North Carolina and one thousand miles northeast of Miami. The largest island, Bermuda, is connected by bridges to seven other large populated islands, draped in sparkling white roofs, as far as one can see. Narrow, spotless streets wind through lush gardens. It was, however, the most expensive place we'd toured. Basic fish and chips were thirty dollars. An emergency power cord for my computer was two hundred bucks. We stopped in Bermuda primarily to wait for a weather window (Bermuda is the northernmost point of the infamous Bermuda Triangle where legend says ships have disappeared, so waiting for a good weather window was prudent!) and, also, to take advantage of WiFi. (We were job hunting and needed the Internet to send out résumés and respond to inquiries.) Sightseeing was a bonus.

Then the wind played a trick on us and cut short our sightseeing venture. We were forced to leave suddenly, because of a mounting storm. If we delayed, we'd be "stuck" ten more days on the island and be relatively broke by the next weather window. The result of our abrupt departure: perfect wind sailed us one thousand miles right into the BVI six days later.

Flying back to Miami was a bummer. It was grand being on a sailboat again, not to mention being out of the van.

Living in South Beach...

Van aside, South Beach Miami is undisputedly a very famous and infamous playground. The rich and famous—let me correct that to say the *young,* rich, and famous—play there. The beach and boardwalk looked like models' runways to us, full of striking and energetic bodies. Throbbing music poured out of the clubs and into the streets on every block. Hustlers hustled their restaurants, their tours, their wares, their drinks at every turn. It was a cornucopia of pleasure—a circus.

As visitors, albeit temporary van inhabitants, we relished the neighborhood. We socialized daily at Starbucks and walked to the beach to feed the wild cats. We took that twenty-five-cent bus to the shopping district regularly, just to enjoy the views.

When it rains, rainbows follow

Sure enough, just back from the BVI and what happens? Not one but two new opportunities. Trusting in dreams pays off. That's all I can say.

A broker searched us out to deliver a sailboat, from Trinidad to Florida in March, one month away. We committed to the trip, another new island for the résumé. And remember the broker who'd met us at the Fort Lauderdale Boat Show while showing his client *Zodiac?* Well, his Seattle client researched why we were his sole recommendation, and called.

The Pacific rolls in differently with every wave, yet seems to pose for photographs on Winston and Cynthia's favorite beach, Windansea, in La Jolla, CA.

We flew to San Diego (yes, can you believe that's where the yacht was?) to meet with the owner. We squeezed in some time at Windansea Beach, thinking of all the adventures we'd lived through, from palm frond hut full circle to San Diego again. Then off to the interview and maybe the job of our dreams, finally.

The ninety-two-foot *New Atlantic* traveled up and down the West Coast from Canada to Mexico. The owner was a fisherman by trade and owned several huge fishing vessels that caught and processed fish sold worldwide. He knew boats. He seemed safe, calm, forthright, and honest. And he was a lifelong mariner. We committed.

Then we flew to Trinidad, the island at the end of the Caribbean chain, almost touching South America, to do that sailboat delivery. We delivered the boat as far as St. Thomas when the engine stalled. It wouldn't start no matter how we coerced it. Granted this boat had sails to propel us north but relying on only sails with no backup engine just wasn't a smart idea. The owner agreed to come to St. Thomas to tend to his broken boat. We flew back to Fort Lauderdale, packed two suitcases, stored our Toyota FJ, and flew to San Diego and our new job.

We left our car in Florida just in case we got fired and wanted to come back. You never know. Some opportunities just don't work out.

Ironically, that couple we really liked, who didn't have a yacht, finally bought one. They called us with a great job offer, but now it was too late. We'd already committed. No, we wouldn't go back on our word and, yes, we'd keep them in mind should this job not work out. But we'd committed and had to give *New Atlantic* a chance. We'd come up for air and we weren't going to blow it.

Nervously we wondered, were we doing the right thing?

Part Three:

Yacht Enough

Our ship comes in before our dock rots.

2012 - Present

Chapter 20
And That's How We Got This Job... Perma-Vacationers with a Salary

Every person, all the events in your life are there because you have drawn them there. What you choose to do with them is up to you.

—Richard Bach

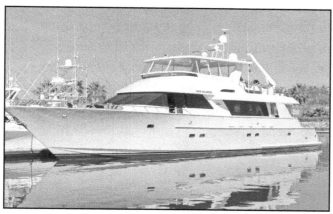

The New Atlantic in San Jose del Cabo, Mexico, the answer to Winston and Cynthia's dream.

San Diego, Cabo San Lucas, Puerto Vallarta, San Francisco, Seattle, San Juan Islands, Victoria, British Columbia, Vancouver City, Desolation Sound, and Vancouver Island
May 2012—2018

Our dream was to simplify life, to be perma-vacationers, with a life of adventure and sustainable salaries. The criteria for that dream: full-time work for a wonderful boss in exciting vacation spots, with generous free time and fair pay. The first step we took: eliminating our "stuff" and the need for our one hundred thousand-dollar salaries.

And now, after weathering one pirate bar, twelve yachts, sixteen owners, including several tyrants, a hundred charters and almost as many vacation spots, three firings, five resignations, twelve hurricanes, life in a van and zero divorces, we landed the ultimate job: crew of the *New Atlantic.*

Finally, we found a wonderful owner who is a good and safe mariner, yacht-savvy yet Jimmy Buffet casual, who understands that yachts require a lot of money. This guy's been running boats, since he was a kid back in Norway, and owns a large fleet of fishing vessels. His expert seamanship shines through when he delays our trip due to bad weather. So many of our previous bosses ignored the weather and got angry when we didn't. His good judgment is refreshing.

In six years of running this yacht, with these Norwegian owners and their family, there has hardly been even a raised voice, much less an argument. We enjoy mutual respect and solid, shared seamanship, total trust, and a strong sense of humor. Our boss and his wife, their Australian shepherd, Charlie, and their extended family are all as good as gold. We are considered members of the family, and the feeling is mutual. Often, we sit with our bosses over coffee or drinks, and eat with them.

Occasionally, we host the boss and one, or two, other couples for a week on the yacht. Often, it's boisterous "boys'" trips fishing off Canada's coast, in the North Pacific. Or, it's the adult daughter and her girlfriends sneaking away from kids and work, to bask in the sun of Cabo. A grandchild's birthday brings the entire family together. Many who come aboard are Norwegian, and they're as easy as they are enjoyable, a far cry from the usual ultra-demands of most of our yacht owners.

Whatever the excuse, beer, wine, vodka and margaritas abound, as do good food, hearty laughter, warm feelings, and mutual respect.

Finally, we found a yacht that is ocean-worthy, reliable, well-designed, and equipped, with all the necessary electronics, mechanics, and systems. A cadre of top-notch engineers, operations experts, satellite specialists, electricians, and plumbers, from our boss's factory ships, are available at least via phone, if not in person. They certainly take the pressure off in times of mechanical, or electronic failures.

New Atlantic has a thirty-four-foot fishing trawler in the northwest that runs alongside us, with its own captain, to host day trips for the boss and his guests. As the mother ship, we feed the sleepy fishermen, listen to their stories long into the night, then send them off at 6:00 a.m. with deli sandwiches and plenty of water. Six to eight hours later, they return with the trawler's icy holds chock full of the day's catch.

Joyfully, the interior of *New Atlantic* is casual and inviting. *New Atlantic* has only one set of dishware and easy to clean/easy-to-store/unbreakable/dishwasher-safe platters. There are no seventeen pillows per bed (only three), or delicate crystal candelabras.

Simple fare and simple presentation are the orders of the day. That's what the owners want. No demanding two-inch veal chops and ninety-eight-point wines on the spur of the moment. Fresh fish (which we catch), potatoes, and carrots, Norwegian style, is the meal of most days, accented with some mayo and sour cream. Crackers, cheese, and a smoothie make up most breakfasts. Huge, fresh shrimp pour from the traps to the boiler to our guests' fingers on the aft deck, for happy hour, accented with a roll of paper towels and plenty of beer.

Minutes ago these crabs were swimming in the Pacific, now their lunch on New Atlantic.

Finally, we again look forward to the owners being onboard, knowing there will be good times, lots of laughs, and no drama. We hadn't had that feeling since *Sweet Life's* wonderful owners, Jerry and Donna. It had been a long dry spell.

But here we are, finally, running the ninety-two-foot *New Atlantic*. With a combination of perseverance, persistence, guts, fate, luck, most probably the flexibility of Cerque du Soleil performers and, rest-assuredly, belief in ourselves, we attained our dream.

The adventures

"In the summer," explains Winston, "we travel to British Columbia's Victoria, Vancouver and Desolation Sound with some of the most beautiful vistas we've cruised. Fall finds us travelling south to Mexico's Cabo San Lucas, San Jose del Cabo, Puerto Vallarta, and La Paz on the Sea of Cortez. Up and down the West Coast every year. (As an extra benefit, when we refuel in San Francisco, we get to visit Jason and the grandkids.)

"On annual deliveries south to Mexico, the yacht motors through herds of spinning, jumping dolphins and many whales making their way south with us. Most are gray and humpbacks, but, once, even a giant blue whale passed by with a wave of his tale.

"We've swum with dolphins, snorkeled with sea lions, and hovered underwater within arm's length of the largest fish in the world, whale sharks. We've floated around huge, mama whales and their calves, and become well-acquainted with two huge, conniving ospreys that insist on perching atop sailboat masts, in the marina near our yacht. (They regularly check out our lifelike osprey kite, which we've flown over our yachts for years.) Excellent fishermen, the birds religiously dive for dinner and always entertain."

Just when Winston and I are satiated with tacos, burritos, juevos rancheros, and ceviche, we're on our way back north to Canada's shrimp and salmon feasts. San Diego sits along the watery highway of our seasonal trips, and we still consider it home. We get time for doctors and dentists and hairdressers, visit friends and family, and squeeze in a Harley ride, or backpacking trip if we're lucky.

Winston always likes to relay the bad parts . . . "We can count on at least one miserable passage leg each year on our two thousand mile trips north. The ten-day voyage can be stretched out to five weeks due to ferocious seas and layovers. On one passage, the Coast Guard required us to call in every fifteen minutes, just to verify we were still safe. (Another season we opted to ship the yacht north instead of driving it there ourselves. Craned onto the huge ship (instead of floated on) and skillfully secured, our yacht and twenty others still faced fifty-knot winds and fifteen-foot seas. At one point, the carrier was going backward!) Going north on the Pacific was not my favorite trip."

A group of islands off Washington's northern coast, the San Juan Islands, is Winston's and my summer base each year. Roche Harbor is a quaint, family-oriented, resort community straight out of the '50s, with log-rolling contests, donut-eating battles and blind rowboat races (yes, the oarsman is blindfolded). We join in the antics every year, hosting a July 4th party for our boss, his family and his friends that includes delectable crab, fresh shrimp, and clams with traditional burgers, hotdogs, potato salad, and corn on the cob. Finger-lickin' good and messy. Bald eagles soar overhead and fish teasingly swim around the docks, daring the youngsters to net them without falling in.

Luckily for us, British Columbia, especially Vancouver, Victoria and Desolation Sound, are close to the heart of our boss. So, we visit them each summer. We've seen the international fireworks competition in Vancouver and Butchart Gardens, in Victoria. We've stood in line in the rain for the renowned fish and chips, at a tiny, wooden stand on the waterfront, and had tea with the boss at the historic Empress Hotel. We've toured the fabulous Parliament Building and enjoyed the thirty-three thousand light bulbs illuminating its outline at night.

Learning from a Norwegian fisherman certainly has its benefits.
Halibut and salmon, the catch of the day.

Adventure with pay . . . that was our goal.

Outside Vancouver Island in Barkley Sound, a seaplane brings a new round of guests eager to fish for king salmon, coho, halibut, and rockfish. These male-dominated fishing trips promise wild times, from our 5:00 a.m. wake-up call to the exuberant afternoon radio plea, "Boil the water! We're picking up the shrimp pots now!" Serving a five-gallon bucket of freshly-caught shrimp cocktails and beer on the deck is topped only by Captain Winston's perfectly grilled salmon dinners and lots of good wine. Then it's off to bed and that all-important alarm setting—week in and week out, for sometimes two months.

I've never handled so much fresh fish in my life. After the boss cleans the fish to perfection, slabs of filets piled high on trays get carried into

300

my galley, as if on conveyor belts. Fishing regulations demand that certain filets are matched with tails, wrapped, vacuum packed, and labeled with the fisherman's name, location caught, type of fish, and the date. That's part of my job. Fishing regulations are strict, and we follow them to a T.

Sometimes, new guests arrive on the same seaplane that departing guests are boarding. That schedule requires some fast work, bedding changes and staterooms spick and span. But, all in all, we look forward to these back-to-back charters primarily because the people—whether CEOs, bankers, family or employees—are all so casual and enjoyable.

Calamities don't matter

"For most of our former bosses," Winston reminds, "calamities equaled immediate crises, yelling, screaming and blaming. Even the smallest inconvenience could cause an outbreak of hysteria. But this boss is different. Nothing fazes him.

"You name it, if it's on a boat, it's going to break, and usually it's when the boat's at sea. We've faced double and triple whammies when it comes to repairs on *New Atlantic,* and yet our boss maintains his cool, even when it's human error—as in ours. He takes everything in stride. Imagine being told, right in the middle of your summer holiday, that the shaft seals are leaking and have to be replaced, which requires the yacht being lifted out of the water and put in a boatyard for weeks. At the same time, you're notified, 'Oh, and the engine is completely out of balance and must be corrected.' And, further, 'All the main batteries need replacing to the tune of thousands of dollars.' Now imagine our boss hearing all this. Through any of it, he keeps his cool. He shakes his head and scowls for sure but not for long. It's a boat, after all. He's a godsend."

Winston and I love this guy. Even family emergencies don't faze him. Sadly, my vibrant, twenty-one-year-old nephew passed away suddenly, one week after being diagnosed with cancer. We not only visited him in the hospital and attended his services in Texas but also spent considerable time supporting my sister and her family. Later, Judith, my closest friend of thirty years, died suddenly in St. Louis. Without a blink of an eye, my boss urged me to go even though it was a busy time on the yacht. I'll forever treasure those unselfish gestures.

The fabulous free time

From the onset of our employment on this yacht, the owner has bent over backward to not only accommodate our needs but sincerely encourage our enjoyment. Never before when working a yacht did we have holidays off—we were always hosting a party or trip—but this family spends their holidays at home and generously lets us enjoy ours privately.

The boss took us to the international America's Cup Sailboat Races, in San Francisco, hosting not only his guests but inviting my son and his children to join us. We motored the yacht out to the racecourse to watch state of the art yachts sail forty miles per hour right by us. It was a real first for Winston and me, not to mention those kids. We've had a personal tour of our boss's three hundred seventy-six-foot factory trawler, one of the largest fish-processing vessels in the U.S. fleet, and met the ship's captain, who's worked on that ship for thirty years. We've commemorated the Norwegian Constitution Day annual parade, with our boss in Ballard, the little city that is the center of Norwegian culture in Seattle. When the Seattle Seahawks won the Super Bowl, the boss even made a special trip to the stadium to buy official Super Bowl shirts and brought them to us in Mexico.

"We wanted adventure," says Winston, "and with this job we sure get it. On our own, we've explored Mount Rainier and Mount St. Helen, the Space Needle, the Boeing plant, and Oregon's Columbia River Gorge, with its kite surfing. We have road tripped to central and western Washington, Coeur d'Alene, Idaho, Montana's Glacier National Park and driven a car down the one thousand-mile Baja Peninsula twice, delivering cars for the boss.

"We've enjoyed having our family on the yacht numerous times in Mexico, when the boss wasn't going to be using it. Andrea and Lassen come every season and explore the wonders of whale watching, dolphin swims, and snorkeling. That makes Cynthia a very important grandma, I'll tell you. Jason and his troop enjoy the yacht when it is in San Fransicso and San Diego."

The only downside

On most of our other yachts there were at least *several dozen* downsides . . . The only disappointing aspect of this perfect job is there is no Caribbean venue. New Atlantic had already been to the Mediterranean and throughout the Caribbean, before we were hired, and the owner wanted now to stay on the West Coast. No Caribbean, therefore no snorkeling in the warm, crystal-clear, coral-filled water teaming with tropical fish. Mexican waters are beautiful, but they just can't compare.

But, then again, this job is our dream come true—adventure with pay, working for a wonderful family, on a wonderful yacht. As far as missing the Caribbean, 'no worries, mon.' On our own vacations, we charter a sailboat in the British Virgin Islands, don mask and snorkel, see clearly and breathe deeply to our hearts content.

Our boss thinks we're nuts. "You work on a boat, you live on a boat, and you're *going on vacation* on a boat?"

Yes, indeed!

Chapter 21
Expect Your Dreams

The simplest questions are the most profound.
Where were you born? Where is your home? Where
are you going? What are you doing? Think about these
once in a while and watch your answers change.

—Richard Bach

You are never given a wish without being
given the power to make it come true.

The Present

When we began this yachting adventure, our friend Judith sent us
a note:

> *Run swift, run free,*
> *over silver sidewalks of the sea.*
> *Salute the moon and sprinkle wine*
> *upon the wind for me.*

We like to think we've been doing just that ever since.

Call us perma-vacationers, living and working 24-7 in places other people visit. We work hard with an adventurous schedule. We are paid well, with lots of time off. It's our dream come true.

"But remember," interrupts Winston, "we kissed a lot of frogs to get here and paid a boatload of dues. We morphed from minimum wage in a grass hut to running luxury yachts, with people asking us every day, 'How in the world did you get that job?'"

We held fast to our dream. We spotted opportunities and dove in. But there's a "yacht" more to the story. For us, happiness isn't relentlessly collecting "stuff." Happiness is our state of mind.

We hope our story will compel you to wonder, "If Winston and Cynthia did it, why couldn't we?

Author Richard Bach wrote in his novel, *Illusions: The Adventures of a Reluctant Messiah*, "You are never given a wish without also being given the power to make it come true. You may have to work for it, however."

That's how we got our dream job.

What's yours?

Winston and Cynthia dance with
joy at the life they created.

Epilogue

After twenty-five years with paychecks in paradise, including twenty years in the yachting industry and six wonderful years on New Atlantic, we decided to try a new adventure.

We're continuing our nomadic lifestyle with no "stuff," but traveling by land instead of by sea. We've taken the helm of a new little RV, aptly named "Yacht Enough." She's enough of a yacht for us.

The transition to fulltime RVing has been easy because of our seafaring lifestyle. "Yacht Enough" is about the size of our crew quarters on yachts, so it makes us feel right at home. Everything we need is at our fingertips, and it all travels right along with us.

We'll slip in lots of yacht deliveries and take people on yacht vacations, too, (email us at <u>wincynbook.com</u> if you're interested), plus lots of Harley rides, while exploring the U.S. in "Yacht Enough." We really don't know where RVing will lead but . . . you can bet we'll remain as flexible as a palm tree.

Stay tuned!

Addendum
Researching Yachting Careers?

If you're curious about a career in yachting, searching the internet is your best bet, and there are wonderful resources available. Assess your skills and decide, first, if you'd like to work as part of a larger crew, or run a yacht with just yourself and one other person, like we prefer. Here are a few sources we've used that might help get you started.

Publications and Websites

DOCKWALK – "The essential site for captains and crew," a monthly online magazine great for beginners. You will be asked to register and can do so under the category "Looking for work." Read DOCKWALK cover to cover to get broad insight into crew business, job postings and yachting issues.

    www.dockwalk.com

The Triton – "The voice of the community of people who earn their living working on yachts," is another monthly magazine covering yachting news, day work, classifieds, business directory and upcoming events, etc.

    www.the-triton.com

Training

Research a maritime training center in your area. Any professional training you do furthers your employment opportunities. There are many organizations providing information, even on which courses to take if you want a certain position on a yacht. Courses range from one day to several weeks, depending on your interests. Maritime Professional Training in Fort Lauderdale offers all levels of maritime certifications and licenses. Winston received his credentials from MPT. On the other coast in San Diego, Maritime Institute provided my captain training. U.S. Coast Guard recreational boating safety courses are also a good resource, and offer all levels of certification and licenses.

Mptusa.com

Maritimeinstitute.com

Uscgboating.org

Crew Placement Agencies:

There are many good crew agencies, most base in Fort Lauderdale. Each has its own guidelines, and some require a fee. Search the web, but here are a handful of agencies that were informative, helpful to us personally and referred us to a few of our crew positions:

CrewFinders.com

CrewNetwork.com

CrewUnlimited.com

LaCasseMaritime.com (Seattle based)

LuxYachts.com

Neptunecrew.com

Good luck on all your adventures, and keep us posted at our website, **www.WinCynBook.com**.

PLACES WIN/CYN HAVE BEEN

Between 1990 and 1994 (while living in San Diego)

La Jolla and throughout California

British Virgin Islands (chartered sailboats throughout all British Virgin Islands)

Hawaii to San Diego by way of sailboat delivery

New Zealand (road trip through both North and South Islands)

California to Arkansas road trip (in a convertible hot rod Mustang!)

From October 1994 going forward . . .

Bahamas
Nassau, Paradise Island - Atlantis
Abaco Islands, Marsh Harbor
Grand Bahama Island, Lucaya
Exumas, Staniel Cay

Turks and Caicos, Turtle Bay

Bermuda

Greater Antilles, Caribbean Islands
Puerto Rico
Dominican Republic, Puerto Plata

Lesser Antilles, Caribbean Islands

<u>British Virgin Islands</u>
Saba Rock Island
Virgin Gorda Island
Tortola Island
Sailed to all the various smaller islands
weekly, i.e. Norman Island, Cooper Island,
Peter Island, Anegada, Jost Van Dyke

<u>U.S. Virgin Islands</u>
St. Thomas
St. John
St. Croix
Hassel Island
Water Island

St. Barts
St. Maarten (both Dutch and French sides)
Anguilla
Antigua
St. Lucia
St. Vincent and the Grenadines
Grenada
Trinidad

Mexico
Baja California – driven full length twice 1,000 miles)
Ensanada
Turtle Cove
Bahia Magdalena
Cabo San Lucas
San Jose Del Cabo
Todos Santos
La Paz
Isla Espiritu Santo
Loreto
Mulege
Bahia de los Angeles
Puerto Vallarta
Barra de Navidad

Canada
Maritime Provinces, New Brunswick
British Columbia, west coast
Vancouver Island, Victoria and throughout
Desolation Sound, throughout

Tonga Vava'u Islands

Fiji

Slovenia

United States
Florida

Key West
South Miami Beach
Miami
Fort Lauderdale
Palm Beach
Daytona Beach
Clearwater
Cape Canaveral (Shuttle Launch)
Panama City
St. Augustine

Louisiana

New Orleans

Mississippi

Biloxi

Alabama

Mobile

Texas

Houston
Galveston
Tyler

Georgia

Savannah

South Carolina

Charleston
Georgetown
Myrtle Beach

North Carolina

Beaufort
Moorhead City

PLACES WINCYN HAVE BEEN

Virginia	Norfolk
Maryland	Baltimore
	Annapolis
New Jersey	Atlantic City
	Cape May
New York	Manhattan
	Sag Harbor
	Montauk
	Hudson River to Albany
Rhode Island	Newport
	Block Island
Massachusetts	Martha's Vineyard
	Nantucket
	Boston
California	Newport Beach
	La Jolla
	San Francisco
	Crescent City
	Catalina Island
	Sausalito
	Petaluma
	Carlsbad
	Palm Springs
	Lake Tahoe
	Napa/Sonoma Valleys
	Monterrey/Carmel
Arizona	Prescott
	Sedona
Montana	Kalispell
	Whitefish

South Dakota	Sturgis
	Deadwood
Idaho	Coeur d' Alene
	Sand Point
Oregon	Portland
	Madras (for the eclipse)
	Newport
Washington	Seattle
	Spokane
	San Juan Islands, throughout
Alaska	Juneau
	Ketchikan
	Sitka
	Wrangell
	Petersburg

National Parks and Monuments

California	Yosemite
	Alcatraz
	Cabrillo
	Channel Islands
	Death Valley
	Devils Postpile
	Golden Gate
	John Muir Woods
	Joshua Tree
	Lassen Volcanic
	Mojave Desert
	Point Reyes
	Presidio of San Fran
	Redwood Forest
	Sequoia and Kings Canyon

Arizona	Canyon De Chelly
	Casa Grande Ruins
	Glen Canyon
	Grand Canyon
	Organ Pipe Cactus
	Petrified Forest
	Saguaro
Nevada	Death Valley
	Lake Mead
	Great Basin
Utah	Arches
	Bryce Canyon
	Canyonlands
	Capitol Reef
	Glen Canyon
	Grand Staircase Escalante and Natural Bridges
	Natural Bridges
	Zion
Oregon	Crater Lake
Washington	Mount Rainier
	North Cascades
	Olympic
	San Juan Islands
	Mount St. Helens
Montana	Glacier
South Dakota	Badlands
	Mount Rushmore
Wyoming	Yellowstone
	Devil's Tower
	Grand Teton
Colorado	Mesa Verde
	Rocky Mountain

New Mexico	Carlsbad Caverns
	Petroglyphs
Texas	Big Bend
	Rio Grand
Missouri	Gateway Arch
Florida	Big Cypress
	Canaveral
	Dry Tortugas
	Everglades
South Carolina	Great Smoky Mountains
	Cape Hatteras
New York	Ellis Island
	Niagara Falls
	Hudson River Valley
	Statue of Liberty
Maine	Acadia
Alaska	Glacier Bay

Waterways

Intracoastal Key West to Norfolk
Intracoastal Key West to Galveston
Colorado River through Grand Canyon (by raft)
Chesapeake Bay
Puget Sound
San Francisco Bay
Sea of Cortez
Atlantic Ocean
Pacific Ocean
South Pacific Ocean
Gulf of Mexico
Caribbean Sea

PLACES WINCYN HAVE BEEN

Historic Highway
Route 66 from Chicago to Los Angeles
US Route 1, longest north-south road in U.S.
US Route 101, Pacific Coast Highway
Mexico Highway 1, Baja California
Trans Peninsula Highway

Motorcycle Trips
Route 66 from Chicago to LA
Arizona
Utah
Nevada
Colorado
New Mexico
California
South Dakota
Wyoming
Idaho

And not finished yet!

CPSIA information can be obtained
at www.ICGtesting.com
Printed in the USA
FFHW010623181118
49394582-53800FF

9 780998 906966